SHAMANIC AWAKENING

"Sandra Corcoran has written a remarkable account of her studies and practice of shamanic counseling. I have had personal contact with two of her teachers, Twylah Nitsch and Oh Shinnah, and she couldn't have found better guides. *Shamanic Awakening: My Journey between the Dark and the Daylight* is filled with fantastic stories into the nonordinary realms, but recent investigation of dreams and other altered states of consciousness lend credibility to her accounts. The author's work is rooted in indigenous traditions and rituals that contain the wisdom and insight so badly needed to help the torn culture of our time."

STANLEY KRIPPNER, PH.D., PROFESSOR OF PSYCHOLOGY AT SAYBROOK UNIVERSITY AND COAUTHOR OF *DEMYSTIFYING SHAMANISM* AND *THE VOICE OF ROLLING THUNDER*

"We live in a time in which increasing numbers of Western spiritual seekers are turning toward non-Western spiritual traditions in search of meaning and transcendence. Sandra Corcoran's book *Shamanic Awakening* is an eloquently written and engaging personal narrative that unfolds in a way to inspire us all."

HANK WESSELMAN, PH.D., ANTHROPOLOGIST AND COAUTHOR OF *AWAKENING TO THE SPIRIT WORLD*

"*Shamanic Awakening* draws you in—a magnet force of symbols, story, and signs. Sandra Corcoran's elegant narrative coils around your heart and awakens you to your energy source—love. Her wisdom births an alternative knowing, alternative dimensions, and multi-universes to explore. The reader develops new eyes, a new heart, and a knowing mind. Experiencing Sandra's book, the reader is left with confirmation that the human mind is sourced far beyond the brain. And not in a place, but in many dimensions. Read Sandra's book and you will comprehend the workings of the quantum mind. And there's more. If you follow her winding path, you may be led home."

REBECCA HARDCASTLE WRIGHT, PH.D., AUTHOR OF
EXOCONSCIOUSNESS: YOUR 21ST CENTURY MIND

"Sandy Corcoran's book represents a very rich and honest account of her experiences with North American shamans, spiritual teachers from Central America, and Andean spiritual masters. . . . In my opinion, Sandy's book is written in a 'panamerican' context, such that her story can be of great help to many spiritual seekers of this continent who are working with the elements that she describes in her book, from her personal experiences."

JUAN VICTOR NUÑEZ DEL PRADO BEJAR,
FORMER PROFESSOR OF ANTHROPOLOGY AT THE
UNIVERSITY OF CUSCO, PERU, AND MASTER OF THE
ANDEAN MYSTICAL TRADITION

"In this remarkable book, Sandra Corcoran gifts us with her personal, magical journey of awakening to shamanism with exceptional skill and candor. Ever cognizant and respectful of the Mystery, she generously includes details of ceremonies and teachings from the many extraordinary teachers that influenced and catalyzed her most profound and formative experiences. A great storyteller, she offers thoroughness and detail in relating her experience."

NICKI SCULLY, FOUNDER OF SHAMANIC JOURNEYS, LTD.,
AUTHOR OF *PLANETARY HEALING: SPIRIT MEDICINE FOR
GLOBAL TRANSFORMATION,* AND *ALCHEMICAL HEALING: A GUIDE
TO SPIRITUAL, PHYSICAL, AND TRANSFORMATIONAL MEDICINE*

"Impeccably honest, deeply personal, and sparkling with jewels of wisdom, *Shamanic Awakening* is not only the story of one woman's remarkable spiritual journey but also an astute introduction into the various practices of shamanism. . . . From the moment I began reading, until I finished the last sentence several hours later, I was unable to put this book down."

ROSEMARY GLADSTAR, COFOUNDER OF SAGE MOUNTAIN
HERBS, AUTHOR OF *HERBAL HEALING FOR WOMEN,*
AND COEDITOR OF *PLANTING THE FUTURE*

SHAMANIC AWAKENING

MY JOURNEY BETWEEN
THE DARK AND THE DAYLIGHT

SANDRA CORCORAN

Bear & Company
Rochester, Vermont • Toronto, Canada

Bear & Company
One Park Street
Rochester, Vermont 05767
www.BearandCompanyBooks.com

Text stock is SFI certified

Bear & Company is a division of Inner Traditions International

Copyright © 2012, 2014 by Sandra Corcoran

Originally published in 2012 by Balboa Press under the title *Between the Dark and the Daylight: Awakening to Shamanism*

Teachings and quotations of Grandmother Twylah Hurd Nitsch used by permission of her son, Robert Nitsch Jr., Wolf Clan Teaching Lodge

Library of Congress Cataloging-in-Publication Data
Corcoran, Sandy, 1951–
  [Between the dark and the daylight]
  Shamanic awakening : my journey between the dark and the daylight / Sandra Corcoran.
     pages cm
  Rev. ed. of: Between the dark and the daylight : awakening to shamanism. 2012.
  ISBN 978-1-59143-180-0 (pbk.) — ISBN 978-1-59143-759-8 (e-book)
  1. Shamanism. 2. Self-actualization (Psychology) 3. Spiritual biography. I. Title.
  BF1611.C747 2014
  201'.44—dc23

                                                      2013036110

Printed and bound in the United States by Lake Book Manufacturing, Inc.
The text stock is SFI certified. The Sustainable Forestry Initiative® program promotes sustainable forest management.

10 9 8 7 6 5 4 3 2 1

Text design and layout by Virginia Scott Bowman
This book was typeset in Garamond Premier Pro and Legacy Sans with Gill Sans and Zapf Humanist used as the display typefaces

To send correspondence to the author of this book, mail a first-class letter to the author c/o Inner Traditions • Bear & Company, One Park Street, Rochester, VT 05767, and we will forward the communication, or contact the author directly at **www.starwalkervisions.com**.

For my daughters:
Callie, whose life put my feet to this path, and
Nyssa, whose life keeps my feet walking forward on it.

Author's Note

In 1991 I was given permission by Grandmother Twylah Hurd Nitsch to teach her profound body of work as a certified teacher of the Wolf Clan Teaching Lodge. The only request she made was that when I shared the charts and teachings in workshops or with individual clients, I follow her instructions and not bring my own changes or interpretations to the work.

Some of our more personal conversations throughout the long relationship I was blessed to have with Gram are not specific to the Wolf Clan teachings. I have tried to be true to those conversations and have shared them in ways I feel portray both respect and gratitude for her wealth of knowledge.

However, all of Gram's writings, including the personalized and universal charts and their teachings, are copyrighted and permission to print any part of her teachings must be granted through her son, Robert (Bob) Nitsch Jr., who is the sole owner and distributor of all her works.

When writing this book, out of esteem for Gram, her personal teachings, and the Wolf Clan Teaching Lodge, I requested that Bob read the manuscript sections dealing with Gram to make sure I had not imparted any misinformation concerning the teachings and to point out possible areas of her work that he would prefer I not include in the book. Bob made adjustments and requested some deletions, but has generously given me permission to use what is included in the book now titled *Shamanic Awakening: My Journey between the Dark and the Daylight.*

For further information on the educational charts of the Wolf Clan Teaching Lodge and instructional books and DVDs, contact Bob Nitsch at: www.wolfclanteachinglodge.org.

Contents

Preface

I experienced severe resistance to writing this book. In fact, when a friend approached me about ten years ago to give it a shot, I told her point blank, "No way." As a teacher and therapist, I am used to being the ear for others' vulnerabilities and pain, but the idea of expressing my own, in the unmasked form of a book no less, had me shuddering at the mere thought. I have worked in the public eye for a long time. I could not imagine how clients and colleagues, or some family and friends, might react when reading parts of my story. After a number of years of bearing witness to myself, however, I realized that these experiences have made me who and what I am—and it is time to acknowledge them. While gathering the courage to go public with the story of my immersion into the mystical and shamanic worlds, I would be dishonest if I didn't admit I still have lingering feelings of uncertainty about how several parts of my life will be received by people who know me in a different context. Others, I know, will take it in stride as they have had their own wonder-filled moments. For still others, I hope the example of my candor gives them greater courage to be who they are, in all the magical and mystical ways that are available for all of us, no matter how far outside the framework of their current convictions or belief system they may be led.

Except for my daughters and brother; teachers; friend Joan; and one other person, Will, the names of family members, friends, and colleagues have been changed for reasons of anonymity. Also, some time periods have been compressed.

I am extremely grateful for my two daughters, Nyssa and Callie, for choosing me to be their mom. The depth of love they have brought to my life and the personal accountability their lives have awakened in me have been enriching beyond anything I could have imagined.

I am most appreciative of growing up in a family that I know has always loved me totally, despite my not-so-ordinary beliefs, and that accepts how I have chosen to live and express those beliefs. I am humbled knowing that so many of the people I have known, in a variety of personal and professional ways, have not been blessed with such an unconditional gift.

I am thankful to have been befriended and mentored by all my teachers: in particular, Grandmother Twylah Nitsch of the Seneca Nation, whose philosophy, humor, wisdom, and grace were amazing mirrors for my own growth and whose body of work provides an endless treasure chest of teachings and insights; and Dr. Juan Nuñez del Prado for the impeccability and integrity with which he has shared the pure and simple (not simplistic) Andean mystical tradition for decades, without embellishment or glorification, holding to their history, rituals, and beliefs.

I am exceedingly indebted to my friend Joan Parisi Wilcox for the endless hours she spent with me reviewing the original manuscript for my book. Her insights, suggestions, cautions, and even critiques were not meant to change my voice, simply to help me gain a clearer voice.

I wish to thank the late Dr. John Mack and Roberta Colasanti for supporting me in exploring the more peculiar aspects of my personal story; and Will Maney, whose own story lent credence to mine.

I am grateful to all those at Inner Traditions/Bear & Company—Jon, Kelly, Jessie, Jeanie, Meghan, Elizabeth, Peri Ann, Manzanita, et al.—who saw the value in my story, and moved it forward with both their guidance and expertise. The respect they have shown both me and my work, throughout the process from acquisition to market, was well beyond my expectations.

I am thankful for the many children, students, clients, friends, colleagues, and mentors who have allowed me into their stories and richly contributed to mine. I would not be who I am today without each one of them crossing my path.

I want to be clear before you enter the pages of this book that I do not consider myself a shaman. The term *shaman* is a word from the Tungusic language of Siberia; it is neither a Native American nor South American term, although it is a term that has entered the popular lexicon. Shamans do not receive diplomas, but the ethics and accountability, study and involvement with the teachings—beyond a weekend workshop—do account for another type of credentialed training. Although I take no issue or umbrage with others in this day and age who call themselves shaman, out of respect for those indigenous cultures in which I've immersed myself, I accept that one never refers to oneself as a shaman, or a medicine person—that decision is left to the People to discern.

I do, however, consider myself a shamanic counselor, which I define as one who combines standard therapeutic practices with shamanic techniques to connect a client to the sensory knowledge present in Nature herself, to tap the wealth of information available in meditative journeying or dream states, and to incorporate rituals and practices to uncover the deep wisdom and potential within oneself. I have used all of these techniques for personal realization and self-transformation over the past thirty years, as well as having integrated many of these same methods into my private practice. Thus, I see my practice as facilitating communication between the unseen dimensions and the physical to help clients restore balance to their inner and outer worlds.

Death was the doorway to my shamanic journey. From each death, be it of a special loved one, an important relationship, or a previously held belief, I was challenged to explore new questions and offered the opportunity for a deeper awareness of the world, a fuller understanding of myself, and ultimately renewal.

As the late Lena Horne said, "It is not the burden one carries; it's how you carry it." What I have come to realize is that although we may not have any influence over life's challenges, we can choose to carry our burdens with grace and gratitude. No matter our station in life, or our individual stories, we all face loss or heartache in our lives. No one's is easier or more difficult than someone else's—grief is grief. As my story makes clear, it took me years to find the gifts in the losses. If you are struggling, and even if you are not, I trust you too will find in the collection of your own life stories the gifts that are yours alone to give yourself.

1

The Vaseline World

It was fall in New England and, although the world was ablaze with seasonal colors as the trees turned, my world was void of all color. The days were getting shorter and as the dark of night slipped in I felt panic, the panic of both not wanting to dream and of awakening to a reality I wanted only to dismiss. My nights, like my days, were too long, too dark. With the death of my daughter six weeks earlier, my world had become coated in Vaseline—nothing would ever be clear again. I was so overwhelmed with my own grief I couldn't deal with my husband's grief or with my friends and co-workers when they would generously call or drop by to see if I needed anything. I felt I had to assuage their grief, and that took too much energy. I felt the constant need to be alone, to hide, to retreat into my reflections. At night I sought solace in my car; driving aimlessly, protected by my self-imposed isolation.

Tonight, the rain was beating down, making the already smeared outer world even less distinct. As had become usual in these nightly sojourns, I had no set direction and welcomed the numbness in my body as a fellow passenger. But tonight my bladder was suddenly pulling me back to some semblance of the physical world, rudely intruding on my space. It was odd to feel my body, as it had become like a lifeless appendage since Callie's death.

Momentarily, my bladder's interruption retreated as my mind once more became consumed with questions about where she was. The priest's picture of children in heaven brought no solace. The doctors' efforts to console me with the fact she was no longer in pain did anything but. She had been just sixteen months old. She couldn't take care of herself. Was she safe? Had she gone into the Light? Who was there to hug her? I agonized over whether I had dressed her for her passage in warm enough clothes and whether the locket I had placed around her neck—enclosing pictures of her dad and me—would keep us fresh in her memory. I questioned if I had sent her off with good company—the handmade Raggedy Ann she had loved so much. In my torment I asked what had I done wrong that I couldn't love her enough to make her healthy, to make her stay, to fix this.

The Vaseline world, the driving rain, my own torrent of tears, my bladder tugging for my attention—everything I wanted to ignore so I could enjoy my new companion, Numbness—suddenly parted like fog as a light intruded. The light stopped me like the crossing guard at the school where I taught. I pulled over and stared at a long, low building with a small globe-shaped entrance light above the door. Inexplicably, the light had penetrated my world and summoned me to stop, and so I had. Taking in my surroundings, I realized I was lost. But even this realization didn't penetrate deeply. I didn't care that I was physically lost; the feeling of disconnect mirrored my emotions. All that mattered at that moment was the light. I wasn't even sure if the building was occupied; I just felt commanded by the light to enter.

There was a lot of activity inside, with people milling about in what seemed like a lobby. They didn't register individually in my brain and no one noticed me. The bright lights of the foyer accosted me. I had been sheathed in darkness these days past, talking mostly to Death, shaking my fist at God,* wondering what life could possibly hold without Callie's

---

*I will use the terms *God, Great Mystery, Source, Universal Intelligence,* and *the Absolute Self* throughout this book. I see no gender differentiation or secular religious connotation as I feel either would limit the totality of the expression. There are over seven billion people on the planet, and they each have their own explanations of what that means for them. For me, there is something far greater than us, an unseen *something* that we are each a unique and intrinsic part of—of this I am sure—and so I use all these terms to refer to that greater essence of what one can feel, but language limits.

presence and the smiles her innocence and delight with the world around her always brought out in me and others.

I looked for a bathroom in which to hide from the lights and the congregation of people, and to take care of my bladder. A few minutes later, when I emerged from the bathroom, I was grateful to find the foyer empty. I was feeling increasingly disoriented, so I couldn't find the door to escape back out into the comfort of the dark night. The panic was creeping in again; I had to hide. Out of the corner of my eye, I saw a turquoise blur. My legs suddenly felt shaky, probably a result of not eating anything since I couldn't remember when. I looked for a chair, but the only one I could see was just inside the doorway of the next room—where the turquoise blur moved.

Even as sat I was not aware I had entered some type of lecture hall, one filled with people listening. My focus was so narrow that all I saw was the turquoise shape speaking up front. It was a woman's voice. Over what must have been several minutes, her words began to penetrate my fog. Her words, which to this day I cannot recall, hooked me and kept me in my seat.

I had no sense of time, but eventually I heard clapping and then saw people rising and leaving. I made my way up to the turquoise shape. I don't know what I expected or what I was going to say, but I wanted—no, I *needed*—this abstract being to know hers were the first words I had heard in days.

The woman was finishing up her conversation with the people who had clustered around her. I tried to take her in, this woman who had been a blur but a moment before. She was wrapped in a turquoise caftan-like dress. She had fine silver braids, three of them to my surprise. On every finger she wore turquoise and coral rings and Native-designed silver bracelets up her arms. It was as if she had become crystallized before me so I could take in her presence, but she did not look at me. Finally there were just the two of us. Although I was standing next to her, she still did not look at me as she said, "Now I understand. You are one of the reasons why I have come. Tomorrow

I will begin to teach you what I know. It is time for you to begin."

Confused, I countered, "I can't do that right now in my life." Trying to come up quickly with a coherent reason without spilling out my pain and collapsing into tears again, I sputtered, "I don't have the money or the time."

Arguing seemed reassuring. Arguing with the Universe had become one of the few daily transactions I could muster these last few weeks. I had stayed night and day with my daughter for eight weeks through the end of the summer of 1983 at Boston Children's Hospital: trying to make sense of the diagnosis, trying to comfort her through the many and painful tests, arguing with the doctors about alternatives, arguing with my family because I refused to go home and get some rest, arguing with the hospital chaplain that God couldn't expect these things of children. I had been living, sleeping, cuddling, and playing together with Callie in the cramped hospital room and outside in the hospital's enclosed garden whenever we were allowed that reprieve. We'd sit by the garden's fountain, watching the water rise, and I would read my daughter's favorite books to her—vigilant day and night to make her world seem normal in this abnormal setting, capturing precious time together.

Now, this strange woman standing before me, who still refused to make eye contact, spoke again. "You will come tomorrow morning. There will be no fee. I am here to teach you another way. You are right—you do not have the time. Your body is a skeleton from the waist up and that is not the promise you made Great Mystery. You have a lot to do in this lifetime and you have promised others you would be available to them. We need to get your feet to that path, now."

I started to argue, but she held up her hand, dismissing my next thought, and promptly turned and left. I stood there for a long moment, bewildered, and realized there was absolutely no one to argue with—even the Universe had left the room.

The next morning I returned. I don't know why. I was hiding in the ladies room, having given in to my sobs once again. Who was I kidding? I couldn't sit through a workshop with other people. And what the hell was the workshop even about? And who was this woman to tell me I *had* to work with her? Who *was* she? This was stupid, useless for where I found myself. I was out of here. I'd never promised her I'd show up, and besides I'd never see her again anyway.

As I blew my nose and stepped out of the stall, there she was. We were two women in a face-off, alone. She stood with her arms defiantly crossed, her back against the door, leaving me no escape. This time her eyes held mine, "My name is Oh Shinnah," she said. "And my first daughter died, too." Her admission struck me as if she had slapped me across the face. How did she know? I had said nothing. "Now pull yourself together and get out there. We have a lot to do." She turned and left in what felt like a repeat performance of the previous night—an obvious dismissal of my coming argument, my fear, and even my pain. This was the first of many times when I realized this woman, who was to become my first Native American mentor, took no prisoners.

During that weekend, I was part of a large group of predominately women who had come from far and wide to hear Oh Shinnah and learn from her teachings. They were nurses, psychotherapists, bodyworkers, and those interested in the use of crystals and alternative forms of energy healing. Working this first weekend with Oh Shinnah was one of her dear friends, another amazing teacher and healer in her own right, Dr. Dolores Krieger. They taught us the use of different types of crystals to cleanse or shift energies in the human biofield, about the subtle energy bodies and chakras, the dynamic use of therapeutic touch, also called TT—the hands-on teaching that Dr. Dee, as Dr. Krieger was affectionately called by her close associates, had immortalized—and, most importantly, how when we chance to change our perspectives we can heal ourselves and offer others the tools to heal themselves.

I found I was hungry for this information, starving actually. It wasn't that I was completely unaware of the healing modalities they were speaking about or of Native American cosmology. In fact, over the past two years, I had begun to read as much as I could find on the Native path. I had received my master's degree just eighteen months earlier, in the blossoming stages of Lesley University's programs on expressive therapies and integrated arts. While studying for my master's on nights and weekends, I had continued my job as a full-time special needs educator. Daily, my special needs students taught me that appearances can be deceiving and there is much more to things than what we see on the surface.

I was already using classroom techniques that were outside the pedagogical box. For example, in a hands-on exploration of the natural world, I would ask the kids to examine the similarities and differences between a simple stone they had found and a chunk of quartz crystal I had brought in. They could then apply this practice in discernment to other subjects, such as their poetry, helping them give voice to feelings that were often difficult for them to access and express. As they wrote about their feelings through their poetry, it opened doorways to deeper personal insights. My hope was that no matter how difficult their individual circumstances, they might better see how their lives had purpose. Thus, part of my curriculum involved introducing the kids to nature from a Native American perspective—the belief that all things are alive with energy and everything in life has a purpose. So, it wasn't so surprising to hear some of what Oh Shinnah and Dr. Krieger were sharing in the workshop. Although I was engaged in their teachings, what I was more acutely aware of during this first weekend was that what connected me to Oh Shinnah was the loss of a child.

I had become pregnant during my last year of graduate school, and despite the hectic pace of finishing my master's thesis and closing out the year with my special needs students, I eagerly anticipated the birth of my first child. Callie arrived by C-section at noon on Mother's Day. What a gift to this new mother. Everything seemed normal to my husband (whom I will call Ben) and me, and the doctors gave no indication there was anything out of the ordinary. She had ten fingers and ten toes, she passed all her postnatal tests, she nursed almost immediately, and she made deep eye contact as if she had something special to share. However, late into the night on the day of her birth, a female physician woke me and with no preparation announced in technical terms, without the slightest trace of emotion, that Callie was a Down syndrome baby. I had gone to sleep sublimely happy in one reality and I was awakened, abruptly and to my mind without compassion, and thrust into a completely different one.

My first conscious thought was, "Why is the Universe doing this to us?" Then my mind screamed in endless white noise. It wasn't until later that morning—in the clear light of day—that I moved from raw shock to educated awareness: I felt fear, not of the unknown but of the *known*. I was, after all, a special needs educator and had a fairly good idea of what I thought the future would hold for my daughter. By later that afternoon, I touched raw anger. It was mostly directed at God. A bit later it was also directed toward my doctors, two of whom came in together to discuss her Down's. Although they were trying to be well meaning, I could hardly contain my anger and resentment as they told Ben and me about possible "options"—waiting lists of couples willing to adopt Down's kids or the types of residential homes for placing such children. I had barely begun to process the diagnosis and now they were being presumptuous in ways that were insulting to my true feelings.

I coldly dismissed them. Were they misinterpreting my fear? I looked down at Callie's tiny sleeping form, admittedly afraid, but this was our baby, our blood, entrusted to our care no matter my own fears and disappointments. It wasn't disappointment in her diagnosis I was projecting, although every parent wants their child to come into the world with no difficulties; it was in fact my understanding of this world, which has its definitions of "normal" and doesn't easily make a place for those designated "special." My mind spun ahead to some distant future where I wondered how Callie would be treated, for I had often seen the disparity in the treatment of the children I taught, even by educators. Would she be able to learn the alphabet? Would she be accepted on the school playground? Would the girl talk in junior high school turn mean? Would she be invited to her senior prom? Would people turn away from her as she walked down the street?

Looking at her now that I had been given the diagnosis, I searched for the many obvious signs of Down syndrome and could find but a few. In that moment, two other thoughts flashed through my mind: her soul was light-years wiser than mine and she would not live to be teased at school. I didn't cling to such thoughts in that instant, and I wouldn't understand them as premonitions until the day she died.

We took her home and I undertook a mission to find out all I could about new modalities and alternative methods to enhance her life and to defy her diagnosis. I was not trying to deny her Down's—I accepted that. I simply wanted her to have every opportunity to experience life to her fullest and happiest. As she grew, I took her everywhere and watched as her constant grin coaxed some others out of their fear of her condition. But more often than I would like to admit, I saw in some folks' eyes their obvious discomfort or need to remove themselves from what Down's generated within them. Those who knew Callie differently, more intimately, referred to her as a "little bundle of light," and there was no doubt that her already developing sense of humor and outgoing personality engaged those around her.

Callie was a light in my life, and her passing from complications after open heart surgery was devastating. Like all parents who out-live their child, we were unequivocally changed by her death. Her immense, although short, presence in my life had brought me enor-mous joy. And now with her death, I lost the relationship with who I had always thought myself to be. I didn't know who Sandy was any-more. That woman had died too.

At this workshop, I knew without a shadow of a doubt it had been

Callie who had led me to see "the light" at the doorway of this building and find Oh Shinnah. Through her death, Callie opened a new door I could choose to walk through or not. Oh Shinnah's teachings would be the first step to start me on the long road of healing my grief and creating myself anew.

2

You Can't Walk Stupid upon the Earth

I had never anticipated Death would become my teacher. I never envisioned the winding road that first workshop with Oh Shinnah would put my feet to. I never imagined the depth and richness of the worlds that existed below or above the surface of the reality where I normally lived. I never dreamed that the strange and mystical places I would come to know or the synchronicities that led me to the edge of myself were my soul's calling to inhabit a fuller self.

Oh Shinnah's teachings were, as she described them, a "confrontation to fixed realities." I worked with her alone and in groups with other women for close to six years. She immersed her group of accomplices—she refused to let us speak of ourselves as apprentices—into the training of Mystery schools past, whose teachings still apply today, and into the countless lessons available from Earth herself. She challenged us to discover how the five elements—earth, air, fire, water, and ether—are not only around us, but live within us and can be communicated with, imparting information to help us negotiate both our inner and outer terrain. She taught us about how each of the four cardinal directions has a distinct purpose and yet they collectively form a personal compass that guides us through our own unique landscape.

For example, I learned to experience water not as a thing but as a living elemental, a tutelary spirit. A pond, a brook, a river, the ocean—each has its own voice and different lessons to impart. Winter water, as ice or sleet, instructs differently than spring water. It takes us within, offering an opportunity for reflection, whereas spring water, as soft rain or morning mist, encourages us to grow like new shoots, to come out to play. Thunderstorms, as one prayer says, "bring the rains that cleanse and that heal," which like our tears, once spent, clear the emotion that brought them on. These teachings were not intellectual understandings, but concentrated practices. Oh Shinnah encouraged us to sit with each individual element—such as water—for an entire year to experience it in all its manifestations.

I was committed to this work because the teachings were providing a container in which to process my pain. However, sometimes during group gatherings with Oh Shinnah I just wanted to be alone. One day, feeling especially sad, I wandered off from the group during a break toward a river that ran through the forested property where we were gathered. As I walked with my memories of Callie, what I missed most was that I could no longer physically hug her. I hummed the song I had sung to her almost every day: Joe Cocker's "You Are So Beautiful." Silly though it may sound, it made me feel close to her.

I came to the rushing river and sat on a wide, flat rock, facing my primary direction—south. That morning I had learned we each have a primary cardinal direction that serves as a gateway to magnetize our personal power when doing the inner and outer work. I felt compelled to make an exchange of my energy with the energy of the river. Reciprocity is a way to honor and come into alignment with what we ask of Nature or of another. I offered the river my water—my tears—and sadness in exchange for its energetic flow, which I felt could help ease the ache in my heart. As I had been taught, I sprinkled a pinch of tobacco (a sacred herb to Native Americans) into the river as a testament to the sincerity of my prayer to the water beings. I spoke my prayer aloud—we had been taught the spoken word has power of its own volition. After making the offering, I moved upstream and sat on another stone, allowing its stored heat to warm me. There is a ritual etiquette at streams and rivers: it is impolite to sit where you leave your offering, or downstream from it, as you don't want to collect the energy of your prayer until the water spirits have had time to work with it. Closing my eyes and feeling the solidness of the rock beneath me, I listened to the rush of the river, trusting my prayer was with the river's spirit, its essence.

The cascading water filled my ears, until eventually its cadence aligned me with what I can only describe as its breath. My chest gently rose and fell in unison with the water's measure; we were one, together in a graceful dance. From far away came an indistinct sound, barely audible. As it grew louder, I could detect a melody and I identified the sound as someone probably playing a flute back at the workshop site. I made note to thank them because their song was beautiful and sweet. As the tempo of the rushing water stepped aside, letting the more lilting sound of this new dance partner cut in, its pulse soon began to resonate to the rhythm of my heartbeat. The tune repeated over and over, until I realized I was humming it out loud. Gradually, the melody diminished, until it was barely a whisper in my ears again, handing me back to the sound of the rushing waters. I felt a deep, physical calmness, and as I opened my eyes I found myself smiling. The sound of a bell pulled me completely from my reverie—I must have sat straight through the lunch break, for the bell was a signal to return to class.

I retraced my steps back to the yurt as the group was reforming and asked my close friend if she knew who had been playing the lovely tune. She said she hadn't heard it. I asked others as we readied for Oh Shinnah, who was sitting on her blanket preparing to resume her teachings, but no one seemed to know what I was talking about. Oh Shinnah had overheard my question and was smiling a bit mischievously. She asked me to share what had happened. I felt uncomfortable and self-conscious as I related what had transpired at the river. She seemed delighted, telling me there had been no flute player, it was the river that had spoken and had, in fact, given me its song. She explained that in her tradition the song would be the first section of my death chant. Each of the cardinal directions would provide, in time, another piece of that chant. When it came time for my death, as I was crossing out of this world into what lay beyond, if I remembered to sing my death chant I could cross more consciously. Crossing consciously, she said, would enable me to not get caught in the illusions of death and so I could travel more quickly to Source.

I was taking in everything she said, amazed at this unexpected information and almost gleeful because death was a link back to Callie. I didn't know if the expression on my face revealed what I was feeling— I wanted my entire death chant *now*. I coveted the song that would help me consciously connect with my daughter. I had no death wish, only a mother's wish. I knew Callie existed in a realm beyond the seeing of my physical eyes, but not beyond the reach of my mystical knowing. Quite possibly, Death was becoming my ally and Great Mystery, it seemed, might not have forsaken me after all.

In the years that followed, I embraced daily practices that brought me a greater awareness of the mysteries that inform the world and the synchronicities that can both surprise and tease us. I felt more sincerely the presence of what some call, according to their persuasions, God, the Infinite, or Great Mystery. What this Source energy is called is semantics; it had become evident to me that there is something wiser and greater than us. Something, I was recognizing, that I was part of and that was part of me. I am not speaking of this essence from a cultural context per se—although at the time I was steeping myself in Native Earth-based spiritual beliefs—or any structured set of religious beliefs. The expansiveness I felt during my experiences was forming a connection to Oneness, and without hubris I was becoming conscious of the fact that this Oneness was self-actualizing as I was because the Oneness and I were the same. These practices were helping me to know this in ways that were mending my soul.

I welcomed each day in ceremony. Every morning I acknowledged

Great Mystery with the first rays of the sun, offering tobacco and setting my intentions for a good day. At full dark I offered cornmeal to feed the Earth Mother for all she had given of herself that day, reviewing with gratitude the easy flow or tougher moments the day had brought. Oh Shinnah had encouraged us to end these daily ritual prayers with the invocation, "Today is a good day to die," the premise being that if this was your last day to live you "could no longer walk stupid upon the earth," as she pointedly reminded us through her many and varied teachings. This was a hard prayer for many women in the group, but it came easily for me—until one day I realized I had been saying it cavalierly. It struck me that my consuming grief was a cop out. As long as I held on to my grief, I didn't have to live fully. I got it—that this prayer was not about embracing death, but rather about embracing life. This sobering insight was an important early step back toward regaining the fullness of my life.

All of Oh Shinnah's metaphysical teachings and our private discussions not only helped immerse me in the vast energy contained in the world around me, which I now more consciously inhabited, but in turn were also stretching me beyond the dark place that had initially brought us together.

I had another major "aha" moment one afternoon in mid-September, almost two years after Callie's death. I was outside at a community garden, picking tomatoes before the hard frost of New England came and stole them away. I stood up to stretch my back, sore from bending to reach the ripe fruit whose weight bent the plants close to the earth. I lifted my face to the early afternoon sun and felt its light and heat caress me. With an impact I can only describe as simultaneously exquisite and excruciating, I realized this was the first time in almost two years I had truly felt the sun. I had the palpable, conscious realization that I could release my grief without losing my connection with Callie. Standing there feeling my body firmly on the Earth Mother, absorbing the energy of Father Sun, grief no longer defined the bond my daughter and I shared. With tears of gratitude, I let go a long, deep sigh I had held in my chest for a very long time. With immense thanks to Callie for having been a precious part of my life, I gave wing, finally, to her passage and gained flight toward who I was becoming. Callie would always and forever be only a breath away. And finally, after two years of companionship, I said goodbye to my old pal Numbness.

I continued to have personal insights through my time working with Oh Shinnah, and there were two in particular that had a dramatic effect on my life: the dreamtime work, which I discovered was something I was particularly gifted at; and the Moon Ceremony teachings, an esoteric set of trainings and ritual practices involving a women's outdoor evening ceremony to align with the energy of the Great Mother Goddess. I have since taught this body of work, sharing it with hundreds of women around the globe, as a means to heal the wounds we as women carry on a historical, cultural, generational, and personal level. I will not pretend performing ceremonies creates an easy, rosy everyday reality or that delving into dreamtime work gives ready answers. They are tools to help us more clearly navigate life's vagaries. The awareness they foster, as in any disciplined practice, demands we be impeccable in our intentions, pay close attention to even the subtlest shifts, and willingly accept personal responsibility to make the changes needed to grow through life experiences.

For me this work was a lifeline, but for some of my family and friends it was presenting a bit of a challenge because they couldn't always understand where this path was taking me. My world was moving in an unexpected direction that was not only unfamiliar but at times alien to those who loved and knew me. But I had made a choice that this was the course of my healing and the path back to a fuller, richer life. I still wrestled with the poignant moments that returned me to my sorrow, and as with any wound, there were times the scab would fall off and the bleeding would resume.

After Callie's death, I had avoided sleep so I wouldn't dream, but during these past few years I had discovered dreaming was a significant part of my personal medicine bag (the bundle that literally and figuratively contains tools and totems of personal power). Each morning I would chronicle my dreams, having been taught our nocturnal visions are as important as our daydreams in manifesting or reshaping the fabric of our waking reality. When we sleep at night, which Oh Shinnah referred to as "the little death," our subconscious holds a stockpile of information in the form of symbols and, at first glance, seemingly disconnected story lines that can help us process our waking world and show us who we are and where we are going. She explained our everyday, third-dimensional reality is ruled by time and space, and what we consider our real world is in fact a world of illusions and even delusions fabricated from what our senses, our culture, our image makers, and our biological and generational history tell us is true. Our ego, which helps us negotiate our everyday reality, doesn't like to be wrong, so we often dismiss our dreams, intuitions, and precognitive flashes as illusions because they are not based in reason or logic.

Well over three years into my studies, our core group of women gathered for a dream incubation ceremony in the hills of Colorado. In dream incubation, the intention is to dream as an individual and at the same time remain open to, and supportive of, the group collective in the dreamtime. Often, people coming together for such a rite find they can share dream content or snippets of dreams. In addition, it is not uncommon for any one person in the group to insert herself into another person's dream to support that person or contribute meaningful information.

On this night, the sky was ablaze with stars clustered across an inky blue-black canvas. Like a group of young children gathered for the first time around a campfire, we giggled as we readied ourselves in our sleeping bags. Once settled, we said our good-nights like one big Walton family. As I stared up at the expanse of the Milky Way, I lay thinking; it had been one of those days where my tears had come out of nowhere. I sent out an earnest prayer to Spirit, "Please assist me to follow my trail of stars instead of my trail of tears." The hard earth under my back seemed to soften and take me to her breast. I snuggled deeper in my sleeping bag and gave over to the land of sleep. As my waking world faded away, my dreamscape woke up.

I feel my feet run up timeworn stone steps in what appears to be a turret-like structure; a dark, ancient castle like you'd see in an old movie. I burst through thick wooden doors at the top of the stairs into a room flooded with light. There are children of all different ages taking instruction at small desks. There she sat! I am overcome simultaneously with joy and panic. Callie appeared to have grown—she looks about four years old. I rush over and scoop her happily into my arms, feeling frantic that the moment is critical for escape. She looks gently in my eyes, as if she doesn't want to hurt me, and says, "Mumma, you're not supposed to be here." I am struck immobile, frozen in place on the stone floor, as I remember the morning she crossed—she had lifted her arms toward me just before she passed out and whispered "Mumma." Shaken, I put her down as the memory flooded back that it had been her first, only, and last word, verbalized aloud as she reached her arms to me on that awful day.

Suddenly, two monks in brown, hooded robes materialize. Without comment, they each take me by an arm and gently lead me away. I strain to not lose sight of the daughter I have just been reunited with. She smiles radiantly, and in that radiance I know without a doubt that when my time comes she will be the first person to greet me when I cross.

The monks take me to the shore of a huge river. A massive, ancient relic of a boat sits at the water's edge, waiting. Silently, the monks guide me on board and then just as silently they turn and leave. There is a row of oarsmen on either side of the deck, their long, broad blades in the water. I sadly stumble to the prow, bundling myself in a blanket I've been offered, feeling devoid of all energy. As the boat moves away from shore, the head boatman says that I can row, as if doing that will lift me from the depths of my sadness. I want nothing to do with him or any of them. I sit shrouded in my silence and my sadness. For a long time the boat moves deftly through the water, with the stealth of a heron as it moves towards its prey. I know that I have traveled to some outer boundary, and I know Callie had been right—I was not supposed to be here.

The boat reaches the opposite shore, and somehow I am lowered onto the sand. I look up to where the boatman is watching me intently and I ask with little interest, almost as if a part of me is obligated to speak the question, "What is this ship called?" As inane as it seemed, once the question was asked, I changed from not caring to being possessed by an imperative need to know the answer. "The Grateful Dead," says the head boatman, although he has not spoken aloud; I hear him only in my mind. A profound sadness, deeper than anything I have experienced since Callie's death, envelops me. I know a window had opened for me to get to her, but that I would never be able to return. I watch the boat fade into a thick mist, which moves with it over the water.

I woke up to the rising sun of a new day, the dream full in my mind. I recognized this was what the Native People call a *big dream,* a vision that is life changing. All morning I struggled with how hard it was to have returned from that place alone. I resisted rejoining the group at breakfast, knowing that they would all be sharing what they had dreamed. When we were called to gather, I went, but I knew it would be agonizing to speak this dream and as such to relive it.

When it was my turn to share, I couldn't look at anyone in the group. My sobs and sighs punctuated the story as I related all that had unfolded. When I finally looked up, Oh Shinnah asked, in an especially kind voice, if I knew what *The Grateful Dead* was. I hadn't put it together originally when told the name of the boat, but now in light of the fact that she knew I had been a Deadhead, a follower of the '60s band the Grateful Dead for many years, I thought this was the most absurd of questions given the depth and breadth of what I had just emotionally shared. I stared at her as if she were an idiot. After what seemed like a long time, she continued, "In Egyptian mythology *The Grateful Dead* is the ship that comes to collect souls at the River Styx for their passage to the next world."

Her words caught me and there was no reply necessary. I understood I had accessed the realms beyond time and space that she had so often spoken of. I had been trying for years to understand what she meant by this, trying to reach these realms consciously, and now I had arrived at the meaning with no real effort on my part. This was merely a beginning point for my belief in, and consciously working within, the dimensionalities that exist beyond our everyday reality and that for me seemed most easily accessible via the dreamtime.

3

Traversing the Middle Distances

Dreaming is not the only, nor even the primary, access to otherworldly realms that exist beyond time and space. Intuition can be a major gateway as well. We are not all called to use the same set of tools—crystals, herbs, accessing dreamscapes, tarot cards, toning to change a vibration, animal totems, the angelic realms, or the laying on of hands—to expand our inner and outer knowing, but we all have the opportunity to enhance our intuition. Trusting our intuition, like working with dreams, comes through consciously working with it to recognize our personal symbols and uncovering through interpretation the messages that might bring a deeper understanding of our situation. To some people, developing intuition comes easy—as natural an act as brushing their teeth—whereas for others accessing it is more difficult and takes greater effort. Some may call this inner flow of information instinct or synchronicity; others, survival mode. Mastering trust in our individual process is essentially dependent upon not only our curiosity but also our belief in ourselves. Learning to trust our intuition requires no teacher, ceremony, or ritual. It's a natural innate ability that only needs to be developed and then to have the self-confidence within one's self to be believed. I had learned this certainty through experiencing my own gifts and by witnessing others develop their own talents in the various groups in which I took part.

Intuition provides you with a personal compass in the shamanic realms. Your imagination and senses are the keys to opening your intuitive doors. In this respect, you can trust your body to serve as a kind of barometer to determine whether your experiences or any teachings you receive are true for you. If you don't feel physically at ease, it's wise to evaluate whether this is a true intuitive knowing or a projection, judgment, or illusion. Oh Shinnah described traversing the shamanic realms as "walking with awareness through the middle distances." Walking the middle distances is a path of true freedom because it is the acknowledgement that you and your energetic intentions can make a difference in your world. It doesn't allow you to "walk stupid."

I still catch myself on many occasions not trusting what I know. We all are human after all and it is not productive to berate ourselves for being less than perfect; however, a crucial part of any shamanic practice is developing sensitivity to, and trust in, our inner knowing. Over the years, all of my indigenous North, South, and Central American mentors taught that learning to walk the middle distances in essence means balancing our luminous being and our shadow self.

Shamanism deals with the world of living energies and includes the concepts of good and evil, or as my teachers referred to these in a less judgmental way, the light and dense energies of our world. Individually, our assessment of light or dense energy should only be directed toward the self. When we exercise our moral judgment toward other people, ideas, or situations, we are usually viewing it from one perspective, our current knowledge, or our unresolved wounds at any given time. As Jung suggests in his book *Memories, Dreams, Reflections,* "We must beware of thinking of good and evil as absolute opposites." Though there are ethical choices for all of us, they arise more clearly when we live without our self-deceptions or self-illusions, and that can only happen when we turn the lens inward. Once we identify and work honestly with the shadow self—our old stuffed wounds and those parts of our being we tend to ignore, deny, or hide from—we can begin to take back personal power. When we do not accept our dense, irresponsible, or fearful parts, they begin to have power over us and create the illusion that we are victims or subject to the whim of others or the world.

Conversely, our shadow self can manifest as a tyrant or bully who tries to manipulate or control others' emotions or take advantage of circumstances. We assume others cannot see our shadow stuff, but in reality our very lives are reflections of it. We project onto others what we won't admit about ourselves. However, once we take the responsibility for our shadow side, we can bring these darker aspects of ourselves into the light. In this way the shadow aspect that is held as our woundedness then has the potential to become our ally. This attentiveness can then lead to a deeper source of personal understanding and a more balanced self, possibly leading to new levels of physical or emotional health and even to heightened levels of awareness or contact with other-dimensional frequencies. The true shaman, in a contemporary sense, is someone who walks the middle distances with integrity, gratitude, accountability, and compassion to attain access to the higher and broader frequencies. We can nurture self-realization by accepting that each turn in life offers us a meaningful learning phase to open to new levels of consciousness. This is a constant test. This is life.

Oh Shinnah used to say shamanism involves "allowing and surrendering." Allowing, she explained, means seeing life from many different perspectives, not jumping to conclusions or judgments. Surrender is giving over to a higher knowing, rather than giving up or giving in to a set of circumstances. Therefore, actively accessing other-dimensional realms to gain clarity or perspective on any given issue is an act of will, but it also requires us to be empty and unattached to an outcome.

Shamanism is about alignment with the universal flow for greater individuation of the Self, and about maintaining your power and consciousness in everyday life so you can work responsibly with the living energies. You are given opportunities to realize your Self through acts of personal will, such as becoming aware of your dreams, trusting your intuition, opening to nature's signs, or listening to the whisperings of your spirit guides. The waking world, the dreamscape, and the world of Spirit are one and the same. The challenge is to not get mesmerized by the illusions and delusions of our everyday reality, for the reality we live is only that which we have chosen to be aware of. Nor should we be ensnared by the tools we choose to use to access the nonordinary realms, lest they become limiting because we give them our power. Energy is a divine and limitless force, and there is never any lack of it. Sensing the world of living energy requires no elaborate rituals or accoutrements. As the late Chippewa teacher Sun Bear once said at a workshop I attended, "If you can't stand stark naked in the middle of the desert without your rattle or feather or drum and do your work, then you are not the power of the work, but merely the owner of a beautiful feather."

Facing the shadow self always means acknowledging fear and, no matter who you are or your role in life, we all have fears. In the world of living energy, we are light beings, which is why in metaphysics the energy body is sometimes called the light body. Our fears create density in our light body that in turn present challenges while working in the realms called the middle distances. Therefore, we must be vigilant when delving into our shadow self and hold ourselves accountable for our actions and reactions. Accountability can literally shift the density harbored in those personal aspects we ignore, refuse, or even only pretend to lay claim to, offering both revelation and rewards. From a shamanic perspective, we cannot truly know ourselves until we stake a claim to venture into those dark recesses of the shadow self. That obviously takes courage because when we look within, we will find we are both light *and* dark—and there is no getting around that for any of us.

Within each of us is the capacity to be both the best and the worst. It is only by choice, moment by moment, day by day, that we live our luminosity. This is what it means to be a spiritual warrior; having the courage to scrutinize ourselves so as to resolve and evolve all parts of our humanness. Holding ourselves accountable is our personal responsibility—it cannot be relegated to another, such as a priest, guru, parent, lover, friend, psychologist, or shaman. This inner alchemy requires us to continually motivate ourselves to get in touch on deeper and deeper levels with Source through the capacities of the luminous "god" within.

The diversified lessons I received from the Native elders I was working with, the special needs children I was teaching, and the clients who would eventually come to me for shamanic counseling provided me with four core perspectives I believe are also central to the work of being human: the work of compassion with self and others; the work of commitment to cultivate and seek one's truth; the work of embracing the magic of life; and the work of being a nonjudgmental mirror for others so they can gain clarity about where they need to heal and grow.

According to a variety of mentors I worked with over the years, Earth is the planet of the heart chakra. We have each chosen our physical body, on this planetary body, to advance our potential—raising our own spirit and therefore the potential of humanity to new octaves of expression. No one person is greater than or less than another; we are each simply in a different stage of self-development. Each of us has the obligation to live the truth encoded within ourselves, tapping those special qualities that make us unique.

One of the pitfalls of traveling the metaphysical path is that the further along you go, the easier it is to become ensnared in ego and the enticements of the mysterious. In retrospect, I realize a big part of my work with Oh Shinnah was learning to own my childish self while also embracing my childlike self. There is a profound difference: the former takes for the self and is resistant to sharing the teachings with others, whereas the latter joyously engages the self and gives of the teachings unconditionally to others. For me, at this point in my growth, a primary challenge in facing my own shadow was in not feeling left out or less than when others were recognized more directly than I was by our teachers. I had to learn that not having the biggest crystal or most beautiful feathers said nothing about my ability to access personal power. Actually, this was a lesson for the entire group, not just for me, and not only with Oh Shinnah, for in any group—metaphysical, spiritual, educational, corporate, or political—the sum of the participants' projections, memories, and degrees of consciousness or unconsciousness determines their actions or direction.

Over the years, I observed most students at one time or another had to leap the twin hurdles of wanting to be the teacher's favorite student and of coveting the teachings for fear someone else might use them to greater advantage. We each had to learn to honor ourselves and to give away the teachings we had been gifted. Sharing them with others so they might be the best they could be was the whole point. That didn't mean we were not discerning or that we didn't have to stay open to taking direction and to honoring other people's perspectives. Still, the deep lesson was to learn to trust our own intuition and to not take someone else's—even our teachers'—word as the *only* truth.

I had by now been mentored for close to four years by Oh Shinnah and had begun to explore other Native and metaphysical teachers. I also explored the East Indian tradition, sitting in *darshan* multiple times with the late Baba Muktananda.* I was inquisitive about the range of teachings—the diverse and possible paths to greater individuation—that various traditions offered. I wanted to hear and experience as many different viewpoints on doing the work of the self as could be made available; not to grow a list of teachings or credentials, but to dig as deep as I could into who I am and why I am here. Although I learned something important about myself from each of them, I kept returning to the constant and bountiful teachings of Nature herself and the sacred path of the Feminine. I realized that it was the female sense of my self that was most wounded and from which I could learn the most. I had started on this path to work through loss, but by now it had become a path to an entirely engaged life. At this point in my studies, my work

---

Darshan comes from the Sanskrit meaning "sight' or "vision." It is an interaction between a guru and devotee with the intention of inducing a higher state of consciousness in the devotee.

was less about releasing grief and more about living as a responsible human being. Part of being a conscientious human being is to honestly look at where your actions or reactions no longer serve the greater good. And, part of being a conscious human being is integrating the Divine Feminine and the Divine Masculine we each hold within into what has been referred to as "the sacred marriage of the self."

Although I had grown through the women's movement of the 1960s and 1970s, through my shamanic work I had become even more aware of how much of my Divine Feminine I had suppressed in order to negotiate this predominately patriarchal culture. The imbalance was not about the lack of fairness in pay disparities for women versus men in comparative jobs, whether women had the capability to lead in the armed services should they so desire, or whether a woman could handle the office of the presidency—those were all no-brainers to me, an obvious yes. My need to explore personal balance was more philosophical in nature, about recognizing and respecting both the anima—the feminine nature of the Self, as defined by psychologist Carl Jung—and the animus—the masculine aspect of the Self. Both need to be valued and worked with by both men and women, as both the masculine principle and feminine principle operate within each of us. Jung defines the potential of our wholeness as our ability to uncover both our shadow and our light—which also includes each of us searching through the distortions those wounds to our masculine or feminine expression have created within us.

Because many Native teachings are based on Earth law and Nature herself, they are rooted in the feminine in the form of the creatrix energy. I had begun my reconnection with the empowerment of the Divine Feminine through these Earth-based teachings and ceremonies, particularly through Moon Ceremony. As noted earlier, this is a series of teachings and a specific evening ceremony honoring the Goddess or Divine Mother energy, and of all the rituals that work with feminine energy, this is the one that most deeply reconnected me to that aspect of myself. Even so, I understood there is no differentiation between male and female energy at the level of Source. There, all is One.

One of the disciplines involved in these teachings is scrying, which facilitates working the middle distances. Scrying uses an object to induce a trance from which you can then access information from the past, present, and future. Although Oh Shinnah taught me and her other accomplices to scry with a variety of crystal spheres, other objects such as the surface of still water, blackened mirrors, or smoke can be used to induce a trance state. Trance states were used by many cultures and religious traditions—from the ancient Greeks to the Egyptian Mystery schools to Native Peoples—as a means to tap into the universal information that lies beneath the surface of our everyday knowing.

Trance scrying is probably best known through the stories of the Oracles of Delphi. Originally the main temple of Delphi was dedicated to Gaea, a primeval female divinity or Mother Earth, although later that same temple became identified with Apollo and the patriarchy. The name *Delphi* literally means "womb." Traces of the temple can still be seen today at the sacred mountain called Mount Parnassus, which the ancient Greeks believed marked the midpoint of the universe. Below the temple are caves and underground passageways through which sulfur springs once flowed. The springs were thought to be guarded by Gaea's daughter, the great serpent goddess Python, and were hallowed sites where people came for the counsel and prophecy dispensed by female oracles, the Pythia. They accessed the middle distances between the human and the divine by going into deep trance states through specific preparations and breathing the sulfurous fumes that rose from the springs. During a consultation, a Pythia would sit upon a special three-legged stool called a tripod from which she gazed on the *omphalos,* the scrying stone that marked the center point, navel, or hub of Earth at this site.*

Another society based on ancient esoteric teachings that utilized

---

Omphalos is a Greek word meaning "navel." Omphalos stones, like the one at Delphi, were considered holy objects that facilitated direct communication with the gods.

scrying to access information is the Sisters of the Violet Flame, and it was into this sisterhood that Oh Shinnah initiated me and others as priestesses. The sisterhood is not a religion, but a spiritual path dedicated to the Great Mother of All Things, the primary creatrix energy. Through this evening ceremony we actively bring forth and acknowledge the Goddess, the feminine aspect of the godhead, and her complementary energy in all things. There are many other groups of sisterhoods around the globe dedicated to utilizing the connection with the Divine Feminine energies in prayer and sacred circles with the intent to help and to heal.

In her teachings, Oh Shinnah shared that the Sisters of the Violet Flame originated in Atlantis and their oral tradition was carried to Egypt with the help of Thoth. Thoth is a central deity of the Egyptian pantheon often associated with writing, magic, and the heart. The ancient Egyptian Mystery schools associated the heart with the seat of the mind. Thoth was also the Keeper of the Emerald Tablets,* which held the secrets to raising one's frequencies to ascend consciously in the physical body. These tablets are seen as time capsules of wisdom that preserve profound spiritual knowledge about achieving personal transformation and even accelerating the evolution of humanity. The Emerald Tablets were part of the course of study we were introduced to as Sisters of the Violet Flame.

Sisters can perform the moon rites for women who have not been initiated into the sisterhood. As part of this ceremony, women gather to do the basic work of owning and releasing their personal wounds, fears, and negativities, and to collectively pray to alleviate some of the chaos and pain that plague humanity. Mother Earth does not want our physical garbage, as it is our responsibility to keep the environment clean. However, she does welcome our emotional garbage and is able to trans-

---

*The Emerald Tablets, purported to have been brought by Thoth from Atlantis to Egypt, have been studied in esoteric and alchemical circles since early Greek and Egyptian times. The twelve engraved emerald-green tablets are said to have been created through alchemical transmutation and are thought to be indestructible.

mute our dense energy into more refined energy that can enlighten and enliven us. My indigenous teachers taught that being proper stewards is an important act of reciprocity. Mother Earth gives us everything we need to live, and in return we honor those gifts by striving to live as conscious and responsible stewards, using those gifts without destruction, greed, or neglect.

Scrying is both a tool of prophecy and a means to gather information for personal transformation. In this ceremony Oh Shinnah had shared that the priestess scrys using a large clear quartz crystal sphere that is cradled in a shallow depression in the earth, like the Delphic omphalos stone, symbolically representing the navel of Mother Earth. Oh Shinnah explained that a sphere, as opposed to any other shape of crystal, is the best source through which to scry because it reflects energy instead of directing it. When scrying, the intention is to release thoughts in order to better receive the potent information which lies beneath the mind's chatter. Scrying is considered a practice of "non-doing." She called this "stopping the worlds."

One night, while leading the evening moon ritual, my attention was transfixed by the crystal sphere, its inclusions catching the red and gold light from the fire. One by one, the women approached the fire, speaking aloud their desires, hurts, fears, and challenges and releasing them energetically with a prayer into a pinch of sacred tobacco, feeding it into the flames. Tobacco, as an herb used in this ceremony, represents the male energy within each of us, as cornmeal represents the feminine. As the ceremonial leader, my responsibility was to use my energy body, not my physical body, to collect their dense energetic projections and fears; gathering them into an energetic bundle I would later offer to the Great Mother for transmutation through the flames of the sacred fire. The concerns and hopes these women voiced were not theirs alone, but common to humanity, and as such, the release benefited not only them but all of us. It was my task to remain detached from any individual woman or from getting entangled in my expectations for what answer each might receive. It was not mine to know how the Great Mother might respond to their requests or how the energetic transmutation might manifest in their lives.

As I gazed into the sphere during this particular ceremony, my awareness was catapulted out of my body, into the night sky, into the stars, and I felt an explosive unification with the cosmos that was at once both comprehensible and incomprehensible. From somewhere far outside of myself and yet deep within me, I heard a woman's voice, unknown yet somehow familiar, speak. "From this night forward you have a new name. When you dedicate yourself and call your name in the service of this ceremony, you are—."

Almost like jerking awake from a dream, I was abruptly back in my body, aware I had heard the name I had been gifted, but unable to recall it. I found myself back verbally leading the ceremonial prayers, as each woman was calling out her name in dedication to this path. We soon finished the ceremony and I experienced no further luminal moments. However, it is not uncommon to have prophetic dreams after this ceremony.

I am standing under the night sky, alone on a hill at the edge of the sea. A warm wind is blowing fiercely, whipping my ebony hair around my face. I have been on this hill before. It is a place I come to pray, give thanks, and ask the gods to help my people, the Etruscans. I am lucid in the dream and aware I have heard that word before, although I consciously know nothing of the Etruscan people. I am in an ancient time; my skin is dark, and my clothing of simple design but fine quality. I know the rocky outcrop on which I stand is sacred ground.

The scene abruptly shifts, and I sense two barely perceptible glowing forms, one on each side of me. They and I morph into individual flames, each of us emitting and sustaining a different tone. The sounds reconnect me to the feeling of cosmic knowing. I understand that the use of sound to raise the vibration of human consciousness is ancient and that sound as a vehicle of cosmic acceleration will persist until the end of times.

I turn to the flame on my left, and a faint image of Callie shimmers through. In my mind I ask her, "Who are you?"

"The Crystal Heart."

I turn to the flame on my right. I make out a face, but I can't bring it into focus. "Who are you?" I again ask in my mind.

"Striver Toward a Goal." I struggle to hear, as the words are less than a whisper.

"Who are you?" the flames ask me in unison.

I reply with total conviction. "Starwalker Woman."

I startled to wakefulness—*this* was the name I had received while out of body during the evening ceremony. The name resonated deep in the fabric of my being and I felt an instant connection to it. I couldn't know back then that Starwalker Woman was to be more than a ceremonial name, as I also couldn't know other aspects of this dream were prophetic. As I continued to walk through the teachings offered within the middle distances, I eventually came to see how the information in this dream would bridge both my past and my future, and how intimately connected everything eventually becomes.

4

Reflections in the Mirror

The Native shamanic perspectives and teachers I was exposed to spoke to me in ways other instruction and teachings never had. For me, they were far richer and honoring of life in general, and encouraging of individuals to start where they found themselves. With the different Native teachers, came their nation's oral traditions of prophecy. Many of the prophecies foretold of a time when people of all colors and creeds would reawaken through traditional beliefs and become better caretakers of the Earth Mother. It didn't take long before I realized these traditions shared several core teachings: three of the most fundamental are that everything is energy, we are responsible for our own destiny, and there is an underlying pervasive Intelligence that informs the cosmos.

I was particularly curious about the South and Central American traditions. Some of them have a prophecy that one day the Eagle will fly with the Condor, the Eagle being the representation of the North America peoples and the Condor representing the South American peoples. I also was intensely interested in ancient sites and civilizations, so much so that I had considered studying to become an archeologist in college. I had caved to the advice of my high school guidance counselor when he suggested women are better off becoming mothers, nurses, or teachers. This patronizing statement feels absurd for me to voice now and it should not have held any validity for me then, and yet I had followed along and studied the psychology of teaching special needs children instead.

In retrospect, I have no regrets in becoming a teacher, and I have since learned that eventually we get to where we want and need to go when we are fueled by our passions. And, those detours we think we have been forced to take, or have decided we needed to take, are often important, as they provide us with the skills and insights that we might never have thought would be required of us. In that sense, being a special needs educator enhanced my mothering skills with Callie. However, as I studied now with these various wisdomkeepers, I was learning the anthropology and archeology of these ancient cultures firsthand, in their voice and not from a textbook. My archeological "digs" were presenting themselves.

In the mid-eighties I signed up for a weekend workshop offered by Tlakaelel, a Toltec elder. Tlakaelel was presenting with Dr. Luis Perez, who had a conventional and alternative healing practice in Mexico that involved the use of crystals and herbs. Tlakaelel was a short, solidly built man with a salt-and-pepper beard and longish black hair. His size was expanded by the amount of energy he exuded. As the class began, he explained that *Tlakaelel* is a title meaning "Counselor to the Council." I was to also learn during work I later did with him that he was the only man in his community to carry this name, which was a great honor. He worked in what he called a *Kalpulli,* a spiritual group dedicated to preserving the Toltec traditions, and the Mexican government had given the group official recognition as a Native religious tradition, something that had taken his people more than five hundred years to accomplish. He was here in the United States to share the tradition and form additional *Kalpullis.*

He told the story of his people, the Toltec Chimimeka. Their history was preserved and recounted through oral tradition from as far back as twelve thousand years—the time of Atlantis. The People, as almost all Native lineages I have worked with call themselves, had been scattered by the catastrophes that had destroyed the island nation of Atlantis. It was a mission of Tlakaelel's forebears to reunify these scattered remnants.

I was no stranger to the myths of Atlantis, as almost all the indigenous teachers with whom I was working believed there had once been a continent called Atlantis, which existed around 10,000 BCE. It was purported to be populated by a civilization that had highly advanced scientific, spiritual, and esoteric knowledge, and although principled in the beginning of their civilization's development, they had become increasingly greedy and materialistic. Legend has it that through experiments gone awry, the misuse of the power of crystals, and the abuse of nature and cosmic energies—such as the manipulation of antigravity and antimatter and the aberrant use of cloning—they had destroyed themselves. The stories tell of how the ring of islands making up this great nation sunk into the sea through a series of cataclysms. There are different theories of where Atlantis was located, although most designate the Atlantic Ocean as the general location (hence this civilization's name). Many indigenous peoples—including the Egyptian, Hopi, Maya, and Andean—believe they are descendants of the remnants who had escaped the great flood that occurred when the earth's axis shifted, leading to the final destruction of the Atlantean civilization.

In the cultural legend of Tlakaelel's people, the survivors fled to the Mountain of the Serpent, located at the central Mexican sacred site of Tenochtitlan.* There they flourished into a culture of extraordinary agriculture, art, and science. About two thousand years ago they sent emissaries out in expeditions to the four directions, in what he called the Four Arrows Migration, to both collect and share knowledge. Under the influence of these emissaries, two great confederations flourished: the Confederation of the Condor, which spanned from present-day Nicaragua south, and the Confederation of the Red

---

*A great metropolis, Tenochtitlan, was razed by the Spanish conquistadors and was rebuilt as Mexico City.

Eagle, comprised of the peoples from north of Nicaragua into what is today the southwestern United States. These confederations were decimated by the European invasions of the 1500s. Once Tlakaelel finished summarizing his people's history, his talk included all of us, explaining no matter who we are or what our ancestry, we are all children of *Teotl*, the Creator. He counseled that if for no other reason than this, we all owe each other mutual respect.

Tlakaelel next described some of the complexities of his peoples' calendars, which similar to the Mayan calendar utilize a 260-day ritual cycle and a 365-day solar year rotation. They are constructed around vast astronomical alignments and mathematical time counts, or cycles. One of the simpler counts is a 52-year cycle that is further divided into four 13-year segments, and at the eleven-and-a-half-year point of each segment there is what he labeled a Jupiter effect, which is when Jupiter, Mars, and Earth align and there is increased solar activity. As a consequence, the sun "grows" and Earth receives a super concentration of energy from solar flares, which intensifies the charge at Earth's magnetic poles, can be detrimental to our physical bodies, and increases the occurrence of natural disasters. This effect lasts for one and a half years, and then the 13-year cycle repeats. The ancestors would perform the New Fire ceremony for five days to mark the ending of a 52-year cycle, to cleanse the dense energies built up during this phase, and to offer revelations for the next generation. If the priests, on the last day of the New Fire ceremony, saw the appearance of the constellation of the Pleiades,* this would herald that the world would continue for another 52-year cycle. As a consequence all the fires in the Valley of Mexico would be relit from this new central ceremonial fire, both in people's homes and in the temples. Tlakaelel pointed out that once we understand that as energy beings we are part

---

*The Pleiades-sun zenith has been considered an important sign since ancient times, signifying the movement of the cosmos and the continuation of growth and renewal. In the cultural traditions of the Maya, Toltec, Aztec, Hopi, Chinese, and Maori, to name a few, the Pleiades constellation is significant in the origin stories of mankind.

of, and not separate from, these cosmic cycles, we could become participants, and not just recipients, in this energetic exchange and in the larger universal flow.

As a consequence of these cycles, he explained, we would see increased climate change and the North Pole would expand southward, while the Sahara desert would expand northward. As the ice cap at the South Pole melted, there would be severe flooding starting along the coasts of land masses such as Australia. Solar flares would intensify, overcharging the Earth's magnetic fields. As a result of all of these changes and others, the agriculture zones and migration patterns of birds and sea mammals would shift worldwide.

Like the Maya, the Toltec believed the universe had been created five times and destroyed four times; each of these five eras was what he called a *Sun*. He said humanity had come through four Suns, and was currently in the Fifth Sun. Each Sun lasted for approximately 6,600 years and was part of a larger astronomical cycle of 26,000 plus years, known as the procession of the equinoxes. All these cycles influenced human evolution in one way or another. In 1947, they began to pass their knowledge on to nonindigenous peoples to help them remember their origins as members of the universal whole and participants in its unfolding. Because we each vibrate at a unique wavelength, and all of our energies are needed for the universe to fully express itself, we needed to begin to see ourselves as co-creators with Universal Intelligence.

Although our individual souls are immortal, as a species we can go extinct. Tlakaelel said that it would be crucial to our survival as a species to correct any personal imbalances and become more conscious of ourselves as energy beings and co-creators over the coming years. By doing so, we could be better stewards of the Earth and learn, as a global community, to accept our differences and take our place within the cosmic brotherhood.

Having just shared the mission and prophecies of his forebears, Tlakaelel asked us, "What is your mission at this time?" After a group discussion, he shared that for him our mission as human beings is to seek excellence through self-development. "Each one of us," he explained, "is a link in the great chain of past, present, and future. Our ability to perfect ourselves as humans will come when man is capable of creating what he conceives from his heart, not from his mind." He elaborated that we are all intrinsically connected to each other and to everything around us. He said that energetically we each carry in our genes the memories of all the generations before us, as well as all of their experiences. Our children will carry forward in their genes the impact of our experiences, which is why our self-development and self-awareness are so crucial.

Tlakaelel said he would lead us through several exercises in self-development and self-awareness, but first we needed to center ourselves. He lit copal, a Central American resin burned much like the sage of Native northern traditions to purify the environment. Next he taught us a centering exercise using the breath, which would be a bridge connecting heart and head, or uniting the heart chakra to the pineal gland, crown chakra. He explained that when doing work with Spirit, there is no division between the material and spiritual worlds. Spirit is imbued in everything, and without Spirit matter could not exist. He then directed us into a posture for a "sun bath," a form of energetic communication in which we would intend to bring the sun's energy down through our bodies to make contact with the energy of Mother Earth and then send it back up to the sun. Because the sun is a star, he explained, this in effect is a communication between our physical template with the Earth and stars, as well as an energetic exchange that is beneficial to the health of our organs. Tlakaelel said each of us is a sun, seeking the Great Central Sun, and the sun of our world is here to remind us of the sun of our inner divine spirit.

He asked us to imagine ourselves as part of the cosmos, to merge our physical energy with the rays of the sun, and to visualize the sun's energy as a ball of light. In focusing our awareness of that light energy down to the earth through our bodies we could begin to awaken the radiance that is encoded in our human form. All energy, he said, comes from space, and all ancient earth-based cultures worshipped the sun, not as a god but as a fount of living energy. Every being absorbs the energy of the sun and stars. Even the movement of the galaxies imparts energy to us. We are a part of the cosmos, and we can tap this power to change ourselves at a cellular level for personal health and spiritual development. Because the universal energies are always in movement, are always changing, so too can we change, shift, and transform our perceptions. Once we do then we can become aware of the essential truth of our existence—that we are the fabric of the universe.

We assumed the sun bath posture—our arms raised, our knees slightly bent, and our faces turned up to the sun—and performed the exercise. I was struck by how I could feel much more than just the warmth of the sun, and how it was becoming easier to feel the energetic shifts when I focused my inner attention to connect to those things beyond myself.

After leading us in additional exercises for heightening awareness, Tlakaelel answered questions and then introduced Dr. Luis Perez, who explained how he used quartz crystals in his healing practice. Quartz has energetic healing properties only partially recognized by conventional science, and the esoteric information Dr. Perez imparted about crystals was similar to what I had already learned from Oh Shinnah. Both taught that quartz crystals have vibrations that can transform an imbalanced energy field. As conductors of energy, they transport negative vibrations from the body while also channeling positive vibrations to the appropriate chakra, subtle-body energy center, or organ system. Dr. Perez said that in his opinion quartz crystals do not have magical properties that give you power; instead they help you focus your own natural energies and innate healing capacities with those of the client. The difference between the approach of Dr. Perez and Oh Shinnah is that he used nothing but clear quartz crystals in his healings, whereas Oh Shinnah used many kinds of crystals as well as gemstones. In addition, in his naturopathic practice he combined the use of crystals with herbs that he had carefully correlated to specific diseases. He also burned copal resin in order to see the "spirit" of the ailments of his patients.

When he had completed his explanation, Dr. Perez informed us we would work individually with him with a crystal of our own choosing. When we finished with him, we would work with Tlakaelel in personal mirror work, so each of us was cycling between the two teachers and would have a chance to work with each of them one-on-one.

We had been requested to bring a quartz crystal to the workshop, and I had brought two with me. I couldn't decide which I wanted to use. At that time, I had a real issue with either-or decision making. What if I made the wrong choice? What if I missed a truly amazing experience because I had chosen one crystal rather than the other? It was with a measure of uncertainty that I finally made my choice.

Next, I needed to decide what I wanted to ask Dr. Perez. He had requested we meditate on one serious question to bring to him. After much thought, I settled on a question about which additional non-traditional healing techniques I should learn to best supplement my current rather traditional body-centered counseling practice.

When it was my turn, Dr. Perez greeted me with a warm smile. He reached out his hand for my crystal. I placed it in his open palm, still unsure if I had made the right choice. It was a six-sided, single-terminated, clear quartz point, not quite four inches long. He held it up to the light, studying it. His gaze alternated between the crystal and me, but he said nothing, remaining silent for several long moments. Finally, placing the crystal on the table between us, he asked, "Do you know what kind of crystal this is?" I was unsure of what he meant, but I surmised he was asking if I knew what its purpose was. I answered, "I haven't worked with it yet, because I don't know what its particular use is." He nodded, seemingly pleased with my answer. He held the crystal up to the light again and pointed out a defined diamond shape that extended over two of the sides. I smiled, feeling excited he was pointing out the exact feature which had originally enticed me to purchase it.

"A large diamond window is somewhat uncommon," he said. "The diamond represents the balance between the spiritual and physical realms. A single quartz crystal with a natural diamond window has a specific purpose—it focuses the life-force energy to reveal the Self. The diamond window symbolizes a portal through which one can see beyond illusionary identities and insecurities. This kind of crystal is a powerful teacher. Only after you have cleansed yourself can you use this type of healing crystal to determine dis-ease or energetic mis-alignments in working with others."

He turned his attention from the crystal to me, scanning me in a way I took to be an assessment of my energy body. Finally he spoke. "Your logic and intellect are strong, but they often inhibit the flow of your natural sensitivities and intuition." Then he bluntly declared, "You argue a lot with yourself!" I chuckled inwardly at his accuracy, thinking back to my struggle around just choosing this crystal. He handed the crystal back to me as he explained that intuition comes from the heart, not the head, although they need to be aligned. He offered the opinion that I was still in the process of healing my heart. I felt he "saw" me, although he gave no indication he knew anything about my life and the death of my daughter. Then he went on to intuitively address the question I had intended to bring him but still had not voiced. "Eventually you will use this and other crystals and common stones in healing work with others. Healing is part of your calling, specifically nontraditional healing."

He told me that if I wanted, he would "awaken" the crystal and align it with my healing energies, but once he did, I would be responsible for this particular crystal for the rest of my life. I could never be frivolous with it, I could never let anyone else touch it, and I could use it only for serious healing. I understood the import of his words, yet it took me only a few seconds to agree to the conditions. He placed the crystal in my left palm and then encircled my hand and the crystal with both of his hands. His eyes met mine and the intensity of his gaze was uncomfortable, almost embarrassing in its directness. Suddenly, I felt warmth emanating from the crystal. It spread rapidly up my arm, until it felt as if the blood was on a slow boil between my palm and my elbow. Although it wasn't painful, the intensity of the heat startled me. Simultaneously, I perceived a rod of brilliant white light thrust upwards from my heart to my head. I wondered if Dr. Perez knew what I was experiencing, but he simply held my gaze and said nothing. Within a few seconds, the sensations dissipated, and he released my hand. Smiling, he said there was nothing further to discuss and with that the session was over.

I returned to the group, only to be called immediately to do the mirror work with Tlakaelel. With no time to transition between the two sessions, I joined him out in the hall where he was sitting with a meditative calm. He appeared to be in a state that I can only describe as having the self-awareness of totally knowing himself. He seemed to be perfectly engaged with both himself and everything around him in equal degrees. I wondered if I would ever be able to achieve that level of personal alignment.

Tlakaelel extended his hand, motioning for me to sit in the chair opposite him. Cradled in his lap was an obsidian bowl, as large as a dinner plate and gracefully concave. It was highly polished, black with flecks of green and gold. It was as smooth as the glassy surface of a calm pond and as reflective as a mirror. I knew it was a scrying mirror, as obsidian is used for that in his tradition. With few words and in a hushed tone, he told me to gaze into the bowl and let the outer world go, to soften my gaze and allow images to arise. I knew exactly what he was asking of me, because I had done similar scrying techniques with Oh Shinnah using spheres. I took a few deep, centering breaths and then leaned over the mirror. I looked beyond the reflection of my face, deep into the inky blackness of the obsidian. Within moments, I heard a buzzing sound, like a swarm of bees, inside my head. I felt dizzy.

I am running, running for my life. The thick jungle vines ensnare me, scratching my legs and tearing at my hair. My chest muscles strain from running so desperately. I have to get to the well. It is my only hope of survival. I can feel hot breath behind me as the distance shortens between me and the dark black fur that can claim me at any second.

As fast as I had fallen into the vision, I was pulled out of it. I returned to this reality, disoriented, breathing heavily, my heart still pounding. Tlakaelel was holding me by the scruff of my neck. He started rubbing my sternum, and soon I began to breathe easier. "What was that?" I stammered. He only smiled. It was the first time I had seen him smile, and it was a solemn smile. He finally spoke, and his words revealed he knew what I had experienced although I had not told him. "You have been claimed. I hadn't anticipated this."

"What does that mean?" I asked, still shaken.

He said simply, "You will be working with the indigenous people of the South, at some point, when the time is right." He offered the opinion that I'd had a few past lives in Central and South America and those parts of my being that remembered would begin to inform me as they awakened. He told me he could see the jaguar was my tonal,* a spiritual link between a person and, in this case, an animal. His tonal, he confided, was the tiger. He told me to embody the jaguar, act out its movements, and see through its eyes. He said he saw I was born with a warrior's heart, and the warrior's path could be hard and lonely sometimes, especially for a woman. He counseled that I

---

*The tonal is the structured energy of the waking state that takes on form and can be perceived when you learn to negotiate the *nagual,* or sleeping state. The nagual is the world of unstructured energy, not bound by time and space, from which the tonal arises. The nagual, also called the *nuhual,* assists us to develop the energies of both the physical and subtle realms. When you cleanse and strengthen your energy body, and raise your frequencies, you can use the tonal as a bridge to the nagual for clear perception in this, and other dimensions.

might find myself in struggles with men, especially life partners. They might misinterpret my strengths as a challenge to their manhood. He said, "Your path will bring you to a threshold that once crossed will lead you to a place of balance and strength where you can allow others to feel strong without the need to diminish or deny your own gifts. Others will not see you as you would like until *you* accept the strength of all you are."

He went on to say I had a propensity for making myself small so others wouldn't feel threatened. Once I saw that making myself small was in fact my own self-judgment and something I did to the detriment of living my personal power, then I could accept without discomfort that I had all of the tools needed to be a balanced warrioress. The battle, he counseled, was not with others, it was solely within me. He explained he did not wish to say more, as he would not be the teacher who would help me awaken to this knowing. However, if I had specific questions about my tonal, he would come through the dreamtime to answer them. He instructed me to leave a glass of water next to my bed at night, for in his tradition the glass of water would serve as a channel through the ethers by which he could access my dreambody and impart information. In the morning, if I tapped the glass I would be able to recall the information of the dream. With that guidance, the session was over. As I got up to leave, I looked back to thank him, as he had given me much to think about. He smiled in a way that made me think he might be about to reveal a secret, but all he did was to turn the obsidian mirror over. There, on its underside, was carved the face of a jaguar.

Because I was so interested in Central and South American traditions and their sacred sites, when Ben and I decided to take a long overdue vacation a few months later, we went to Cancun, on the Yucatan peninsula. I had always wanted to visit the Mayan ruins and Cancun would put us close to Tulum, Coba, and Chitzen Itza. Back then, Coba had yet to be excavated in any substantive way. Many of the stone temples and stelae—the tall, stone markers that inscribe stories in bas relief—were still hidden under the dense jungle growth that had reclaimed the site. Chitzen Itza, a well-excavated site even then, had the reputation of being a powerful, mysterious, and magical ruin. The grand step pyramid El Castillo, the stellar observatory El Caracol, and the great Ball Court, where it was purported the game was played to the death, are magnificent examples of Mayan science, architecture, and culture. Tulum, located in what today is referred to as the Mayan Riviera, is quite small in comparison to those other sites and sits on the edge of the sea. At the time I visited, Tulum was not as popular an attraction as Chitzen Itza was, but I had a longing to see it.

In the mid-1980s, the Yucatan was not yet the overbuilt tourist destination it has become. But even back then there were already entrance fees, souvenir hawkers, and tour buses at the more well-known sites like Chitzen Itza, but not at Tulum. Tulum is strategically built on a cliff above the sea, receiving the first light of day from the rising sun, and served as a port and redistribution center for other sites within the Yucatan. At that time you could drive right up to the grounds, and when we arrived there at dawn the site was nearly deserted. The sun was starting to burn off the morning mist, providing a view to the bluff at the far side of the site, where El Castillo, the structure that served as a lookout and ceremonial temple erected to Chac, the Mayan rain god, was located. I could see the Chac Mool, a stone statue atop the stairway, where the figure Chac sat reclined with his head tilted to one side, knees raised, and where a large, flat altar stone serving as a tray, allegedly used for sacrifices, rested across his stomach.

I had forgotten my camera back in the car and Ben had graciously gone back to retrieve it. As I walked into the ruin, I could see the low stone wall, broken at points, but which the guide book said had at one time surrounded the entire site except for the sea-facing side. At each of two corners along the extension wall were small stone enclosures that had once served as sentry and offering posts. Stone temples and rock outcroppings studded the area, and I could faintly smell the sea air and partially glimpse the turquoise ocean just beyond. As I ventured still farther into the ruin, I noticed barely perceptible furrows that ran here and there like pathways through the grass. I crossed one of the slight depressions, heading toward a temple that had caught my eye because of the red handprints on its upper stone concourse. As I approached it, the scent of copal wafted toward me. Suddenly, the inside of my head was filled with a buzzing and I felt a dizziness that was more severe than what I had experienced while scrying in the obsidian mirror. I felt like vomiting as the vertigo intensified, pulling me down into darkness.

All around me dance men, women, and children, some wearing next to nothing or simple white garments, others clothed in tunics richly colored and elaborately decorated. These more regal celebrants wear headdresses of macaw feathers, and their ears, noses, and arms are adorned with gold and jade. They are chanting in celebration of the birth of their new god-king. The temples are arrayed with flowers, and the air is pungent with the smell of food cooking for the coming feast. One of the dancers reaches his hand toward me, and as I go to take it I am jerked back through time and space.

I found myself on my knees, trembling and inexplicably my cheeks were wet with tears. A slight, elderly man had hold of my arm. His soft brown eyes and weathered face were comforting. He whispered in my ear, "You must move now. You are in a burial area. If you come with me, you will feel better." He helped me to my feet. As I arose, I began to regain my sensibilities, and realized how diminutive he was, barely coming to my shoulders. He led me over to the temple with the red handprints that I had been heading towards. I knew the name to be the Temple of the Frescos from what I had been reading. Within the temple were murals depicting Mayan gods and fertility rites; he explained to me that in this temple one was given instruction on birth, death, and rebirth.

We walked on to the Temple of the Descending God, where I could see the carving of the god descending head first, as if being birthed, and looking somewhat like a bee. (Bees were significant to the Maya because of the importance of honey.) Deep within, barely visible, were what appeared to be small offerings. The scent of freshly lit copal wafted out of the small temple toward me. Even in the confusion of my current state, I found that mysterious because there were bars on the temple entrance blocking access. We stood there together silently. After a few minutes he said, "You are very sensitive to the energies here. You have crossed the dimensions of this place. You must be careful and prepare yourself when walking into sacred sites, here and at other places, in other countries, where you will eventually go." He pointed to the temple as he continued explaining. "This is where the chosen one came to give birth to the next god-king. There would be a great celebration of his birth, and that's what you were witnessing." I simply nodded. Like Tlakaelel, he somehow had witnessed my vision although I had not related it to him.

This unassuming elder went on to say ceremonies still took place here, hence the copal, which was "burned as an essence to transport us to work with, and gain access to, our ancestors." He predicted I would come back to the "southern lands" often, learning the traditions of some of these cultures in which I had experienced past lives. As I saw Ben approaching us from across the grass with my camera, the elder gently touched my arm and turned to leave, uttering words that sounded like "*lac ish.*" When I asked what the word meant, I thought he replied, "I am you." (Later I learned this Mayan phrase, *I Lak' ech,* usually translates as "I am another yourself.") My experience and our discussion had all happened so quickly, although while with him it had felt like time did not exist. After he had left, I was startled by the realization that he had not been speaking English and yet I had known everything he said to me as if he were speaking in my native tongue. This was the first time I spontaneously understood the Mayan language, a language I do not know, nor understand. Surprisingly, it would not be the last time and years later I would find myself translating Mayan for a group I brought to "the southern lands."

5

Gifts of Remembrance

My work with Oh Shinnah was slowly coming to an end. I had found a place to lay my grief and new worlds had been opened to me. At this point in my life, on a personal front the pressing question was whether I could become a mother again. Over the past few years, I had tried. Although I felt certain that having another child was my true path, I never wanted it to be predicated on the longing for the child I had lost. However, I discovered becoming pregnant again might not be possible for me, as I had suffered several miscarriages and had survived the excruciating rupture of an ectopic pregnancy.

Knowing my concern, Oh Shinnah shared a personal teaching with me—a conception and birthing ceremony, one she counseled I should not undertake lightly. She cautioned me to "sit and pray on it," which meant being clear about my intention: was my desire to be a mother again a want or a need? I spent almost four months sitting and praying on my desire, until I came to the certainty that for me another child was a want. The need was realizing I must surrender to Source: not my will, but Thy will.

I understood that just because I faithfully carried out the preparations and the ceremony, the result would not be guaranteed. Great Mystery was in charge, and I had to detach from the outcome. If I were to become pregnant, I wanted to participate fully in what Oh Shinnah was offering, which meant I would be making a choice not only to fulfill the conception and birth ceremonies, but also to undertake an additional four ceremonies that would be carried out once the baby was born and during the first seven years of its life.

I was blessed in the conception ceremony, although I did not know it at the time. Close to four months after I had completed it, Ben and I traveled to see friends who had recently moved to California. During our stay, I did not feel well. I was continually dizzy and nauseated. My girlfriend, Renny, insisted I see her doctor. The only problem was she was relatively new to the area and only had a gynecologist, not an internist, although she insisted any doctor would benefit me in the state I was in. So off we went.

Once at the doctor's office, the nurse took my history, which was substantial given all I had been through in the last few years. When it came time to see the doctor, he wanted to do a pelvic exam. I fumed, thinking, "Isn't this just like Los Angeles! Why the hell does he need to go there?"

Staring at him between my legs, I was stupefied to see his eyes well up, and I thought to myself, *Shit! Now what? I don't even know this guy and he's reacting.* He looked up and said in a gentle, polite voice, "Sandy, you are at least three and a half months pregnant." I was thoroughly confused, as I had been having my menses for the past three months. "How can that be?" I asked incredulously. He said, "Sometimes the body protects what it doesn't want the mind to worry about." Now I welled up both out of my joy of finally being pregnant and this man's very human and sage comment.

When I discreetly shared the news back in the reception area with Renny, she was overjoyed. Her young daughter, Lynn, who was with us, and who delighted me then and still delights me today as a grown woman, announced loudly and unceremoniously to everyone in the office that I had a baby in me. She repeated the news to everyone we came across, in the elevator, at the door leading out of the building, and straight out into the parking lot. Although no one she told knew me, their smiles warmed me, deepening my gratitude at this long-awaited moment.

As my pregnancy progressed, I talked, read, and prayed daily to this little one. Others urged me to have tests done for genetic abnormalities, but I chose not to. Although I understood they had loved Callie and their advice was out of their concern for me now, I did not share their fears or worries. I also did not have tests to determine the baby's gender, although I thought it must be a boy because I was carrying so differently from my first pregnancy. We already had decided on a boy's name. As for a girl's name, Nyssa floated in and out of my mind, although I had no idea where this name came from as I had never heard it before.

I focused on paying attention to my body and staying healthy. I ate what my body craved: blueberries in cream in the morning, peanut butter and tomatoes on English muffins in the afternoon, and lamb chops or salmon with greens in the evening. This screwy dietary pattern never waivered and persisted for months. I also began swimming almost daily to support and exercise my swelling body. One day, while swimming laps in the backyard pool, I noticed there were tiny blue orbs drifting in the air outside the fence that surrounded the pool area. They were translucent, a diffused cerulean blue, varying in size from a billiard ball to a softball. I could easily see they were not reflections off the water. Oddly, I felt as if they were watching me, but they dissipated into thin air before I could figure out what they were.

About six weeks later, the orbs materialized again as I was leaning back into the side of the pool, basking in the sun and feeling blessed with my pregnancy. This time there were white orbs as well as blue ones, and there were many more of them than the first time. Some hovered around the water's edge, while others floated in the garden area outside the fence and up in the trees. I wasn't scared or even startled, although I was surprised by how many there were. I actually felt joyful, like I had when I was a child blowing bubbles and watching them float on the wind.

My comfort level may have been because of my years of working with the elements of nature—earth, air, fire, and water. I intuited the orbs may be some form of nature spirit. While working with Oh Shinnah and as part of my one year of work with the earth element, I and others had completed an herbal certification program with herbalist Rosemary Gladstar. In my work with the earth element and in the herbal world, I had many times experienced a vibratory connection with the devic kingdom (the etheric realm in which nature spirits exist) and sensed their presence, but I had never actually seen them take physical form.

The late Dora Kuntz (who was also known early in her career by her maiden name, Dora van Gelder) was a master teacher of the elemental kingdoms and spoke widely on the fairy world. She taught, as did many of my Native teachers, that the transcendental world is as real as the physical world but the mechanized nature of our society separates most of us from nature and prevents us from perceiving nature's octaves of vibrations. However, we can train our senses to see beyond our phenomenological reality to the noumenal dimensions of fairies, angels, and other beings. Dora described how the elements of earth, fire, water, and air are associated with various beings: earth with gnomes, elves, and fairies; fire with salamanders; water with undines; and air with sylphs. Each devic group holds the consciousness of the element in which they live.

I decided to put my training to work in the immediate and see if I could connect with these orbs. Since I was already in water, I chose to attempt contact with the orbs through the water spirits—the undines. I expected only an energetic connection and nothing more. But the breeze suddenly stopped, although the leaves on the trees continued to flutter. The air felt thick, not with heat, humidity, or any atmospheric-related sensation, but with what I can only describe as presence. The world around me got very quiet. Without warning and with no apparent source, hundreds of golden, iridescent light beams rushed across the surface of the water toward me. Fear gripped me as I shouted, "Stop!"

The shimmering beams halted at my command about a foot from my expanded belly, and I would swear I heard them *and* my baby laugh. I was astonished, but I didn't have long to observe them for as fast as these light rays had come, they vanished, as did the orbs.

After this surprising episode, I was reminded yet again that there are realms of existence that defy scientific explanation.* Questions flitted through my mind. A healthy skepticism is certainly valuable, but wouldn't dismissing everything that does not have a logical explanation preclude us from ever discovering anything new? Does giving in too quickly to fear limit the greatness of who we really are and what we may be capable of experiencing? How can we evolve if we are not willing to question our certainties? Wasn't it only a mere five hundred years ago that most Europeans believed the world was flat? And more recently, until the advance of stem cell research, that it was impossible to regenerate body tissue? Although I was uncertain of what the orbs were and of their meaning, I was confident my baby would one day have its own relationship with the water fairies and the realms beyond. A few years later, I would be proven correct, when it became apparent that on this day my child and the elementals had not only met, but they had in fact become fast friends.

As delivery day neared, I was clear I did not want to give birth in

---

*As I write this book, the orb phenomenon has become a metaphysical study in its own right. With the advent of digital cameras, they are particularly easy to document visually. The orb phenomenon is to the atmosphere what the crop circle phenomenon is to the land. Open-minded theologians, physicists, and researchers—such as Miceal Ledwith, D.D., LL.D.; Klaus Heinemann, Ph.D.; William Bloom, Ph.D., of the Findhorn Foundation; and William Tiller, Ph.D., professor emeritus of Stanford University— have formulated theories about the orbs. In their book, *The Orb Project*, theologian Miceal Ledwith and physicist Klaus Heinemann include photographs of this phenomenon collected from around the world. The phenomenon cannot be explained by conventional science, but as with crop circles, the authors hypothesize that "the lack of a visible understanding of what the orbs are, does not necessarily preclude a lack of their existence." They speculate that the different colors of the orbs may be "associated with vibrational frequencies of the dimensions from which they come, some of which may be approaching the quantum field of the sixth plane."

the hospital because of the unpleasantness of my previous experience. But my doctor, a woman I deeply admired and implicitly trusted, insisted if I wanted to deliver VBAC (vaginal birth after Cesarean) or if a situation arose where I would need to deliver through Cesarean section, as I had with Callie, I would have to be in the hospital. I didn't push the issue further because there was a more important matter for which I needed her support—the birthing ceremony. I explained to her how important this ceremony was to me, and she listened intently without judging me. Although I could tell she had no medical framework for my request, she didn't refuse me and left it open for further discussion. However, she warned me if she was not on call the night the baby came, none of her colleagues would agree to it.

I am not at liberty to fully share in print the birthing ceremony and its many levels of preparation, although I did verbally go through the steps with my doctor so she could know all the particulars. I explained to her that I would need to use traditional Native white sage to smudge the birthing suite, as smudging cleanses dense energies. Aside from war zones and sites that have been environmentally desecrated, such as Chernobyl, there are few places more energetically dense than hospitals and prisons. At first she refused my request because there would be oxygen tanks in the birthing suite, but eventually she acquiesced as long as there was no open flame near the tanks. I also requested no one but she, Ben, and the attending nurse be allowed in the room. She agreed. Further, she agreed that if all went well with the birth and I felt strong enough afterwards, I could sign myself out of the hospital within hours of the delivery so I might recover in the sanctity of my own home. Surprisingly, although my doctor seemed okay with this last request, my family and a few friends thought me certifiable.

Finally, I asked something of her I knew, in those early days of the growing HIV epidemic, would really challenge her comfort level—would she catch the baby bare-handed instead of gloved? I wanted the baby blessed with the sacred powder *hoddentin,* the pollen collected from cattails. Oh Shinnah had explained that the *Tineh*, the People's word for what we call Apache, used hoddentin as protection for their warriors, and a small pouch of it was given to every newborn to bless them on their path. When the baby emerged, my doctor would dip her fingers in the pollen and anoint the baby's fontanel, third-eye area, heart, and soles. When I finished describing this part of the ceremony, my doctor remained silent, then, with eyes locked in trust, woman to woman, she agreed. I was grateful, for I recognized she was giving of herself, both as a physician and a woman, in ways that were far outside the bounds of her medical and personal paradigms.

I went into false labor three times, but thankfully on a night when my doctor was on call my contractions came in earnest. After I was settled in the birthing suite, I periodically saw the faces of nurses and orderlies peeking through a sliver of an opening in the curtain covering the window of the birthing room door, and I wondered what that was all about. I learned later my doctor had posted a sign on the door: "Birthing Ceremony. No admittance." Obviously, this birth had become the talk of the hospital.

Our daughter, Nyssa, came an hour after sunrise. As I said previously, although this name had come to me unbidden and I had never heard it before I was pregnant, I had looked it up during the pregnancy in baby naming books and had been surprised to find it there.* It comes from the Greek and means "beginning point" or "striver toward a goal." The memory of the long-ago dream of the three flames came back to me. In that dream, the second flame had identified itself as "Striver Toward a Goal." I recognized now the dream had been a promise of this child, a new beginning. I marveled that there is so much we do not know, so much we are asked to take in trust, and way more than we will ever comprehend until it has come to pass.

---

*In some of my Native traditions it was taught that a child-in-utero carries a unique vibratory frequency. The mother feels this vibration and senses the name that corresponds to that frequency and best encodes the energy appropriate for the child's incarnation in this particular life.

Once home and in the routine of raising our daughter, I occasionally thought of the additional ceremonies I had promised to perform with her over the next seven years. I was a bit worried that they were an obligation based on my desires and not a choice Nyssa would make for herself. I did not want Nyssa to feel anything but joy in this life and I knew, as with any child born into this world, her soul's contract was between her and God, Great Mystery. Until the age of three, children are open receptacles and the experiences to which they are exposed will mold the rest of their lives. For most children the world shrinks by age six, when they start elementary school and are indoctrinated, in spoken and unspoken ways, about what is acceptable and what is not.

Western cultures have a propensity to strip children's imaginations, although imagination is one of the most magical characteristics of being human. Children are socialized into believing imaginary friends exist only in their fantasies, nature is alive only at the biological level, and "normal" means existing only inside the societal box. For most, their doors of perception close early on, and their sensitivities to and awareness of unseen worlds are called into question. Whereas some parents encourage their children's capacities through conventional activities and education—such as music, painting, martial arts, sports—or spiritual training in their particular faith, my wish as a parent was that Nyssa would stay connected to the luminal realms and not have to reestablish that connection as an adult, as most people do, if they ever do at all. The goal of the future ceremonies I would perform with her was to help her access and value this awareness, and later make it her own, should that be her desire.

Time passed, and over the next year and a half I would complete my work with Oh Shinnah. There naturally comes a time with any mentor, no matter how thankful you are for the personal growth achieved through their teachings, when you have to stand on your own, living what you have learned and making it your own. Although mentors, teachers, and spiritual guides offer the best of who they are, they are also, like the rest of us, very human. Oh Shinnah's teachings had renewed my faith in life and in myself. Through the death of my first daughter and the birth of my second, I had been offered a gift back to my own remembrance. The teachings had revealed a new path, awakening me to levels of awareness that had gratefully ushered me between the dark and the daylight.

6

Making It My Own

I had completed two more of the series of ceremonies I had committed to prior to Nyssa's birth, and one month shy of her third birthday in 1989, we prepared to go back to the west coast to visit our friends and while there perform the fifth ceremony—the baptism in the Mother Waters. As part of the instruction of the fifth and sixth ceremonies, the child is baptized in both oceans, the Pacific and Atlantic. According to Oh Shinnah's previous instructions, if it is a boy, he is baptized first in the Atlantic—the Father Waters—and then in the Pacific. The order is reversed for a female. The first baptism must be conducted before the child turns three; the second, before the age of seven. The specific purpose of these last two ceremonies is to synchronize the right and left hemispheres of the brain so the child can optimally balance the conscious and subconscious minds, for both logic and intuition are equally vital in decision making.

About six weeks before we left for California, Nyssa and I were invited to an end-of-the-year party for all the teachers at the school where I had previously taught. The gathering was at the lake house of one of the teachers. My colleagues had supported me years prior through Callie's death, and though I no longer taught at the school, they celebrated my joy at having Nyssa. We sat outside, where some of them played with Nyssa, allowing me the uninterrupted time to catch up with my colleagues.

At one point, I nonchalantly turned from my conversation to see what Nyssa was up to. I panicked when I couldn't see her anywhere. Intuitively, I rushed to the lake's edge. There she stood, waist deep in water, shoes and all, taking off her dress and giggling. Nyssa had a command of language well beyond her years. She looked up at me with total delight and said, "Not my fault, Mommy. They made me get in the water." I didn't think the *they* she was referring to was an attempt at making an excuse for her actions. The words registered, as she had frequently spoken about her imaginal friends. At that moment however, all that was important was my demand that she come out of the water immediately. She obeyed, but justified herself by explaining matter-of-factly, "The water fairies said come play. They'll protect me." I was caught up in my "mom" fear and admonished her that I didn't care what the water fairies wanted, she was never to do that again.

Later, when I had calmed down, and upon reflection, I realized I had to find a way to be a protective parent and keep her safe without shutting down her sensitivities to other realities. On the one hand my concern was especially relevant because we would soon be leaving to do the ceremony in the Pacific Ocean, and on the other I did not wish to close down access to her inner gifts of knowing, as that is precisely why I was doing these ceremonies with her.

In California, we decided to perform the baptism ceremony in the early morning hours so we would have more privacy. While I'll describe only relevant parts of the ceremony, at one point Nyssa would need to walk a cornmeal path to the ocean's edge with her dad and me on either side of her. The father carries dirt from the land from whence they've come, and the mother clear water from the same area. Nyssa would need to cast a crystal, a flower, and piece of bread into the water. These offerings represented, respectively, clarity of life purpose, gratitude for all the earth offers, and feeding the Mother Waters. She was amazingly poised, accepting without complaint everything she was instructed to do, which I hadn't thought possible for a three-year-old. She just got it. After making her offerings, she made the choice for baptism by immersing herself three times in the ocean. Although the waters were calm and she wasn't far into them, this *was* the Pacific so we stood ready at the shoreline just a few feet away, diligently watching, in case we needed to get to her side quickly.

When she had finished by walking the cornmeal path back out of the water, a young man and his son, who had stopped to watch, approached us. With an attitude of respect and saying he did not wish to intrude, the man related that he had been moved by what he had witnessed and had recognized it was something very sacred to us. He then explained, with a bit of confusion in his voice, that he had stopped with his son to watch because, although he didn't understand what was going on, he knew it would be important for his son to remember someday. He then sheepishly revealed his six-year-old son had said he had seen golden light beams dancing all around my daughter on the water as she immersed herself. "Maybe it was a reflection of the sun off the water," he said, struggling to offer a logical explanation for what his son had seen. I only smiled and thanked him, as there was no need to go into any detail. It was clear this man and his son had received all they needed to know in that moment. I noted, while still feeling cautious and protective, that perhaps Nyssa's comments back at the lake house were true; maybe the water spirits did watch over her.

When we returned home to Massachusetts, an unexpected event rocked my world. After six long years of learning to deal with death, it was about to test me again. From the depths of sadness, I would once again be shown death always holds hands with life, and the exchange between life and death has the potential to bring forth something new.

My parents had just returned home to Cape Cod from visiting one of my sisters who lived in Montana. Mom was worried because Dad was in pain and short of breath, and upon getting a check up, he was diagnosed with pneumonia. I took Nyssa for the weekend to visit. My father was very pale and labored to breathe, and it was clear, although he smiled wanly, that he was in tremendous pain. When I offered to do hands-on healing, he agreed, even though he was uncertain about it, not understanding what it entailed. He was a literal guy, having been an elementary school principal and having impressed upon his five children the value of logic and education. He had never understood why I had given up a good job as a teacher, with its predictability of benefits and pension, and he had no point of reference for my new work as a non-traditional counselor.

I was a trained bodyworker, but I was surprised as I worked on him when I felt a lump at each place on his body where my hands were drawn. They shouldn't have been there. As I felt the bulges I could also sense his unspoken fear, which prompted me to finally ask him what he was afraid of. He didn't hesitate to answer, but his answer came as a surprise: "I am afraid I will die at a young age like my father."

His father had been sixty-three years old when he died from stomach cancer. My father was now sixty-four, so I reminded him, maybe a little too lightly, "You're safe! You're already a year older than Grandpa was." He offered a weary smile in response, but both of us knew something was really very wrong. Since I wouldn't let my mind fully go there, I tried to lighten things up even more by offering a private joke between us, "Give your fear to Sookie." Sookie was the childhood "friend" of his father, my grandfather. Like most Irishmen of his generation, Grandpa had been full of stories of the Little People, and Sookie was one of his most memorable. My dad and I laughed in the moment thinking of it.

Grandpa had first shared the story of Sookie with me when I was about seven years old and having recurring nightmares. They were of vague nocturnal visits, and they terrified me, although I could never clearly remember who was in the dream or what happened. I only knew that on many nights the fear propelled me out of bed and screaming down the hallway. One weekend after one of these night terrors, Grandpa had visited and taken me for a walk out of earshot of my parents, who thought he filled my head with too many wild ideas. As we walked in the woods behind the house, he pointed out trees, robins, and squirrels, and said solemnly, "All of these are full of life. There are many different kinds of life in the world and there are even some beings you may not be able to see with your eyes. When I was a little kid, a small being named Sookie came to help me when I was afraid in the night. When you get afraid at night, you can ask Sookie to come help you, too. He can stay in the wall behind your bed. He looked like a short pale elf to me, but he might look different to you. Or, he might not even show himself to you at all." My grandpa was the chief of the fire department in a nearby city. I couldn't imagine my grandfather, with his thick crop of white hair and weathered hands, ever having been a kid, never mind ever having been afraid. Nor was I all that sure I wanted to invite into my room a short pale elf that could move through walls.

However, because of the constant nightmares, falling asleep and staying asleep had become a real issue, so I had taken his advice, inviting Sookie to watch over me at night. I never saw Sookie, but whenever I woke up frightened and called on him, I imagined he was close by, which made me feel somewhat protected. Although the nightmares didn't stop and were no less terrifying, the thought of Sookie provided me some comfort for close to two years. He left when I was nine, the same spring Grandpa died. I brought up Sookie's memory now, hoping my dad could feel some small amount of comfort, as I had as a kid, or at least see the humor in the retelling of the tale. Dad and I shared other stories as I worked on him that summer afternoon, but we avoided any further mention of his health.

Once back home and still concerned about my dad's health, I went to see a new mentor, an elderly woman I had been studying with for only a few months. Maya Perez had been born in Guyana, South America, and was a spiritual mystic, a person who uses mediumship to help others.* Maya defined mediumship as the ability of a person to be an intermediary between the unseen worlds and this one. Mediums

---

*At birth Maya had been born with a film-like substance from the amniotic sac, called a *caul*, over her face. Many cultures believe this veil has spiritual significance and endows the child with mystical gifts.

can channel information from souls who have crossed over and collect information for individuals, from that person's past lives. She called this reading the Akashic Records. She explained the Akashic Records as being a storehouse of energy imprinted in a dimension of consciousness that contains every soul's journey—past, present, and future. *Akasha,* the primary substance out of which everything is formed, and *Records,* because they are repositories of mystical knowledge.

A very direct woman, although one of great sensitivity, she was teaching me about the healing vibration of the psalms, numerology, and prayer. Maya believed that "with positive thoughts, we mortals are able to do great work for the fulfillment of our personal destinies." She taught that we each come to the earth plane with a unique vibration that is suited to what we must learn here. Furthermore, year by year, based on the vibration of our name and the numerological significance of that year, we are in a different personal learning cycle. She was convinced the power of prayer helped us to stay connected to our inner and outer light. She said specific psalms from the Bible can be used to uplift or balance our light frequencies and dispel imbalances when used in conjunction with meditation, other kinds of prayer, and personal discipline.*

Maya told me Dad did not have pneumonia and needed to be in the hospital. She cautioned he was in a nine-year cycle and that he might die, but she also explained that "no one really dies; they just walk into a different vibration of consciousness." She said my dad was fearful because he still had so much he wanted to do on this material plane and he was concerned about what would happen to my mother should he die. I asked how I could help him, and she said all I could do was to pray and hold him in the light, because either living or crossing over was his choice to make. She told me that each of us comes into the physical as a vibration of light, and every cell within us holds that light. Our

---

*In her book *Born with a Veil,* Maya speaks in more detail about the energy of the different psalms.

thought forms and experiences, she explained, can block the recognition of our greater lightness of being, but we all reincarnate many times to grow in the awareness that we are divine light beings and part of what she called "God's expression." Maya believed a physical illness was a spiritual lesson, not a punishment, and even if we died from that illness, we would learn something about our inner light before we crossed over. She felt my father was going through that process now.

From her perspective, when we die we go through the universal fires, which are energies that cleanse the light body, although if we are fearful we might mistake them as the fires of hell. The soul can sometimes get stuck in the journey through the universal fires if one has not forgiven oneself for things done during one's lifetime. "We can believe in a higher power," Maya said, "but still might choose to not act right. We must forgive ourselves for the way we chose to learn our lessons." Forgiveness is the gateway from the universal fires to the "river of life." Going through the river of life is like a baptism, she explained, helping to raise our vibration and further heal from the wounds we received, or inflicted, while in the material plane.

There are two additional stages to the death journey, she said: "getting off the cross" and "ascending to the twenty-second vibration toward God realization." To get off the cross, we must move through the "seven points of the subconscious self and the following seven points of the superconscious self." Once off the cross (explaining it as a metaphor that symbolizes the illusion of the time-space continuum created when our divine expression finds itself Earth born), the soul is finally free of its wounds and we can begin our ascension back toward merging with God realization, which she claimed was at the twenty-second vibration of the soul's evolution.* In her words, she felt this fully realized vibration is what Jesus was trying to teach us by example during his life and at his death. She said, "That is why

---

*Maya never fully explained to me the details of the twenty-second level of the soul's vibration, providing only the most basic information about the fourteen points necessary to get off the cross.

we all continue to reincarnate—so we can continue to learn. Every aspect of existence has a divine purpose and all events we encounter on our own evolutionary path have a purpose within the divine." She concluded that it was my dad's destiny to decide what unfolded next for him in his divine evolutionary purpose. As for me, she counseled that I continue to pray that his highest light inform him as he made these choices.

Although I understood what she was saying, it didn't seem that only praying for him was nearly enough, and I was very worried that my family would lose him. When I expressed that feeling, Maya said, "Worry is a sin because it means you do not have faith." She asked me to "have faith in the contract being worked out between your father and God, which ultimately is to evolve to know we are part of God and God is part of us." I countered again, saying that I was not ready to see Dad go. "We never lose each other, Sandy," she responded. "That is the myth of our separation. Every person who has ever lived or will ever live lives in you. Everything is in each one of us." Although I knew what she was telling me was true, I didn't want to imagine that our family would not have our dad there always.

Over the next few days, Dad's breathing worsened. The antibiotics weren't working. He went for more tests, which revealed he did not have pneumonia—he had lung cancer. What's more, it had metastasized from his lungs to his bones and brain. He was admitted to the local Cape Cod hospital. I realized how frightened he must have been because he was willing to try any technique to bring some level of comfort to his pain. In one of my visits, I had brought along some meditation tapes I had made for relaxation and pain reduction. He wanted to listen to them immediately. He told me the following day he liked them, they did help some, and even his roommate was getting comfort as they listened to the meditations together twice a day. As nice as it was to hear that the tapes had brought him some relief, anyone looking at him could see he was deteriorating quickly. Three days later he was transferred to Massachusetts General Hospital in

Boston, where he awaited more tests before he could begin the radiation therapy the doctors were now suggesting.

Although his pain was obvious, he seemed to ignore it because he was so preoccupied with getting his affairs in order, especially making sure Mom would be taken care of in every way, not just financially. My sisters and brother and our families visited him daily, as did his mother and his siblings. My mother kept vigil around the clock, but by the fourth day she was near exhaustion. That afternoon, I suggested that she and the other family members who had gathered by Dad's bedside take a break and get something to eat, and I would stay with him.

Once alone with him, I asked if there was anything I could do to make him more comfortable. The gravity of his response caught me off guard. "Sandy, I have believed in God my whole life without question, but I am scared to die. What if there is nothing beyond this place? And if there is, what will it be like?" Although Dad and Mom were devout Catholics, like almost anyone who knows they may be facing imminent death, he was probing his belief about an afterlife. That did not surprise me. What did was that he would express such profound feelings to me, since my spiritual path had taken me so far afield from the religion in which I had been brought up.

I took a deep breath before I answered. "Dad, I believe when we die we cross into some form of light vibration. I trust this light represents our soul's essence and is part of all we are, part of everything that has gone before us, part of the essence of creation—God. I believe that as we are returning to the light of the All That Is, our time spent during this life passes in front of us like memory balls and we can get caught in those illusionary scenarios that were our fears and hurts, instead of aiming straight for the light. I think the essence or energetic imprint of those we loved here, like Grandpa, will be there in the light to welcome us home, although I have no real idea what that home might look or feel like. I don't think we have a clue until we're there, but I think it will be perfect."

I paused. I had possibly pushed too far, and now I was about to go further. "And, Dad, you can do something I can no longer do. From that place, you can give Callie a hug for me." Tears welled up in both our eyes, and Dad's energy shifted. He became more alert. "I can do that!" he whispered. Ever the go-to guy, Dad's next statement didn't surprise me. "If I die, knowing I have a meaningful purpose to fulfill, I'll be less fearful."

Two days later, heavily on morphine because of the profound pain, Dad died. It had been only two weeks since he had been diagnosed. Although we are a tight family, each of us dealt with the devastation of the loss in our own and different ways. For me, Dad's death was not only about the loss of myself as child, but also the loss of a trusted confidante. He was the one I always had turned to—to talk through life's confusing moments, to learn how to push past my limitations, to argue life's injustices, to regain a sense of humor when life seemed too dark. Through Callie's death and now through Dad's, I was learning birth and death are the bookends of our human existence, and we can never have total dominion over them. All we really have control over is how well we fill the space between them.

7

Getting Wet Noodled

Within two months of Dad's passing, that space between the bookends of birth and death was augmented for me by a new mentor. Over the previous two years I had heard people in the shamanic community talk admiringly of the Seneca elder Grandmother Twylah Nitsch. I saw in a local New Age newspaper that she was offering a workshop in Boston, and because I was curious about her teachings I telephoned the center to sign up. I was told by the receptionist that she had needed to cancel her workshop. I almost hung up, but spontaneously asked if there was any way I could contact her. The receptionist said she had a number scribbled in the margins of the workshop brochure, but had no idea where it would ring in to. I took down the number for future reference.

As I put down the receiver, my attention was drawn to a group of crows in the backyard that suddenly were raising quite a racket. I took that as a sign, because I had been taught a sudden shift in energy is meaningful. I decided to play a game with myself, pretending the crows were insisting that I call Grandmother Twylah without delay. I picked up the phone, dialed the unidentified number, and instead of hearing a connecting ring I heard a lighthearted voice say hello. I was momentarily caught off guard before I asked, "Who is this, please?"

"You called me, honey. You should know who you are calling. It's Gram. Who is this?"

"My name is Sandy," I blurted out.

"Oh, honey, it's about time you called. You need to come up to see me. We need to start our work."

"Huh?"

"Yep," she continued, giggling, as if this conversation were an amusement. "I have time in two weeks. Come up to the reservation then, and we can start to do what we need to do." She didn't give me time to respond. "I have to go now. Four Winds until I see you."

I heard a click as she hung up the phone. I stood there, staring at the receiver in my hand for a long moment as the crows' caws shifted to cackles in what sounded distinctly like laughter. I thought, *Here we go again.*

Once the perplexity of the conversation had passed, I felt excitement at having been extended an invitation to work with Grandmother Twylah. I called my friend Ann, whom I had become close to through our mutual work with Oh Shinnah. I related the conversation and shared my excitement. "I think I'm supposed to go with you," she announced. I did not know if it would be okay, but I immediately welcomed the idea and told her I would ask. It would be good to have a companion in the work and share whatever happened. So, a few days later, I called Gram Twylah to ask if Ann could come with me. Her reply was simple, "The more, the merrier."

Two weeks later, Ann and I set off on what was to be the first of countless nine-hour drives over the next seven years to the Cattaraugus Reservation outside of Buffalo in western New York State to be with Gram in her little house and receive her big teachings. When we arrived, Gram Twylah greeted us with a hearty embrace. She was in her seventies, smaller than I would have thought from the energy she exuded over the phone, and wore her thick white hair gathered into a single braid that looped up the left side of her head and was held in place with a silver barrette. Taking her in for the first time, it was not her demeanor that attracted my attention, but her energy. It was immediately evident she was a woman full of laughter and generosity of spirit. Her blue eyes sparkled and her laughter rang out infectiously as she welcomed us into her home. Ann and I had brought gifts of loose tobacco, coffee, a jar of honey, and fruit. Gifts are a traditional way to pay respect to a Native teacher, and Gram Twy (as she had asked us to call her) warmly accepted them.

She instructed us to put our luggage upstairs and then meet her in the living room. We had no sooner seated ourselves when she began to relate part of her tribal and personal history. She said the philosophy she would be sharing came from her ancestors, the Seneca, who are part of the Five Nation Peace League, also called the Iroquois Confederacy. She pointed across the room to the bronze bust of a woman of great beauty. It sat alone, atop a piano, with an aura of dignity. With great pride, she said this was her mother, Blue Flower. Even though this was just a statue, it was clear to me that Gram was making an introduction.

She told us she and her mother had shaped the oral teachings of her People into a body of work that could be shared with others through the Wolf Clan Teaching Lodge. The teachings had been entrusted to her by her maternal grandparents, Moses (who was a well-known medicine man) and Alice Shongo, and her parents, Raymond Hurd and Maude Shongo Hurd (Blue Flower). She said it was important for the traditional wisdom to be passed on "so that seven generations hence could live the continuum of the seeds of my People." Like so many of the other indigenous elders I had sat with, Gram Twy was not covetous of the teachings as belonging only to her People; her heart was open to all people who came to learn and grow from them.

We moved to the kitchen, where Gram prepared tea. It was the kitchen that would serve as our primary classroom over the coming years. I, and whoever showed up for a teaching session, would sit with Gram around the gray Formica-topped 1950s-style table. It would become covered with our charts, colored pencils, and notebooks that were filled with questions or observations that had come up between these teaching sessions. We always kept a thesaurus nearby. Gram felt every word, each audible sound, has its own vibration, so it was important we always speak the word truest to our meaning. The words we choose solidify our thoughts into form, influencing how another person might receive our ideas or expressions based on how those vibrations impact them. Even this awareness became a part of her training, provoking long discussions as we searched for the "most true" word.

As we listened to Gram Twy's stories and teachings, we drank copious amounts of tea while we filled pages with notes. Sometimes only Ann and I would be there; at other times, we were joined by other students or Native elders who had made their way to her kitchen to learn specific teachings from Gram. Sometimes we would laugh at life's incongruity; sometimes we would lament our pasts; but always we plied Gram with hundreds of questions. Gram was always up to the challenge, more often than not reacting with the glee of a childhood playmate who could make us cry uncle as we collapsed with exhaustion at the end of each day. When our eyes glazed over and when our brains could take in no more information, she would triumphantly announce she had "wet-noodled us."

As we sat around the table that first night, with our cups of hot tea, Gram shared her Seneca name: *Yeh-Weh-Node*, "She Whose Voice Rides on the Wind." She introduced us to her constant companion, Gagan, a white dog that was part she-wolf. Then she began to tell us the methods she would use to teach us in the coming days, explaining that we would start with three charts, which she called wisdom wheels. The first chart, the Cycles of Truth, was based on the universal principles of truth that become the adventure that we each have when we come into physicality. The second chart, which she called the Pathway of Peace chart, uncovered our personal gifts of birth and our latent talents, both of which define how we approach our individual Earthwalk. The third chart worked with animal energies as reflectors of the quality of our earth connection, and was called the Creature Teachers chart.

Many myths and most all indigenous cultures, not just Native

American, speak of the mystery and communication between human beings and Nature's kingdoms. As had been taught by other northern Native teachers I had sat with, such as Oh Shinnah and the late Chippewa teacher Sun Bear, animal energies carry medicine or attributes that could improve our connections to the self, Great Mystery, and all life on Earth. Called *totems,* and often seen as spiritual guardians, they can symbolically represent a tribe, a clan, or an individual. When Sun Bear taught his body of work, there was an animal that corresponded with each month on the wisdom wheel that made up the year and matched up with one's individual birth month. When sitting with Oh Shinnah, we were led to approach each of the kingdoms—animal, winged, fish, and insect—to see which species from each category was associated with our centering energy and could provide a lesson or direction as we went through life. Gram shared how the characteristics of each creature of Nature can provide the wisdom, behavior, or lessons to teach us something vital about ourselves. Each animal's qualities represent a contribution that can help fulfill us as a whole person.

Gram continued to explain that she and her mother, Blue Flower, had formulated the teachings around the form of a circle, or the Medicine Wheel. The teachings on the three charts we would be introduced to were based on the ancient philosophy of the original inhabitants of Turtle Island (the Americas), who used the philosophy gained on the Medicine Wheel as a tool for self-understanding and self-direction toward wholeness. According to Gram, moral consciousness is based on love and respect, in a kind of spiritual and physical marriage that produces harmony. "As the People grew spiritually and physically," she said, "a tool emerged called the Medicine Wheel of Earth Energy." It is a wisdom road, she explained, representing how all things are united and move through rhythmic cycles. The walk around a Medicine Wheel represents the totality of one's life's process, both seen and unseen, as a gift manifesting from *Swenio,* the "Creation that comes from Original Source—the Great Mystery."

The Seneca believe that the Great Mystery created everything, lives in everything, always was, and always will be. Therefore, the light that lives within every entity is part of the Great Mystery. The teachings on the Medicine Wheel provide us a doorway through which we can access the lessons that Creation offers.

She shared one of the Wolf Clan teachings that from the moment we take our first breath we face four opportunities: challenge, change, choice, and commitment. "In every moment," she said, "these opportunities can help us find peace within our sacred space. We suffer all kinds of Earth lessons that are caused by fear and create stress, but we can use those lessons to awaken ourselves to who we really are physically, mentally, emotionally, and spiritually. Fear arouses stress and influences our feelings." She explained that inwardly stress affects the spiritual self and outwardly it affects the physical self. Once we tap our inner knowing and confront our fear and the stress it induces, we do not drain our precious life-force energy.

Gram explained that most all of the future teaching charts we would eventually be introduced to were also based on the form of the Medicine Wheel and that in working with the teachings we would be able to accelerate our own personal growth by more deeply exploring our sacred point of view and personal value system, both of which also affect the greater whole. Our mission in life is to realize and express our full potential. To do that, we must continually confront the unconscious parts of ourselves and courageously face the challenges that will inevitably arise in life. Only we can make a choice to commit to change.

What I had come to understand through my studies over the years concerning the teachings of Medicine Wheels was that although their structure was used universally among the tribes to reestablish harmony, the way they were used individually was based on the particular value system of the tribal teachings. Among the elders the term *medicine* does not refer to healing, but to wisdom. To walk the Wheel is to view life from many wisdom perspectives, gaining freedom and clarity for life choices. The essence of the Medicine Wheel is movement to promote change. Further, their teachings can aid us in developing those as yet untapped resources we can use to find greater balance and to promote personal growth. In this way the Medicine Wheel honors the cycles of life and the cycles of nature, and each stage around the circle or the Wheel becomes a preparation for the next lesson.

People have gathered together for thousands of years to connect with Spirit, receive guidance, and heal using this sacred structure. The large Medicine Wheels constructed on the ground with stones, as seen at sacred tribal sites in states such as Wyoming and Montana, or the form of the Medicine Wheel used for these teaching charts, as I understood them, were essentially used as a spiritual tool to align with the Mystery and to assist each of us to better understand the nature of the Self.

Gram explained that what we would learn from the teachings contained in these three charts could empower us to tap into our unlimited creative capacities. Living our true expression with compassion and gratitude helps move us beyond our dysfunctional patterns so we can more fully own our personal power. Gram said we could not live our power and relate to others with respect if we did not first know ourselves, including our gifts and challenges. "There's no need to seek perfection," she said, "for at the Spirit level everything already is perfect." Seeking perfection is one of the delusions of the earth plane. Fear reveals where we still need to grow, whereas our gifts of birth show us how to overcome the stress that revelation creates. Failure to find the cause of our fears gives energy to the effects, which include prolonged pain, lack of self-confidence, confusion, and so forth. In that sense we are seeking growth, not perfection.

As Gram's explanation wound down that first day, a fragment of something Carl Jung had written came to my mind: "He who looks without, dreams; he who looks within, awakes." I was ready to awaken to whatever awaited me in Gram's teachings.

The next day, Gram led me to the living room to work privately.

As I settled onto the couch, she sat in the easy chair across from me. She said, "The most important question each of us should ask ourselves every day is—am I happy where I find myself?" She asked that question of me now. Instead of answering directly, I launched into a review of the past six years and what had brought my feet to this path, beginning with the death of my first daughter. She listened intently. When I finished, she said with gentleness of voice, "I, too, lost a child."

My God, I thought, *was this to be my connection to another of my teachers?*

She continued, "The gift your daughter offered you through her death was the choice to put your feet to a new path. You had promised the Infinite within yourself to walk this path, and you have obviously accepted her gift, because here you are." Gram generalized for a moment, saying, "If people had more gratitude for both life and death, then they could more easily negotiate the uncertainties of their lives with conviction and waste less time with the things they cannot control."

Without diminishing the import of what I had just shared, she returned to her original question and asked me directly again, "Are you happy with where you find yourself?" She went on to explain briefly, "Life is not about always feeling happy, otherwise we would not be challenged to grow. However, we become happy when we find meaning in our lives, and often what is holding us from happiness is that a sense of purpose is missing from our lives."

I took my time considering the question and answered as honestly as I could. "I am happy being a mother and working within the teachings, but I am not fully satisfied with my life on many levels." Gram nodded and said the work we would be doing together would shine light on any personal changes I needed to make to be able to commit to greater happiness and further my purpose in life. She told me that although we would do the detailed work with the personal charts in earnest the next day, she would open the door to those teachings through the preparatory work that we were about to do now. We began with the Pathway of Peace chart, which revealed my seven personal gifts of birth (personal attributes) and my six latent talents (personal challenges).

Almost two hours later, Gram said that this was enough of a beginning for this particular chart for the day, and we would shift to the Creature Teachers charts with Ann, who had already completed her personal chart. Once situated back at the kitchen table, she handed me a deck of cards portraying a collection of animals, birds, and insects, each of which held different qualities and expressed different Native teachings or meanings.

I recognized these as the Medicine Cards, a book and divination deck using animals that Jamie Sams and her collaborator, David Carson, had created. I told Gram I owned this deck and had already used it to discover my totem animals. I also shared with her that I had written Jamie and requested an explanation of four others—two additional animals (jaguar and raccoon), a winged (blue heron), and an insect (praying mantis)—that I had wanted details on because they were not included in her original deck and I was working with them. Gram said she thought they were good additions for the deck. She also said that as these animals had already spoken to me, I should keep using them when I did other types of intuitive card spreads. However, she explained that she had a different way of using the animal cards and I should not be attached to the animals I had previously identified, I should go along with her now because Spirit would impart new information in this moment that I could learn from. Further, if one of the animals I had previously chosen came up now, I should pay particular attention.

I shuffled the deck, spread the cards out on the table, and chose a card. She had already laid out the Creature Teachers chart, and she directed me to place each card I drew on one of the nine positions of this chart. She placed the first card in the east position, turning it over to reveal the animal, and gave me a brief explanation of both the animal's meaning and its significance at that position on the Wheel.

We repeated this process until I got to the seventh card, which would be placed in the center position on the chart. She stopped me from drawing this card and explained that if I wanted to one day teach this body of work as a certified teacher of the Wolf Clan Teaching Lodge, she would automatically put the wolf card there. In her tradition, the wolf represents the teacher and the pathfinder. My response was immediate. "No thank you, I don't choose to put wolf in that position. I don't want to be a teacher anymore. I think there is something else the Universe wants me to do." With exaggerated seriousness, I chose the next card and flipped it over. It was the wolf.

Gram collapsed with peals of laughter. When she regained her composure, but still grinning, she said, "Sometimes, honey, there is a clear path. If Spirit offers you the gift of teaching this body of work, it will become your responsibility as to how you choose to accept that gift." While Gram giggled and shook her head, I drew the last two Creature Teachers cards and we ended that portion of our work for the day. It was late and we were all full from the day's teachings, so after one last cup of tea and some lighter talk, the three of us retired for the night.

Sometime during the night I thought I heard howling far off in the distance, and its persistence began to pull me out of my sleep. As I was stirring to wakefulness, I had a flash of the dream I was coming out of.

I am sitting in a clearing in the woods. It appears to be daybreak. Approaching me silently are two wolves, one gray and one white. I am not afraid and they are not menacing. They each sniff one of my hands, and then lick them.

That is all I could remember, and although I listened carefully for the sound that had awakened me, I heard no howling. In the morning I shared with Gram what I had dreamed. In an interpretation similar to what I had learned about dreamwork from Oh Shinnah, Gram said that seeing white animals was generally a message from the world of Spirit. The gray wolf was of this world. Given that I had pulled the wolf card as my centering card the previous evening, Gram thought that the ancestors were welcoming me to the work and that I would have the opportunity to share it in my waking world should that be my desire. Furthermore, she said that the howling I thought I had heard was Spirit's way of waking me up so I could remember the dream.

When we resumed our work later that morning, Gram explained in more detail about our personal charts. While I won't go into the details and depth of this rich body of work, an important aspect of my chart was that my primary gift of birth came through the lens of purple, the color of the dreamer and counselor, which was further emphasized through the energetic gifts of my birth month, May. The attributes of May are harmony, prophecy, philosophy, and sensitivity to sound—all energies that could assist me in living my truth and enhancing the power of my dreamer and counselor skills. From where other colors and words fell on the chart, Gram said she could tell not only that I was a dreamer, but that I was a shamanic dreamer. A shamanic dreamer is one who can traverse the terrain of the dreamworld, understand its symbols, and assist others in retrieving messages from their dreams. She suggested that investigating this gift on deeper levels would enrich my work as a shamanic counselor and dream decoder.

Gram then spontaneously cautioned me, offering a prophecy of her own, "Even though you have the gift of understanding the dreamtime, you will disregard the counsel your dreams provide and give away your power to a deep love. You won't listen to the information from your dreams when you need it the most." Her prophecy didn't register with me at that time; it couldn't have. It was not until almost two decades later, while reviewing old journals to write this book, that I came across Gram's prophecy and realized how right she had been. I was feeling the current pain and betrayal of divorce from my second husband. And as I read her prophecy, I reflected on a recurring dream I had during my marriage and how I had purposefully chosen to ignore its content.

I had never recorded this dream, not wanting to give it form, but each time I had it I would awaken wracked with sobs. My husband would awaken terribly concerned, asking me what was wrong. I always minimized the dream and the apprehension it created in me by answering the same way, "Oh, it's just a dream, nothing's wrong." Despite all my years of teaching and counseling on the power and gift of the dreamtime, I had continually ignored this nocturnal message, which I had felt if honestly and openly addressed, might end in the dissolution of our relationship. In making my choice not to act on the potently accurate information the dream was imparting, the end result of what I most feared manifested anyway. Truth has a way of eventually coming to light, supporting the innate clarity that we so often try hard to ignore. I saw now that, all those years ago, Gram had been right.

When we had completed our work for that weekend, as Ann and I were preparing to leave, Gram momentarily left the room and came back with her hands behind her back and a twinkle in her eyes. That twinkle always meant she was up to something. She said she had a gift for each of us. She opened her hands, and in each was a small wolf fetish. One was of blue-green turquoise and the other of black obsidian with a turquoise arrow running up its body. Our eyes lit up. I felt this extraordinary teacher was honoring us for the attentiveness with which we had taken in her teachings during this first meeting.

"Take the one that belongs to you," Gram said, nonchalantly. Both Ann and I knew, from the weekend's teachings with Gram and our past work with Oh Shinnah, that turquoise is symbolically associated with healing and obsidian with dreaming. And, because this weekend's work had made clear my birth gift was reading dreams and Ann's was hands-on healing work, our preferences should have been obvious. However, our little-girl insecurities came out and we were indecisive because we each were attracted to the fetish associated with the other's gift. Seeing our hesitation, Gram teased, "Well, whose is whose?"

Sheepishly, we admitted we were drawn to both fetishes. "See," Gram continued, "people covet what someone else's gift is and think in claiming it, naming it, or using it, they can expand their own power. But expanding our personal power comes when we stand in the truth of who we are; respecting and utilizing our personal gifts and honoring others for their gifts." As Ann and I took the wolf fetish associated with our individual gift of birth, we realized this was Gram's final teaching for this weekend—simple, yet profound.

8

Moths to a Flame

Every visit with Gram was a unique experience. Sometimes the teachings were cultural in nature, imparting the history and beliefs of the People. The Seneca People, for example, were seen as the philosophers of the Five Nation Peace League. She told us her family had been teaching the philosophy since the 1700s. She also shared that within the Seneca Nation there were clans or traditional social groups and families based on matriarchal lineage. The clans were represented by certain animals or birds, and each was responsible for a different body of information that would educate and benefit their community. Although every indigenous culture is different, they share cultural values based on Earth awareness, have universal stories about Earth's past, and relate similar prophecies about the future.

At other times her lessons were metaphysical, teaching about the different uses of crystals and healing herbs, or working with the sacred energy of trees. The lessons were often extremely specific. For example, in the work with trees, we learned the healing properties of specific kinds of trees, how to commune with them energetically to receive their information, and which species was identified with us individually as our sacred ally or centering tree. Gram said, "Trees are called the *Standing Ones* and they are also part of the planetary family. They act as a life-support system to provide many things to humankind and to remind us of the great Tree of Life." She also introduced us to other teachings and charts that would help us expand our self-awareness and further our unique gifts. One of these centered on reading stones and another gave ways to help us navigate through the debilitating stages of fear.

Gram talked often about how the sun and light influence Earth Law. One aspect of Earth Law is that we come to Earth to experience the creative energies of nature while also learning to become responsible users of that energy, ultimately coming to the realization that we are masters of our own creations. Counterintuitively, feelings of lack and limitation can foster our creativity because they provide us with the incentive to grow. Fear is an instant warning system, alerting us to feelings of where we sense lack or limitation in our lives. Gram felt that fundamentally fear is born out of a lack of self-awareness. Our challenge is to stay within the vibration of our core, or center, and creatively work with our fears until they become stepping stones to greater levels of self-understanding. As self-understanding is heightened, we more easily feel nature's unconditional love, which, as one example, is symbolized through the sun's warmth. The sun is a living entity that metaphysically is a gateway to what Gram called the "Eternal Light of Peace."

Like my other Native teachers, Gram said the sun enlivens Earth's physical and spiritual energies, creating harmony between these two celestial bodies. It also fosters harmony within the self. Another means for us to achieve harmony is by living with love and respect for ourselves and others. We are asked to do this even in the midst of turmoil and chaos. When we are in harmony, we are connected to, not separate from, the living cosmos. Gram felt that although we are all capable of living this way, most of us do not.

The human condition of disharmony led us to a discussion of prophecy and Earth changes. According to Gram, the history of the earth will span seven "Worlds." The first three Worlds have come and gone. When the First World ended, the Earth was cleansed by the fire of the sun. At the end of the Second World, life on the Earth was destroyed by meteors, resulting in an ice age. The destruction of the Third World came through water, which led to the demise of the Atlantean civilization and is the great flood of the Bible. The people who survived suffered greatly and were dispersed all over the earth. Humankind was reduced to an infantile level of consciousness and to the most basic of survival skills, spawning separation and control through war and religion.

Within very recent history, we have moved from the Fourth to the Fifth World, although we are still under the influence of the Fourth World and not fully feeling the influence of the Fifth. During the Fourth World, religion became a primary controlling factor, distancing humankind from Great Mystery by fostering the concept of a God who is separate from us and in Gram's words is "male, two-legged, and up in the clouds." However, Gram felt this entire process is necessary for human beings to evolve, to live their destiny, and to finally come to realize the inherent oneness of the cosmos. The Fifth World, according to Gram and many other teachers, began at the Harmonic Convergence, on August 16, 1987.* This unified gathering was the first synchronization of this many individuals coming together in prayer and ceremony to shift the evolutionary path of humankind toward unity consciousness, which is the realized energy of the Fifth World.

I had led an evening Moon Ceremony gathering with my group that night, joining our prayers with other like-minded groups and individuals around the globe. The circle was large, but to a person everyone seemed to be in a centered and calm place, which isn't always the case in this ceremony as individuals usually unburden themselves of their fears

---

*In 1987 author and visionary José Argüelles beseeched 144,000 people to come together to conduct ceremonies or to gather at sacred sites to pray and meditate for the fulfillment of the prophecy of Quetzalcoatl. The prophecy speaks of the thirteen heavens and nine hells. The final cycle of the nine hells ended on August 16, 1987; the first cycle of the thirteen heavens began on August 17, 1987. Thus began the projected twenty-five year culmination of the 5,125-year great cycle of current history, as well as the 26,000-year cycle of evolution, both of which were slated to end on the Mayan calendar date of 2012. Tens of thousands worldwide heeded this call and participated.

and frustrations. That evening, however, everyone rose above their own issues and directed their energy and prayers toward global understanding and acceptance of each other. The energy of global unity supported what Gram was explaining: that once the energy of the collective consciousness reaches critical mass, humanity can began to live more from the heart and soul than from the mind and body.

In Gram's opinion, the twenty-five years following the Harmonic Convergence would be a period during which we could realize our full potential of illumination and so have the ability to take our place as a planetary family in the cosmos. This time span included the widely cited Mayan transition date of 2012. During these preparatory years, we would experience deep personal and collective fears, witness vast injustices around the world, and be held accountable for the far-reaching cultural and environmental destruction we have caused through our greed. "These tribulations," Gram said, "are not punishments, but keys that can unlock our hearts, so that through love and respect we can accelerate personal growth, unite globally, and become proper stewards of the Earth, eventually taking our place in the galactic unfolding." Gram felt that if we all did our self work, by the end of this preparatory period we could each shift our frequency enough so that together we could transform our reality, both on our planet and as part of the fabric of the cosmos.

Gram continued with the prophecies by telling us the elders predicted that during the Fourth World people would migrate from the east to the Americas. They would have only a superficial understanding of the interrelatedness of all things and so would greedily search for personal power. They would be dominators of the environment, digging first into the earth, then the oceans, then the moon. The predictions were that when they started to dig into the sun and use its secrets—such as harnessing nuclear fusion not for the benign purpose of creating heat, but for a violent one such as creating weapons of destruction—that violation would trigger the next cleansing. Illumination, she said, is possible during the Fifth World, which would herald a time of collapse of the old paradigms, environmentally, politically, economically, and religiously.

The elders said that the Fifth World would be announced by a specific blue-hued celestial body, called the Blue Star, that would show itself in the Milky Way. There is a prophecy held by the Hopi People that speaks of the Blue Star Kachina,* which they also call Sirius, the bright star in the Canis Major constellation. Oh Shinnah had spoken about this, and it is related in Frank Waters's *Book of the Hopi* that the Hopi prophecy declares, "when the Blue Star Kachina makes its appearance in the heavens, the Fifth World will emerge." The Hopi will enter a new cycle of consciousness when Saquasohuh (Blue Star) Kachina removes his mask during the ceremonial dances in front of the uninitiated. At that time they will stop their ancient ceremonies, as the emergence of the Fifth World will require new rituals. According to Gram Twylah, the appearance of the Blue Star would usher in a world of higher consciousness whereby we humans would recover the "Uniworld" and finally accept our responsibility for caring for it. Gram felt we were living in exciting times, and we had each chosen to be here at this momentous time in the Earth's and

---

*The Hopi prophecy speaks of the Blue Star Kachina as both a kachina dancer, Saquasohuh, and a celestial body that will appear in the heavens and affect Earth's vibrations; some theorists have surmised this as future cataclysms and others as ushering in a higher consciousness. In 2010 an amateur Russian astronomer, Leonid Elenin, discovered a solar body that was labeled comet Elenin. NASA tracked this object's trajectory as it approached Earth, suggesting that its orbital track would bring it close to Earth and we would witness it as a blue tailed comet. It had been suggested by some that Elenin was the Blue Star Kachina. NASA didn't endorse this theory. They shut down their buzzroom.nasa.gov website on March 30, 2011, after speculation from various groups made NASA uncomfortable. Besides linking Elenin to the Hopi prophecy, certain groups also suggested it validated the widely prophesized Mayan end date of December 21, 2012. However, on August 19, 2011, a massive solar flare and coronal mass ejection hit the comet resulting in its disintegration. Despite all the speculation surrounding Elenin as the Blue Star and the misinformation circulated by many leading up to the 2012 Mayan end date, historical figures and sources—Nostradamus, St. John, Sumerian texts, Hopi prophecy, and even "remote viewers" from a 2008 US special forces project run by the Farsight Institute—have spoken of a blue light or a blue hued celestial body that will lead to significant Earth changes.

humanity's history to experience our part in and contribution to this reawakening.

Gram equated the Fourth World with what she called third-dimensional reality, which is bound by time and space and experienced predominately through our physical senses. When our reality is locked only into the third dimension, we limit our frequencies and this restricts us from experiencing the breadth of knowledge available in the higher realms. In contrast, the Fifth World is one of fourth- and fifth-dimensional reality,* which is unbounded and where humans can expand their awareness to access other inter- and multidimensional realities. It is my understanding that these higher dimensions carry more refined light frequencies so the negativity or denseness of the third dimension vibration cannot penetrate into those realms.

Many indigenous peoples, and those comfortable with the idea of other dimensions, already have a sense of their interconnectedness with the cosmos. However, those who have a more limited belief system—in which superiority, ownership, cultural control, and unchecked growth and consumption dominate—tend to struggle with this perception. Those who refuse to deal with the density of their actions or reactions, or who remain unaccountable for the negativity they willfully generate, will remain bound to the third-dimensional plane, continuing to experience chaos and lack. Gram suggested that at the end times those who inhabit the higher frequency dimensions will be invisible to those who remain on the lower frequency plane.

Gram predicted, as have others, that from December 2012 onward, many of us will have the opportunity to begin to live in this fourth- and fifth-dimensional awareness, conscious of, yet separate from, the chaos of the third-dimensional experience. She said of those who will vibrate

---

*Through the teachings of J. J. Hurtak, who founded the Academy of Future Sciences and wrote *The Book of Knowledge: The Keys of Enoch*, the fourth dimension is defined as "the consciousness threshold that must be crossed when entering and leaving three-dimensional *perceptual time and space*" (Hurtak's italics). He further defined the fourth dimension as, "A time-coordinate in addition to length, breadth, and depth of conventional space."

at that more refined wavelength, "In that future, they will simply know and be." She suggested we would begin to know that these challenging yet transformational times were upon us because we would be able to see different spectra of colors beyond what we normally have been able to perceive. Other signs would be both the discovery of new animal species and the increase in mutations in the animal kingdom.

Maya Perez had told me something similar: that we are all here at this time to learn how to hold the higher vibration of our potential. She felt that because we are spiritual beings, as spirit we had lived the expression of crystals, minerals, trees, the wind, fire, animals, even angels—everything was held within our field of knowing at the highest level. As a result, "in every incarnation, each of us has the capacity to learn to be more humble and to walk in the awareness of the light we actually are." Maya felt strongly that everyone who has incarnated at this particular time in Earth's history is here not to walk away from our problems but to work out in this lifetime where we are still asleep, especially as concerns the environment and our connection with each other. She said that "we are here now so every thought form and action that our souls have experienced since the beginning of time can be healed."

She suggested that between the years 2010 and 2025 the "doors will start to close" and we will either ascend in consciousness or remain in suffering. Those who do not learn to raise their vibration and ascend in consciousness will have to continue coming back to the "the density of matter," a period that she suggested may last another 30,000 to 40,000 years. However, those "who make it through the door will be able to know what's happening in third-dimensional reality without having to experience it." By learning to live with humility, love, faith, and discipline, we can expand our conscious awareness and attain the vibration that shifts us through the door, because "we each have the capacity to be the bright lights that we really are."

I remember asking after hearing this information, "Maya, how do we stay in faith and raise our vibration when there are so many atrocities happening all around us?" She smiled and said, "You don't lose what you don't have. You either have faith or you don't. It is through faith our desires are manifested. Faith is neither passive nor conditional."

Gram and Maya related their beliefs back in the early 1990s, and as the years have unfolded I have seen many of their predictions play out, but not all. Native perspectives on prophecies and time differ from Western viewpoints in how they are perceived. Native people experience time as a cycle where the center is timeless and becomes the steady or present around which cycles of change are observed. Prophecy is formless, so events aren't inevitable because our choices moment to moment determine our experiences. From the Western perception, time is about past, present, and future: thus within the form of history there is implied a beginning, middle, and end. Because of this mindset, many people have postulated an end to the world rather than a transformation of consciousness that makes possible a new worldview.

I suspect that the Mayan end date of December 21, 2012, signaled the disintegration of the paradigms that have ruled and conditioned us rather than the end of the world that was suggested by some. Time as we have known it is collapsing, or compressing itself into shorter and shorter waves, as described by the late Terrence McKenna in his Timewave Zero theory; the day to day is speeding up, although the month to month as noted on a calendar has not changed. Cycles are repeating in ever faster loops. We are in a process of consciousness quickening.

The natural disasters and the man-made ones; the financial collapse of national economies; the constant wars over religion, ethnic superiority, and political systems; and economic need or greed are showing us that our way of operating on personal and global scales no longer makes any sense. Many of us have become ignorant in our use of free will, acting willful only to meet our own needs, and so we have created the conditions that support the ego's inability, or its resistance, to let go of what is separating us from the inner purpose of our higher selves, which is to awaken.* For me, the Mayan prophecy is an expression of evolutionary consciousness, where we have the opportunity to attain our soul's central aim—enlightenment. I believe life is chaotic because we are transitioning from the values of this present age to take on new, shared values supporting the greater good of the planet and ourselves.†

I am merely speculating, but on the winter solstice of 2012 the Galactic Center, Alcyone (the central star in the Pleiades constellation), and our sun were all in alignment in the dark rift of the Milky Way. The dark rift in the Milky Way is seen by some indigenous people as a birth canal, and the Milky Way itself as the Great Mother. It takes our sun approximately 26,000 years to revolve around Alcyone, and as such this star figures prominently in Mayan and Toltec cycles. The processions of the equinoxes and the Hindu concept of *yugas*‡ both speak of 26,000-year cycles and describe reoccurring human cycles of development. The energy that was birthed through the Great Mother by this alignment with the Galactic Center resulted in an influx of electromagnetism and intergalactic plasma§ that may serve as energy to transmute personal and collective consciousness. Perhaps this influx will have the potential to birth something unique within humanity, both literally and psychologically. And possibly that birth of new energy and opportunity for higher levels of consciousness, predicted and celebrated by

---

*Eckhart Tolle, in *A New Earth,* points out that the extent of the ego's inability to recognize itself is staggering. He states, "The ego will do exactly what it condemns others for. When it is pointed out, it will use angry denial, clever arguments, and self-justification to distort facts. People do it, corporations do it, governments do it." He further states, "Awareness is conscious connection with universal intelligence."

†Carl Johan Calleman, Ph.D., writes in his book *The Mayan Calendar and the Transformation of Consciousness,* "The difficulties, or even catastrophes, in the time ahead will have much less to do with natural disasters than with the social, spiritual, and psychological consequences of the old values coming to an end as a result of a change in consciousness."

‡Jospeh Selbie and David Steinmetz, in their book *The Yugas: Keys to Understanding Our Hidden Past, Emerging Present and Future Enlightenment*, share that the great Swami Sri Yukteswar explained that "the cycle of the yugas is caused by influences from outside our solar system that affect the *consciousness* [authors' italics] of all mankind."

§Plasma is one of the four states of matter along with solid, liquid, and gas.

many people on December 21, 2012, was in fact just that, a birth. As we proceed through 2013 and beyond, as with any newly born beings or visions, we will need to move through the various stages of growth that bring greater self-realization and collective consciousness. We have hopefully developed a better awareness of how our personal choices can, and will, profoundly define humanity's challenges moving forward. I see both the Hopi and Mayan prophecies as both an opportunity to restructure and a seeding time, not as an ending or catastrophic time. And I see the accelerating global social climate and cumulative effects of shocking world events as tipping points to quicken our ultimate transformation. Common sense tells us that the Maya couldn't predict how mankind would awaken to and manifest this energy moving forward after the December 21, 2012, prophecies. That is up to all of us. And, quite possibly the lifting of the mask spoken of in traditional Hopi prophecy really symbolizes the lifting of the veil, needed by all of humanity to all finally grasp and face true unity consciousness.

Indeed we are at a choice point where we have to crystallize as a species a truth that the many prophecies have disclosed—we are not limited, physical human beings, but divine, multidimensional beings. From that knowing, we will be more capable of becoming open to the voice of God within creation because we finally find God's voice within ourselves. With the verity of seeing God in each other, we will not be able to act unconsciously toward each other. Although we live in a world of infinite possibilities, multiplicity is not a contradiction to unity; the "many in one" will be the reality of the new world—the Uniworld of which Gram spoke.

To me, this does not suggest a political "One World Order," but the reality that we share basic human needs—food, water, shelter, security, health, education, and, most importantly, love—and that we serve ourselves best by working together in unity. I am not so naïve as to not realize that we face very real and complex challenges as globalization tethers nations and economies together. However, with the world population experiencing more and more disparity at all levels, the answer can only lie in social equanimity and social accountability. It is true, as my teacher Maya pointed out, we cannot walk away from the problems we have created, either personally or collectively, for the time to advance a unity consciousness, more than ever before, is now upon us.

As a preparation for this shift, most of the work I did with Gram over those earlier years focused on personal transformation as the primary way to cleanse my dense energy cords and reclaim the gifts of myself. Such personal effort is crucial for each of us because we must become balanced within ourselves before we can add to the greater whole. The indigenous saying, "You can't know where you are headed unless you know where you have come from" reflects this necessity. Part of that work involves recapitulating memories and the personal impact of outside influences.

During one visit with Gram, Ann and I were discussing our families—our roles in our families, events that had fostered fears and desires, the persistence of generational patterns—when Gram stopped our discussion. She asked us to go out for a walk, separately, and meditate upon an unfulfilled desire from our childhood that may support one of the purposes of our life's mission. Once we identified the unfulfilled desire, we should make an offering of tobacco to the land and pose our question aloud to the universe about how we might best realize that desire. We should then continue walking until we felt we had received a clear answer. When we did, we should search the ground immediately around us for a stone that "spoke" to us. She said that we had to complete this exercise before she could teach information through a stone reading, which would further reveal our individual potentials.

Always eager for a new lesson or creative learning experience, I went out to sit in the morning sun and recapitulate my past. Many events bubbled to the surface, some significant, some trivial. Eventually, I settled on a particular dream about the unfulfilled desire I wanted to query the universe about. It was a dream I had repeatedly as a child— about Peru, a country and culture I had always been interested in. It was a mystery to me that I always had such a strong desire to visit there. In the dream . . .

I am standing on a high mountain peak that overlooks a city of stone that is surrounded by mountains and skirted by jungle. A wide silver ribbon of river wends its way in the valley below, along the base of the mountains and into the jungle. The rays of the rising sun are hitting the rooftops of the city's stone structures. Huge red and yellow flowers, with thick green foliage, grow on some of the roofs, whereas other rooftops appear to be covered in bright feathers of various colors, and still others are thatched with straw. Water flows in rivulets through carved channels that run between the buildings and the steep stone stairways that wind through the metropolis. The stone city steps up the side of the mountain on a tiered landscape. Smaller huts dot the valley farther below, where animals graze and crops grow. In the golden hue of dawn, the site looks magical and ethereal.

I am with a small group of other young people, both boys and girls. We have been trained for seven years for this fertility rite; not just a rite of sexual coming of age, but one that is designed to carry forward the life of the community. The girls, young virgins, have been instructed by the elder women priestesses; and the future warriors, also virgins, by the elder male warrior-priests. The boys wear yellow feathered shirts and gold disks, which represent the sun, on their foreheads attached by a thin band of gold. I know the color of their shirts signifies both kernels of corn and their "seed." We girls each wear a white feathered skirt and a necklace from which hangs a gold crescent moon that wraps under our exposed breasts. Tied around our foreheads and falling down the backs of our heads is some sort of headdress made from red knotted cords that holds back our long, black, free-flowing hair. We are all barefoot.

As the sun crests the mountain directly across from us, we begin to dance. This dance is offered only at specific times within the cycles of the earth and sun. We gracefully move to the rhythm of panpipes and the rising rays of the sun, as both the man-made and cosmic sounds are the music. The dance has a deliberate choreography, our movements an energetic expression of gratitude to the sun, mountains, and land.

In the years since first having this dream, I had recognized the mountain site in my dreamscape from images in geography and history books. It is the sacred citadel of Machu Picchu, which had been rediscovered when Yale archeologist Hiram Bingham came upon the ruins around 1911.* The mountain above the ancient city where I had dreamed I was dancing is Huayna Picchu.

Now, as I walked through the woods, feeling the sun warm the top of my head, I wondered what Spirit might tell me about this dream's significance and any influence it might have for my future. Even as I offered a pinch of tobacco to Mother Earth and posed my question to the universe, I realized that in some sense I was already defeating receiving any answer because I believed I would never go to Machu Picchu. Almost in contradiction, immediately following that thought a second realization came to me—I might never understand the dream unless I actually went there. I had no sooner thought this when I literally tripped over a stone. I bent to pick it up. It was a roundish gray rock the size of a small plum. Short, fine black lines formed triangles that marked its surface, and one side had a pea-sized indentation. The stone was so indistinct that I wondered how it could hold any special meaning; still, I thought it best not to ignore the fact that I had tripped over it, so I took it with me.

When I returned to the house, Ann was already there, sitting at the kitchen table with Gram. I grabbed a cup of tea and joined them.

*Controversy surrounds Bingham's discovery, although he might have been one of the first white men into the ruins. Indians say they had come upon and frequented the site well before Bingham arrived. They tell stories of gold and silver artifacts in many of the temple caves, although in the years after Bingham's expedition had explored the ruins, they could no longer be found. However, he brought fame to Machu Picchu, opening the door for archeologists and scientists to study the ruins and tourists to visit.

Gram asked us to tell her our question, but not the answer we may have received. She had us place our rocks on the table. Ann's rock appeared spectacular to me. It was multicolored and palm-sized, with many angles and inclusions. Gram saw multiple animal faces and geometric symbols on its surface, and she interpreted each of them. She next scrutinized the lines and indentations, offering her interpretation of those, and when she was complete, Gram set Ann's rock on what she called the Stone chart, which she'd already placed in front of her on the table.

She then read the Stone chart, telling Ann many wonderful things about her capabilities and what she could accomplish with patients in her healing practice. As she spoke, I felt self-conscious, wondering if my rock was up to par. It was so plain. It didn't have a quarter of the markings and faces that graced Ann's. Although Ann and I are sisters of the heart, I would be foolish to deny there was a bit of competition between us. We had spoken of this openly in the past and the insecurities it brought up in each of us. I felt that insecurity now.

When Gram examined my rock, there were only three sides on which it could sturdily stand. There were eight small triangles scattered over its surface and the pea-sized indentation, which I worried might not be all that auspicious. Gram fingered the indentation and called it a mouth. Great, I thought sarcastically, assuming that was something negative. As she often did when she felt us slipping away into our own feelings of doubt or self-pity, Gram asked, with that distinctive twinkle in her eyes, "Why are you still whining about what you think you don't have?" I was taken aback by her seeming reprimand. I felt exposed in that vulnerable moment and became defensive, assuring myself and then Gram and Ann that I wasn't whining about anything. That obviously was not true to anyone, especially me, and I admitted, "I guess my rock really didn't bring any clarity to my dream question." I should have known from her twinkling eyes Gram was baiting me for yet another of her teachings—or should I say *my* teachings.

"Well," said Gram, pointing to the tracing of my rock on the chart, "the lines drawn from the stone's three stable faces across the Stone chart hit these points. This first line," she explained, pointing to it, "lands in the Age of Improvement and hits the seventh gate on the Wheel, which signifies that part of the answer to your question is about overcoming the obstacles that stand in the way of you loving yourself. The second line moves into the Age of Learning and hits the point of action you need to take to honor yourself, which is accomplished by activating a new, yet undiscovered path. This third line moves to the quadrant of the Age of Wisdom and hits the dreamer and counselor section of the Wheel. You are a dreamer and need to counsel yourself on how to get where you want to go, especially by visions shown to you in the dreamtime. These tiny inverted equilateral triangles are symbols of inspiration. And because there are eight of them, this tells me that you will be in service to others teaching the information and inspiring them through what you gain in your new quest. Trust your intuition, Sandy. Don't fall into servitude to any teachings or teachers. Make the teachings your own. And finally," she said, pointing to the pea-sized depression, "this represents a mouth and how you will communicate the teachings once you have made them your own." Gram then said, "Many moths will be called to your flame, Sandy, so don't sit there bemoaning what you feel is not easily available to you. Make it happen." With that twinkle in her eye, she said, "So, what do you think now?"

Well, okay then, I thought to myself. What I said was, referring to Peru, "I hope I can get there someday, although I don't know how I will do that."

"Hope has a big hole in it," Gram admonished me. "Don't hope, *trust*. Trust in Great Mystery. Trust in yourself, and when it's meant to be, you will find the way to get there and the right teachers to work with. Take it into your dreamscape."

We had already talked a great deal about the dreamtime, and I now asked Gram to speak more about dreaming. From our many and varied previous discussions, I understood dream language is our soul's way of making our deepest desires known so we can remember our promises to ourselves and act to fulfill them. Dreams can also reveal our fears and self-limiting beliefs or patterns, and help us understand them so we can restore balance to our personal world. To merge our inner spirit with the timeless flow of the dreamworld offers us a greater sense of connection and expansion that can bring us inner fulfillment and peace.

Gram expanded further on some of what I knew, outlining the many types of dreams: precognitive dreams that alert and warn us; conscious dreams in which we are lucid and active participants; cross-over dreams that take us into multidimensional or interdimensional spaces; past-life dreams that can help us understand karmic patterns experienced in our life-stream; and clarity dreams, which have the potential to liberate us from attachments and tensions that hold us from our infinite expression and that can ultimately offer us the freedom to become aware as we are transitioning at our death. She counseled, "Dreams are an important source of spiritual and practical guidance. Always express gratitude for the message of the dream. The ancestors believed Great Mystery offered the gift of the dreamtime to every creation; it is a gift of peace."

Gram stressed that we need to feel the energy of each dream, even our nightmares. The feeling of the dream is ultimately where its guidance lies. If we neglect our dreams and ignore the feelings they elicit, we will miss an important link between our inner and outer worlds. Dream awareness helps inform us and disentangle us from our daily concerns as we learn to control the dream and realize that we have choices in our outer life. As Buddhist priests have long suggested, "It is not the dream that commands the dreamer, but the dreamer who commands the dream."

Gram went on to say that dreaming is the best preparation for dying, whether that means the end of your life or only to some part of your life. Oh Shinnah, Maya, and some of my other teachers had expressed similar opinions. Oh Shinnah used to call the dreamtime the *little death*. I understood this to be an analogy. If we can emerge from our dream state, awakening to each new day understanding we have fresh opportunities and choices, and are not ruled by the limitations or conditions that we have come to believe define us, then similarly at the moment of death, as we return to the *bardo*,* we can learn to awaken to the realized Self, instead of emerging into another lifetime. Shamanic traditions throughout history, no matter the culture involved, employed the dream state to access different aspects of consciousness. Generally the shaman uses the dreamtime for two primary purposes: to heal, which does not always mean curing but can include simply shifting the energy of the person, offering them a healthier perspective on an issue given what was divulged in the dream; or to gain information from the spirit world.†

I had been learning from my indigenous mentors that dreams help us hold on to our vital energy. They are supersensory and don't always make sense at first glance. The greatest gift of a dream is that it can put us in touch with the deeper parts of ourselves—connecting us with our ancestors and linking us to our personal stories, our past, present, or future—because our dreaming minds release us from the limitations of time and space. Because in our dreamstate we are not tied to time and space—as we are in the conscious state we generally occupy in our waking world—we have the ability to transcend the physical and function

---

*The bardo in Tibetan traditions refers to the states of existence between lifetimes. Some Buddhist schools speak of six bardos or intermediate states. According to Chogyal Nam-khai Norbu (simplified here) these include: the waking state, dream state, meditative state, dying process, the arising of visions as a consequence of one's karmic experiences, and finally the search for rebirth or reincarnation to confront karmic seeds.

†In *The Dreaming Universe*, Fred Alan Wolf examines the psychological and scientific elements of dreams. He has linked research about the Greek Asclepius dream temples with modern research about telepathy and lucid dreaming. Asclepius was the Greek god of medicine and healing. At the Asclepian healing center in present-day Turkey, "requestors" would undergo ritual purification and then spend the night in holy chambers, called *abatons*, where they would experience dreams and visions they would later discuss with a healer-priest. Their dreams were often a source of healing because they contained symbols, personal facts, or metaphors relevant to the cause of the affliction. Wolf theorizes that "dreaming is the basis for consciousness, and that it is through dreaming that we are able to manifest a sense of ourselves. This sense of our self is imperative to our own survival." Wolf came to feel that "the dream is a laboratory of the self," an opinion shared by the late psychiatrist Dr. Montague Ullman and well-known psychologist Dr. Stanley Krippner, both eminent dream researchers.

in the higher realms.* And again, because dreams are not bound by time and space, dreams can help us to untangle from the complexities of our lives—those things that might be holding us from both personal and transpersonal awareness.

These discussions and teachings from an indigenous perspective were not that far afield from the work of modern dream researchers and therapists, especially Carl Jung's dream theory. One of the distinguishing points of Jung's theory is that dreams express both personal content, whose symbolic expressions can support individuation, and collective universal content through archetypical symbols, reflecting images that lie beneath the surface of human conscious awareness. Dreams can uncover information that the conscious self has ignored, denied, or repressed. Therefore, the natural wisdom lying below the facade of our everyday reality, deep in the pool of our human collective unconscious, can help us to tap universal insights, intuitive knowing, and opportunities for self-realization. In his book *Memories, Dreams, Reflections,* Jung recounts an experience of a dream from which he awakened with a pain in his head and a feeling of concern for one of his patients, who he later learned had committed suicide by shooting himself. Jung writes, "The collective unconscious is common to all; it is the foundation of what the ancients call the 'sympathy of all things.'" He concluded that "the unconscious had knowledge of my patient's condition."

I came to understand that dreams are a gateway to inner truth and self-development, and that journeying into our dream space is a journey into the *I* of our Self. As that *I* becomes capable of controlling the dreamstate, the experience of dream lucidity helps us to understand that we are co-creators of our destiny in our waking state, because we are not just part of the universe, we *are* the universe. As I recapitulated the unfulfilled desire expressed through my Machu Picchu dream, the

---

*In *The Book of Knowledge: The Keys of Enoch,* Dr. J. J. Hurtak writes, "Higher Evolution generally programs man to accept the realities of the higher universe by taking man's subjective consciousness body out of his physical body during a dream cycle for education through a visual light experience."

walking meditation exercise, and personal information concerning Gram's reading of my Stone chart, I found I had a new purpose: if it was in the best interest of the evolution of my work and the destiny of my soul to go to Machu Picchu, I would figure out a way to dream myself to Peru.

9

Down the Rabbit Hole

My work with Gram was not only furthering my understanding as I grew on my personal path, but also was helping me mature from an insecure student to a teacher. I had received the wolf card while working with the Creature Teachers chart at our first meeting, and now two years later I was finally accepting the gift of teaching this rich body of work to others. I was sharing many of the indigenous teachings—such as Oh Shinnah's Moon Ceremony training and work with the elementals, and Gram's Seneca Earthpath energy charts and dream interpretation—in my private counseling practice and while facilitating group workshops.

At the same time that I was enjoying all that was manifesting in my life, I also had to deal with everyday challenges, one of the most serious of which was the impending end of my marriage to Ben. The doctors at Callie's death had suggested couple's counseling because they knew over one-third of couples who lose a child do not end up staying together. Over the years, as the doctors had predicted, Ben and I had expressed our grief and dealt with our loss in completely different ways. Now, we sadly both knew our sixteen-year marriage was coming to an end.

At the prospect of soon needing to go at it alone and needing increased income, I took a second job as part-time director of an after-school educational and enrichment program serving at-risk children from the community and local homeless shelters. My own education was enriched on many fronts—by my daughter Nyssa, the educational programs with the at-risk children, my clients, workshop participants, and shamanic teachers. Although disheartened about the impending end of my marriage, I had a full and satisfying life in which to absorb myself.

That said, I was brought crashing back down to the level of the physical when, in the spring of 1991, I was diagnosed with a breast lump. My doctor wanted to biopsy it immediately and she set me up with a surgeon. The process was moving way too fast, and I was petrified as I went in for the surgery one week later. As I was going under anesthesia, the doctor, an older, conservative, and emotionally distant surgeon, leaned over me and asked me a question that was completely out of character: "Sandy, is there anything I can do to make you more comfortable?" I didn't immediately answer him, for, as the anesthesia was taking effect, the bright circular lights above were unnerving me. I was fleetingly remembering back to when I was six years old and had my tonsils removed. I had fought the doctors to get off the table and had to be physically restrained as they put the mask over my nose to administer the gas. I remembered the intense circular light staring down at me being the cause of my fear then. Without quite knowing why, and trying to calm myself, I now responded groggily to the doctor, "If my dad were here, he'd sing 'When Irish Eyes Are Smiling' and then I would know that everything is going to be okay."

Without hesitating, the surgeon burst into the song, and the last thing I noted before I drifted off was the nurses turning to look at me with raised eyebrows and astonished eyes over the blue masks that hid the rest of their faces. When I came to later in the recovery room, one of the surgical nurses was by my bedside waking me and, still obviously mulling over how the surgeon had acted out of character, she confided, "We've never seen him do that. He's usually so serious." I didn't know how to respond. I was just grateful for his song, for to me it was a message from my dad that I would be okay. Later, fully cloaked as his serious self again, the surgeon came to tell me that the tumor was benign. Thank you, Great Mystery.

Although I had grown more comfortable with the unusual and unexpected in both my everyday and more metaphysical experiences, the next turn of events was about to send me down the proverbial rabbit hole. I found myself tottering on the edge of my known reality, and it was to Gram that I turned to regain my stability. I've shared some of my out-of-the-ordinary experiences encountered while exploring the conflicting truths of my changing paradigm, but what I eventually would have to confront over the next ten years was the death of what I still concretized as my defined framework of reality. A life transformation affirms two things—life will never look the same, and you will never look the same at life.

A few months after surgery I began to experience severe panic attacks. I thought maybe they had come on because of the impending divorce, or maybe from the release of the pent-up anxiety about thinking I might have had breast cancer. The attacks would come without warning and were often preceded by a buzzing sound in my head. My heart beat so hard and fast that I feared it would explode out of my body. I broke out in a cold sweat and my whole body shook uncontrollably, with my legs wobbling so badly they often wouldn't support my weight. I wanted to run screaming, much like I had in my childhood during the night terror dreams. Oddly, I would often smell a strong scent of what I can only describe as wet cardboard, which intensified my panic. The episodes began to intensify and could happen at any time—while I was driving, sitting reading a book, walking down the aisle in the grocery store, or outside playing with Nyssa.

I sought medical reasons for the attacks, but after all kinds of tests, doctors found nothing physical to explain them, and the Xanax they had prescribed did nothing. A psychotherapist I consulted suggested maybe they were precipitated by unresolved fears of Nyssa dying early in life, as Callie had. Although that was always an unspoken fear, I knew it was not the cause. Family suggested maybe it had to do with the impending divorce Ben and I were discussing, but I knew that wasn't it either. The panic felt primordial and disconnected from anything in my routine life. I didn't know how to approach what might be causing these episodes, but what I did know was that they were becoming debilitating and I had to do something about them.

Because I still experienced unexplained night terrors, I began to examine possible connections, both through my dreams and in shamanic meditative states. If all the answers are within, something had to surface to help me understand what was happening. Strangely, what kept coming to mind was my response to a movie, *Invaders from Mars*. I had become obsessed with this 1950s sci-fi movie when I was a kid. It was continually played on a local Boston television station, and I had always made it a point to watch, even though it scared the bejesus out of me. I would hide behind the green sectional sofa in the living room and watch it in its entirety with fingers spread over my eyes.

I have always been fascinated by worlds beyond our own. As a kid, I loved watching the night sky, naming constellations, and marveling at unidentified lights and their movements. I had read with great interest about the Air Force UFO investigation Project Blue Book when I worked as an assistant librarian in high school, and more recently I had read scientific and metaphysical books about the likelihood of life in other galaxies. I had been drawn to the *Star Trek* TV series of the '60s and '70s, and some of Steven Spielberg's movies in the '80s, my favorite being *Close Encounters of the Third Kind*, which I had found uplifting. I entertained the information from these media and literary sources as possibilities and others as sort-of-out-there theories, but for some reason I had always felt a mixture of both fascination and terror when watching *Invaders from Mars*.

This 1953 sci-fi movie is about a young boy, David, who is awakened by a thunderstorm and looks out his bedroom window to see a spaceship land in the hills behind his house. With fear and confusion, he watches it disappear into a sandpit. He rushes to his father, a scientist, who goes out to investigate. But he doesn't return until late the next morning, and his personality has changed, becoming cold and distant. Also, he has a small cut on the nape of his neck. Over the next few days, David observes as friends and others from the community get sucked into the sandpit near his home, only to return acting oddly and exhibiting the same small red scar on their necks. David finally convinces the town's doctor and a local astronomer to believe him that something strange is going on out in the woods by the sandpit, and they go to the military for help. The military decides that an invasion from Mars is under way and prepares to attack the flying saucer and its occupants.

Meanwhile, David and the doctor are captured by the aliens, who look like green-scaled humanoids with large slit eyes, and they are taken to the underground tunnels where the spacecraft is hidden. The military finally rescues David and the doctor, and the movie ends with David in bed, a montage of memories running through his mind. He awakens, and frightened by the raging thunderstorm, he runs to his parents' room, where they comfort him, telling him he was only dreaming. The question left hanging at the end of the movie was whether David was experiencing a repetitive dream, having a premonition of the future, or remembering an actual event that everyone else seemed to have repressed.

The absolute fear that movie instilled in me was nothing compared with the shock I felt as an adult, when out of the blue, a few weeks into using my shamanic techniques to uncover a cause for the panic attacks, I had a waking episode the likes of which I had never experienced before. I wasn't asleep; this was not a lucid dream. It was not a hallucination and not even a DMT experience. (It has been suggested that DMT, dimethyltryptamine, which is a natural chemical released in the pineal gland, can, if not inhibited by other enzymes, create profound sleeping dreams or waking hallucinatory states much like an LSD experience.) Nor was this a case of hypnagogia. Hypnagogia is one of the many levels of a relaxed state of consciousness that is experienced prior to falling asleep. Many artists, lay people, and scientists, such as Albert Einstein, have experienced and recorded this state as an intuitive bank of information and a source of creative, psychic, or artistic details. No, without a doubt, this was not any of those.

It was a beautiful, warm August night. I awoke to a blue glow lighting the entire bedroom. The bedside clock read 3:15 a.m. With a panic I didn't fully register, I bolted upright to the awful smell of wet cardboard, which immediately terrified me. I could not shake Ben awake. I sensed a presence in the room, turned to my left, and saw a short, pale humanoid-type figure with a large head. His face was dominated by huge, penetrating black eyes and a small mouth, and he had very thin arms. He was dressed in a pair of denim coveralls, making this scene even more absurd and surreal, despite the fear rising like bile in my throat. I recognized him as what is called a *Gray* in the literature about extraterrestrials. I thought, *This can't be real!* But I knew I was not dreaming, and this was not a projection, although in my terror I wished it was a dream because then I could wake up from it. Most disturbing of all was he felt familiar, way too familiar.

I was rendered immobile. I could not even scream. In my head I heard the words, "Everything will be all right." It took all of my willpower to take my eyes off the eyes of the pale-skinned creature at my side, but I felt my attention being commanded to the foot of the bed where I sensed this voice was coming from. There stood three exceptionally tall beings that appeared humanlike and had a faint glow or reflective energy around them. Unlike the Gray, they were beautiful, with staggeringly blue eyes and blond hair. Their presence and the palpable energy they were emanating soothed me—it's as if they sensed my incredible fear and wanted me to trust they would not harm me.

Their mouths did not move as they spoke inside my head in one voice, although it was clear they were three separate beings. Through telepathy, they explained they belonged to the Legions of Light. They told me it was time for me to remember and that I would begin to recall contact episodes from my childhood, and in the future would have conscious interactions with them. I was not to fear the contacts. They said there are many types of galactic beings currently on, living within, or visiting Earth at this time. Earth's peoples have been contacted by these various civilizations for thousands of years, for the purpose of both advancing the evolution of civilization and as preparation for humanity becoming part of the Legions of Light. They explained these encounters with humans often cross generations in a family group. As they communicated that, in my peripheral vision I saw Nyssa floating down the hallway. Because I was immobilized, my screams were only in my head. I tried desperately to move, to get to Nyssa, but I couldn't. The Golden-haired Ones telepathically repeated, "Everything is all right."

The next thing I was aware of was looking at the bedside clock, which read exactly 4:30 a.m. The beings were gone. I could move again. I raced down the hall and ran out to the porch, as it was the direction I had seen Nyssa go. Nyssa was standing in the backyard in her nightgown, her long hair flowing as she twirled on bare feet. She was giggling and looking up into the early morning sky. My heart was racing as I scooped her up and checked her physically to make sure she was unharmed. I asked her if she was all right, holding her tightly and showering her head with kisses. She looked at me with innocence and excitement. "Mommy, they took me on the starflasher bed! They let me drive it! They said I would need to remember how to do that. They showed me the Bee People on the Pleiades, and the Crab People on Arcturus."

What the hell was she talking about? How did she even know those words? I collapsed to the ground on my butt with her still in my arms. She was oblivious to anything but her enthrallment with what she had experienced as she continued to look skyward. Then she turned to look at me, a very serious expression on her face. And leaning toward my ear, she whispered conspiratorially, "But we can't tell Daddy. He won't understand."

It took all of my willpower not to call—who? The police? No! Maybe the FBI? Ridiculous! I couldn't tell Nyssa's dad—she was right about that. Not only would he not understand, he would think I had gone totally over the edge, especially in light of the panic attacks. Or, what felt worse still, he might simply laugh it all off. Maybe I could call

Gram Twy? I didn't know who else to call. What had happened felt insane. Having no control over the encounter scared the hell out of me.

I have little memory of the rest of that morning, except Nyssa sitting happily drawing pictures of what she had experienced. Agitated and distracted, I waited until what I thought was the reasonable morning hour of seven o'clock before I called Gram. Still shaken and babbling, I rushed through the story. "I know this all sounds totally nuts," I said, "and I can't imagine you would believe me, but I needed to speak to *someone* about this!" Gram listened patiently and then said matter-of-factly, "None of my students have yet approached me on this subject. I have much to say to you, but you need to be patient until we can meet in person. I have time in two weeks, come up then. This is not a simple subject." Two weeks! *Gawd*, I thought to myself, *that's an eternity*. I thanked her for listening without judging, and we said our good-byes.

Two very long weeks later, I traveled alone to see Gram. Although I asked a thousand questions, she wouldn't answer any of them until we were sitting out under the stars that night. Then she engaged the subject directly. She asked me what else I remembered about contacts other than what had happened that frightening night two weeks ago. I told her although I was fascinated by the possibility there may be other galactic civilizations, I had no memories of other encounters, although I could recall those nights as a child when I would wake up in terror. I had chalked those experiences up to childhood nightmares. I also shared with her the times as a child when I thought bright lights had occasionally appeared to descend close to me while I walked through the woods at the top of my street during childhood explorations and I would lose track of time. In retrospect, I had passed those incidents off as acts of a child's active imagination. I told her that upon seeing the creepy little gray guy during the incident two weeks ago, I had immediately felt something about him was uncomfortably familiar. Although I didn't divulge this to Gram at the time, I didn't want to remember those eyes; the draw of his eyes made me shudder.

Gram was looking at me intently, and I got the feeling speaking about this subject would expose something vulnerable in her, too. She said, candidly, "The Star Nation information is not a story." After a pause, she explained that Native peoples have a rich history of communication with the Star Nations and she, too, had her own personal experiences. Most of the Peoples of the Americas had passed down not only legends about the Star People within their tribal lore, but also their personal experiences of how these beings had come to offer help, guidance, and instruction in times of need. "They are still assisting humanity to this day," Gram said. She described how the wisdom of the Star Nations is in every culture, not just the Americas, although different cultures and tribes honor the Star People in different ways, according to their traditions and histories.

Gram Twylah's discussion mirrored some teachings I was simultaneously receiving from a Nakota (Yankton Sioux) teacher I had only recently begun working with. Gram Twylah had introduced me to Grandmother Kitty, whose Native name is *Dee Keel She Wa*, "Dark Sun She Walks" (referring to the corona of the sun during an eclipse). Twylah felt that a dream I had shared with her and a series of events that had followed needed to be addressed by someone who carries the *chanunpa*, the sacred Native pipe, which Gram Kitty did. Gram Kitty was also a Lakota peace elder and Sun Dance grandmother for fourteen years.

In private discussions with me, Gram Kitty had related that the Lakota speak with reverence of White Buffalo Calf Woman, who is said to have come to Earth as a falling star from the star cluster known as the Pleiades. She brought with her seven sacred ceremonies to the People and the sacred bundle holding the first chanunpa, which is to this day in the safekeeping of the Looking Horse family. The union of the pipe bowl with the pipe stem represents the union of Mother Earth and Father Sky, and in Kitty's words, when these two parts of the pipe are joined in prayer the pipe becomes "a living being." She told me that all the bands of the Sioux People had received help from the Star Tribes after times of cataclysms—once after a great Earth shift that caused the sun to rise in the west, and again after the more recent shift known as the great flood, when the earth flipped again and the sun returned to rising in the east. She said the People sometimes see the Star People when participating in their sacred ceremonies such as the Hembleciya (a vision quest), the Inipi (a sweat lodge ceremony), and the Yuwipi (a healing ceremony). And, that they believe these star beings come from stars, possibly other planetary systems, and constellation clusters such as the Pleiades, Ursa Major, the star Sirius, and the Orion constellation. Gram Kitty believed that we are all "Starseeds" but that "people are so full of who they think they are that there is little room for them to grow and remember who they really are."

I also remembered things Oh Shinnah had told me about the Star People. She had sat on many occasions with the late Grandfather David and his wife, Grandmother Nora, of the Hopi People (the Peaceful People) receiving their teachings on legends and prophecies. She shared with me that the Hopi kachina ceremonies and the Apache Gan, or mountain spirit dancers, relayed spirit messages that came from the *Katsina* (the Star People). Kachina dancers represent messengers between worlds, seeking to bring the spiritual world into physical manifestation. The Hopi have oral stories, ceremonial dances, and stone glyphs that encode their history, going far back into the distant past describing a great destruction that occurred upon the earth. In one accounting of Hopi history, the Katsina came in metal cylinders to collect the People so they might survive the deluge threatening the earth. Another version recounts how after the earth was destroyed by water the People came up from a *sipapu,* or place of emergence, which is symbolized by the small hole in their *kivas.** The survivors were assisted by the Ant People, a benevolent off-planet race that aided humans during that cataclysmic period and who had come to Earth on flying shields.

Within their oral traditions, Native People hold that each tribe has

---

*Kivas are usually round subterranean pit-houses, accessed through a hole in the roof and used by the Pueblo communities of the Southwest for ceremony.

a Star Race counterpart that helped form their culture, spiritual beliefs, and sacred ceremonies. Standing Elk, a spiritual elder for the Lakota nation, speaks of their teachings coming from the Pleiades; the Pawnee and Hopi speak of Sirius in their creation stories; other traditions speak of the Orion and Andromeda systems as their source.

Gram Twylah now spoke about the bright star Sirius and its companion star, Sirius B.* She explained her People had legends of contact with the inhabitants of this star too. The Dogon tribe of West Africa, who call it the Dog Star, and the People had known about this star long before Western astronomers had photographed its existence back in the 1970s. The Dogon creation myths have described the DNA-like pattern the binary star system makes within its elliptical orbit as the two stars rotate around each other. They believe Sirius to be the axis point of the universe, where all matter and all souls are formed.

The Dogon say that their culture was seeded by the Nommo, a race of amphibious beings who come from the Sirius star system. In contrast, Gram's belief was that the beings were dolphin-like in that they were able to communicate telepathically both as a single mind and a group mind, as she believed Earth dolphins can.

What Gram was sharing with me also mirrored research and accountings in books I had been reading from many cultures—such as Egyptian, Mesoamerican, and East Indian—that have legends of beings who came from other star systems to impart helpful information, provide refuge to humankind during or after Earth-based catastrophes, mine the planet for its rich resources, and construct great edifices, many

---

*Sirius, a binary star system, has consistently been associated with the dog in ancient cultures around the world, and in the mythology of many civilizations it is named as the place from whence the ancestors came to seed their knowledge and brought with them a mysterious force. Some Native tribes refer to Sirius as the Wolf Star or Dog-face Star, and the Tsalgi (Cherokee) people name Sirius as one of the stars that guards "the path of souls." In Chinese astronomy it was called Heavenly Wolf. In ancient Egyptian mythology the star Sirius represents the goddess Isis, who was responsible for the birth of consciousness throughout the universe, and the glyph they use to represent this on their monuments is that of the dog.

of which today we label sacred sites. The Mahabharata, one of two Vedic epics, depicts what the Hindus called *vimanas,* believed to be the stellar vehicles in which beings came to Earth. This sacred text recounts a time when humans witnessed terrifying aerial clashes between competing extraterrestrial groups who navigated the heavens in vimanas and used weapons that strangely resembled lasers to destroy vast sections of land, much like a nuclear weapon would today. Excavations started in the 1920s by R. D. Banerji, an officer of the Archeological Survey of India, uncovered two large sites, Mahenjo-Daro and Harappa, in the Indus River Valley that support this theory as both the sites and the skeletons uncovered within them are extremely radioactive.

Ancient Egyptian legends speak of *tep zepi,* meaning the "first time," as an age when "sky gods" came down to Earth on flying boats bringing wisdom, laws, and technology to the populace through a royal line, later called pharaohs. It is said they provided the technology that went into building the Pyramids of Giza. Hieroglyphs and reliefs within the Giza pyramid chambers depict sky boats and even beings who look strangely like some of the extraterrestrials reported today.* Further, legends suggest that during tep zepi the god Ra, who could bend sound, light, and color, traveled to and from Egypt in a "solar boat." Glyphs on the ceiling beams at Abydos show many images that resemble a variety of advanced modern day aircraft.

The 12th Planet, written by the late Zecharia Sitchin, Hebrew biblical scholar and researcher of ancient civilizations, provides evidence from ancient Sumerian sacred texts and stele glyphs of an extraterrestrial race called the Annunaki, who he stated come from a planet called Nibiru. He designates this as the twelfth planet in our solar system.

---

*In December of 2010, delegates to a convention at which Dr. Ala Shaheen of the Cairo University Archeology Department spoke were surprised to hear him comment that there might be truth to the theory that aliens helped early Egyptians build the pyramids. When questioned by Marek Novak, a delegate from Poland, about the possibility that the pyramids might still contain alien technology or even a UFO, Dr. Shaheen answered vaguely, "I cannot confirm or deny this, but there is something inside the pyramid that is not of this world."

Sitchin suggested that because of Nibiru's immense open elliptical orbit, it travels close to Earth every 3,600 to 3,900 years—its gravitational pull causing great instability to Earth's axis. Sitchin postulates that the Annunaki, who are referred to as the Nephilim in both the Bible and Torah, first visited our planet 450,000 years ago.

Like other theorists, Sitchin felt the oldest and largest interdimensional portal is in the area we now call the Middle East, and it was used particularly by those otherworldly civilizations who sought minerals and other resources they had depleted on their home planets. In eons gone by, these cosmic travelers interacted with the root races, who mistook them for gods because of their advanced knowledge and technological skills. Sitchin writes that "about 300,000 years ago, the Annunaki engaged in genetic engineering to upgrade Earth's hominids and fashion *Homo sapiens,* the Adam. In that they acted as emissaries for the Universal Creator—God."

Many famous Renaissance religious paintings depict stars, beams of light, and manned flying objects, which raises speculation about what the artists might have seen. For example *The Crucifixion,* painted in 1350, clearly shows a spacecraft with astronauts inside flying above the crucified Christ. The 1486 painting *The Annunciation with St. Emidius,* by Carlo Crivelli, and the 1710 painting by Aert de Gelder entitled *The Baptism of Christ* both show depictions of spacecraft that appear much like what witnesses note today. For the past fifty-five years, the Vatican has appointed theologians to explore the implications of life on other planets and has its own astronomical observatories around the world to map the galaxies. The late Monsignor Corrado Balducci was a member of the Curia of the Roman Catholic Church, a prelate of the Congregation for the Evangelization of Peoples and the Propagation of the Faith, a leading exorcist of the Archdiocese of Rome, and the author of several books and interviews examining the issues surrounding extraterrestrials. In an interview recorded with Balducci he states "that life may exist on other planets is certainly possible. . . . The Bible does not rule out that possibility. On the basis of scripture and on the basis of our knowledge of God's omnipotence, his wisdom being limitless, we must affirm that life on other planets is possible." He also wrote that "Extraterrestrial contact is a real phenomenon. The Vatican is receiving much information about extraterrestrials and their contacts with humans from its nuncios (ambassadors) in various countries, such as Mexico, Chile, and Venezuela."*

As interesting as these historical, anthropological, religious, and indigenous stories and references were, none of them did much to alleviate the confusion I felt from my recent encounter. It is one thing to read and speculate on this subject, yet another to research material to prove or debunk its validity, but it is something entirely different to have one's worldview shattered by an experience of this nature.

As if everything she had already shared with me wasn't enough, Gram told me about a race of beings who always appear in groups and whose colors correlate to what they are here to teach. They exist on interdimensional rings or bands of light that surround our physical planet and vibrate at octaves or frequencies higher than what our physical eyes can detect. They come and go through etheric portals or dimensional doorways as teachers and observers, sometimes shapeshifting into forms that do not frighten those who see them. Gram also briefly discussed the Tall White People, old entities or Star People, who for thousands of years have used Earth as a way station as they traverse the galaxies and who can occasionally be observed by certain individu-

---

*Monsignor Corrado Balducci passed in September 2008, early into gathering information for this book. However, Father José Gabriel Funes, leading astronomer and Director of the Vatican Observatory, stated in a 2008 interview, "Just as there is a multiplicity of creatures over the earth, so there could be other beings, even intelligent (beings), created by God. This is not in contradiction with our faith, because we cannot establish limits to God's creative freedom. To say it with St. Francis, if we can consider some earthly creatures as brothers or sisters, why could we not speak of a brother alien? He would also belong to the creation." Catholic News Agency. "Believing in Aliens Not Opposed to Christianity, Vatican's Top Astronomer Says." May 13, 2008, http://www.catholic-newsagency.com/news/believing_in_aliens_not_opposed_to_christianity_vaticans_top_astronomer_says/.

als as guardians of gateways to parallel universes; and another civilization from Pleiades, who are tall and blond, like the Golden-haired Ones I had seen at the foot of my bed. Of these beings she said, "They recognize their responsibilities and they came to you so you would begin to recognize the extent of yours."

She told me that in her belief the Star People are here to help make us become more self-aware. Furthermore, people from ancient civilizations, such as the Atlanteans, purposefully interacted with various intergalactic and interdimensional travelers who came through portals or vortexes, and who have been visiting since the dawn of civilization. She said these portals—energetic openings that make travel between the dimensions and worlds easier—are located all over the earth, often under sacred temple sites and connected by energetic ley lines around the globe. Gram reminded me that after the collapse of the Third World, the civilizations of the Fourth World no longer possessed the technical knowledge and ability for intergalactic communication their forebears had. Since the 1940s, she said, we have been remembering these contacts, which has resulted in our rapid technological advancement. The question is whether we can use this technology responsibly. If we can, we will finally be admitted into the Star People confederation. She offered her opinion that the reason so many people in recent decades have been recovering memories of encounters with star beings is because they are preparing us to remember we are star beings ourselves.

I listened to Gram, mesmerized, and finally asked, with respect, if she ever had experiences with the Grays or any other star beings. She was cautious in her reply. "I personally feel the Grays could be us—humanity—come back from our future to warn ourselves of how we are destroying the earth and breeding heart energy out of ourselves. The reason our future selves take such an interest in us is that although we are currently losing our heart energy—as we make choices that dishonor and disrespect each other and the earth—they are aware we still have the ability to come from the heart. Heart energy is akin to the feminine energies and is connected to birth, nurturing, and forgiveness and to the heartbeat of the Earth. There is no gender differential, for in our divine state we are neither and both masculine and feminine, the pure essence of Spirit. We still have time in the now to change. I think they are seeking to help us so that future reality can be changed, for they know what we, as well as they, have lost. There is always an exchange—*their* return to heart energy and *our* awakening. The opportunity they are offering us is to shepherd in an age of peace."

I sat quietly for quite a long time, thinking about everything Gram had just shared. She was obviously musing on all of this, too. She broke the silence to share a more personal story. She confided that once while she was in California on her way to Joshua Tree she had passed a being she considered not of this Earth. She described him as close to seven feet tall, with pale skin, sparse blond hair, and startlingly blue eyes. She said he held her gaze for what felt like a long time but was actually only several seconds, and through his eyes she understood that many of these beings are already here on Earth, living among us. That thought renewed her faith that humanity had a future, she said.

It was very late, and as Gram drew the discussion to a close, we went in for a cup of tea before bed. Although my mind was swimming from everything she had told me, I felt my sanity had been restored. I was immensely grateful to have such a wise woman as Gram as my teacher and friend. Before we retired, Gram shared one more thing. She ardently believed we are all from different star systems and those frequencies encode us when we emerge into this physical earth plane. She felt we each incarnate on Earth to regenerate as grounding rods or connectors to the Star People confederation and to remember who we really are.

After this visit with Gram, I never experienced another panic attack. She had provided me a context for the shocking encounter with the beings at the foot of my bed. As my experiences and memories increased over the following years, I would call Gram to discuss the events, dreams, or happenstances specifically around the star beings to get her opinion or counsel. She told me she was delighted with these discussions as she had been instructed to speak openly on the subject only when one of her students brought it up first. She asked me to write down all of these conversations and give her copies, as often the information came to her in the moment that I was asking the question.

That there are higher levels of creation or conscious beings more advanced than us was not the question, for I had always believed that there could be. What stimulated me, despite so many people continuing to deny the reality of contact, was the consideration of the amazing opportunities that await humanity once contact with star beings is verified. I wondered what octaves of beingness we might be able to reach both within ourselves and as a global community once we know for sure we are not alone in the cosmos.*

Since childhood, I had toyed with the idea that other planetary beings existed and now I trusted the veracity of my own experiences. Over the coming years, I would feel less alone in this strangeness as I found myself increasingly in the company of people from all levels of education, various cultural backgrounds, and with diverse religious convictions who believed they had either seen or been contacted by extra- or interdimensional beings. Today, it is no longer a topic I have to prove through research or defend as possible. Although when I discuss this subject more openly now with people, their reactions still run the gamut—from excitement and belief to curiosity or fervent disbelief to outright laughter and even scorn; however, my experiences have made it real in and for me.

---

*Dr. J. J. Hurtak writes in *The Book of Knowledge: The Keys of Enoch*, "The higher levels of creation are not simply states of consciousness, but actual realms of vast crystalline cosmoses, universes, and worlds, which are modeled into the most minute parts of the human microcosmos." He also believes, "Each person is a star but in a different harmonic octave within a larger star nodal point."

10

The World
of Living Energy

True to one of Gram Twy's predictions, I met a man who introduced me to the Andean path and with whom, as part of a large group, I first journeyed to Peru. Although our work together was short-lived, through him I met other teachers who took me deeper into the teachings. I started learning the Andean tradition in 1991, and over the next twenty-two years I would journey often to Peru to immerse myself in the south-central Peruvian mystical tradition, especially that of the Q'ero people. My mentors were Americo Yábar and Juan Nuñez del Prado. I received many profound teachings and participated in many ceremonies during these decades, but the following two chapters will focus on only a few experiences with Americo: one relates to my connection to the cosmos and another relates to teachings imparted through the act of forgiveness. During my Andean studies, I met many like-minded people and two women in particular who have become lifelong friends. One is Joan, a writer and confidante who assisted me in reviewing the original manuscript of this book. She and I traveled many times throughout Peru in the mid-90s as we studied together with the Q'ero. The other woman, whom I will call Mary, became an important healing partner in a clinical practice we developed together.

Mary and I synthesized many different streams of metaphysical knowledge with our counseling expertise to create a healing modality we called the STAR Process™: STAR is an acronym for *Soul Transmissions And Retrievals.* We realized we had work to do together during the first weekend we met, at an Andean workshop in the United States. In conversation after a fire ceremony, we discovered we were both psycho-therapists with metaphysical and shamanic backgrounds. What's more, as we talked about the ceremony that had just concluded, I revealed that during it I felt I had "downloaded" information that could be helpful in my healing practice. Mary admitted she too had a similar experience. As we shared our information, we realized we each had been given a piece of a larger body of work that could provide a more effective and faster process for clients to address their issues and problems. Within weeks, we had formulated the STAR Process soul retrieval technique.

Soul retrieval is a millennia-old shamanic healing technique that seeks to recover aspects of the Self to which a person no longer has conscious access. The concept of soul retrieval has changed little through the centuries, attesting to its potency as a healing paradigm. It approaches healing not only from a physical perspective, but from a spiritual one as well.

In the realm of shamanic healing, the energy body is perceived to be comprised of many layers of luminous vibrating energy filaments.*

---

*In the late 1990s, Russian physics professor Konstantin Korotkov developed the gas-discharge visualization (GDV) technology to image the biofield in a way that can distinguish the differing energy signatures of the physical, mental, emotional, and even spiritual energy bodies. This technology can also image life-force energy from plants, animals, and other organic entities and substances. GDV is being used in many different fields, including medicine, biology, botany, psychology, and agriculture. It allows researchers to view imbalances in these different energy bodies that may be influencing an individual's well-being, showing both the area of the body that is out of balance and the organ systems involved. In 2009, Korotkov took GDV photographs of people in the final stages of dying. At the point of death, the area around their stomach, called the *qosqo* in the Andean tradition, was the first to lose the light of the life-force, followed by the head, groin, and heart, in that order. This technology has been accepted by the Russian Ministry of Health for use in health-related fields, and it is in use around the world by physicians, health care practitioners, scientists, and researchers.

Our energy bodies are affected by personal experiences and our actions or reactions to those experiences. These responses leave imprints of either refined or dense energy that can affect one or more of our energy centers, also called chakras, or one or more of our subtle bodies—the emotional, physical, mental, psychic, and spiritual bodies. If we are not conscious of those imprints, and are not cleansing dense energy and replenishing our energy body with refined energy, then we can become distanced from the universal Source. In addition, we have less access to the multi- and interdimensional states of the Self that can further link us to Source.

It was clear to Mary and me in the work we had been doing in our individual private practices that many clients no longer recognized the voice of Source within themselves. This was creating a break in their belief in themselves and inhibiting access to actualizing many of their personal gifts. When we have life experiences that challenge, threaten, or traumatize us, we retreat into a stance of protection and survival. This can cause "soul loss," which is the inability to access some aspect of our core Self, causing us to fall out of alignment with the infinite possibilities of our essential nature—our soul connection. Hence the need to recover the forgotten aspects of our Self, which in shamanic terms is called *soul retrieval.*

Soul retrieval re-empowers or reactivates us, allowing us to reclaim the gifts or awareness encoded in our DNA structure. Soul retrieval healings have the potential to restructure our DNA because the mind-body connection re-informs our cellular structure creating a new environment in which to exist without the prior conscious or unconscious stress. Our soul connection through our re-informed DNA offers us a spiritual tool for advancement because we are no longer held hostage to the limitations that inhibit personal growth or personal change.

Since I started offering soul retrievals for clients close to twenty years ago, there has been a growing body of evidence that our thoughts and emotions influence our physiological state and even our DNA. Physicists, biologists, organic chemists, and neuroscientists have done the research that shows that DNA is affected by influences external to us, such as the environment, and internal, such as our thoughts and beliefs. These can determine gene expression—which genes are turned on or off—and so have a direct influence on cellular function.*

In her leading-edge research, neuroscientist and pharmacologist Dr. Candace Pert suggests that when we suppress emotions, our cells and even our DNA change in a way that can foster disease.† She writes that "the emotions are the link between the physical body and nonphysical states of consciousness, and the receptors on every cell are where this happens!" David Hamilton, Ph.D., in his ground-breaking book *It's the Thought That Counts,* provides scientific evidence that "the human states such as happiness and optimism can actually change your DNA." Originally a clinical researcher for a large pharmaceutical company, Hamilton had discovered through research into placebos that there is a brain-heart link by which thought causes changes in the microstructure of the brain and in the chemicals passed to the cells, down to a sub-atomic level, that can create physical changes in the body.

The Institute of HeartMath, a nonprofit health and consciousness research foundation, has found through its experiments that "an energetic connection or coupling of information occurs between the DNA in cells and higher dimensional structures—the higher self or spirit." Furthermore, the heart is a major generator of the biofield and "serves as a key access point through which information originating in the higher

---

*Bruce Lipton, Ph.D., is a cellular biologist whose groundbreaking work helped develop a new field of study called epigenetics, which shows how genetics (DNA) does not control biology in the way previously believed. As he discusses in his book *The Biology of Belief,* environmental signals operating through the membrane of the cells partially influences the expression of genes. This breakthrough in the understanding of human biology redefines the mind-body connection, suggesting that as we change our perceptions and beliefs, these new messages reprogram our genetics. Lipton has even made the leap that we have an immortal spirit, and our spiritual beliefs are as important as biochemical signals to the workings of cells.

†See in particular her books *Molecules of Emotion* and *Your Body Is Your Subconscious Mind.* The quotation is from her most recent book, *Everything You Need to Know to Feel Go(o)d,* page 31.

dimensional structures is coupled into the physical human system (including DNA)." The "states of heart coherence generated through experiencing heartfelt positive emotions increase this coupling."*

Another case of science catching up with ancient medical and spiritual practices relates to mindfulness meditation. Brain studies with meditators, even beginning meditators, showed actual structural changes can occur in the brain in as little as two months.† These changes correlated to enhanced function in certain areas, increased brain wave coherence, and improved functional efficiency of synaptic connections. A Harvard University study published in 2008 found compelling evidence that the physiological response to meditation, yoga, tai chi, or repetitive prayer positively affects DNA. The scientists proposed that the Relaxation Response—which is achieved through meditation, yoga, qigong, or prayer—may counteract cellular damage from chronic psychological stress‡ The study demonstrated that meditation is a powerful tool not only for physical health and improving subjective measures of quality of life (such as happiness, self-confidence, and so forth), but also for positively influencing our DNA. Dr. Herbert Benson of the Benson-Henry Institute Mind/Body Medicine; Jon Kabat-Zinn, director of the Stress Reduction Clinic and Center for the Mindfulness in Medicine; and psychologist Richard Davidson from the University of Wisconsin have all shown through their research or studies how meditation has the capacity to effect change within the human biofield. A further study called Mind-body Genomics published in the open-access journal PLOS ONE by Sue McGreevy, May 1, 2013, furthers this theory that the relaxation response through meditation ". . . produces immediate

---

*This particular study is reported in the 2003 article, "Modulation of DNA Conformation by Heart-Focused Intention," Rollin McCraty, Ph.D.; Mike Atkinson; and Dana Tomasino, B.A.

†"Alterations in Brain and Immune Function Produced by Mindfulness Mediation," *Psychosomatic Medicine Journal of Biobehavioral Medicine* 65, no. 4 (July/August 2003): 564–70.

‡Found in "Say Om: Doctor's Find Meditation Affects Your Body," by Laueren Cox, ABC News Medical Unit, *Public Library of Science* (July 2, 2008).

changes in the expression of genes involved in immune function, energy metabolism and insulin secretion."

We are more than our brains—mind is not an epiphenomenon of our brain but exists beyond it—and our commitment to restructure ourselves (beyond our enculturation, ego-wound reactions, and self-limiting beliefs) is now proved to be possible not only in terms of our spirituality and psychology but also in terms of our physiology. These are merely a few examples of what epigenetic and other kinds of advanced research are showing is possible as we awaken to the reality of the mind-body-spirit connection. These findings support the beliefs and experiences of indigenous healers and current shamanic practitioners.

Mary and I formulated a flexible structure we would use in the STAR Process, working as a team offering soul retrievals to clients both locally and nationally. We discovered that in a single session we could help a participant heal in ways that had previously taken months or years of therapy. Again, although healing does not always mean curing, a soul retrieval was giving clients a different way to frame and deal with their previously conscious or unconscious memories and experiences. For the next few years, we would work together with the STAR Process paradigm, co-teach workshops on the Andean tradition, and lead groups to sacred sites throughout Central America.

After being introduced to the Andean tradition in the United States, where I'd met Mary and Joan, I made my first trip to Peru in early 1992. It was on this journey that I met Americo Yábar. The Q'ero, whose traditions were my primary study, call Americo a *chakaruna*, a living bridge between traditions. Americo has been initiated to the highest level of the Q'ero tradition, and he passes his knowledge on with a poetic and dramatic flair. Americo teaches how to work with *salka,* the undomesticated energies that imbue the Pachamama (the Andean word for Earth Mother), the cosmos, and other natural forces. He is a master of the "left side" of the *mesa.* The mesa is similar to a Native North American medicine bundle, a ritual bundle containing sacred objects, often taken from nature, that are meaningful to the mesa carrier and are used in healing work and ceremony.

A practitioner of the Andean tradition is called a *paqo*, and in the Q'ero tradition every paqo carries a *mesa*. There are many ways paqos acquire power objects for their mesa, but the two primary ways are when a teacher gifts the power object during or after an initiation or when paqos recognize that an object is personal to them while working the path. The mesa has two primary uses, for healing and for communicating with the spirits. The "left side" of the mesa, called *lloq'e* in Quechua, the indigenous language of Peru, is associated with healing, intuitive perspectives, and the magical realms, which are also called the nonordinary realms. In contrast, the "right side," *paña,* is more focused on energetic relationships, communication, and accessing the mystical realms. Paqos must learn to bridge both realms to work effectively, although they tend to specialize in the skills of one side of the mesa or the other.

Americo took our group of intrepid travelers to the high-mountain village of Mollomarka, where his ancestral home, which he called Salka Wasi, was being refurbished. It was the first time he had taken outsiders there, and it was an amazing experience of first contact for both the locals and us. We were housed in a large mud-brick, thatched-roof house. There was barely any electricity and no plumbing. We had brought a few solar showers with us, and to our disbelief the villagers produced a full-size porcelain toilet, which they set up in a tiny private addition inside the building for our use. It wasn't connected to any plumbing and it kept falling over, which I found hysterical when it happened to others and not so funny when it happened to me. We had brought in some food and were able to supplement it with Andean staples—potatoes, large-kernel corn, and coca tea.

We stayed for five days and we felt honored to be so generously received by these humble people, experiencing their culture and working with several of them in ceremony. During our stay we observed three baptisms of children in the surrounding village, the clipping of the ears of the llamas in their herds, and a ceremony to the Madonna that took place in what had once been a tiny chapel on a small hill at the edge of the village.

Americo had invited a Q'ero elder, don Sebastian, to work with us. Don Sebastian had walked over the mountains from his village for three days to join us. We didn't actually meet him until our second evening, when he suddenly appeared in the doorway of the large room in which we were all staying. We were hanging out, some people talking, some doing bodywork on each other, some reading by flashlight. It was dusk and the room was lit only by a dim electric light in the dining area and a few candles, so no one noticed that don Sebastian had arrived. Another woman and I were headed toward the doorway when we saw him. He greeted us similarly, first her, then me, by placing his hands on our shoulders and pressing his forehead against ours.

As our foreheads touched, a brilliant white light expanded within my head and I felt myself momentarily propelled out into the Milky Way, connected to the vast cosmos, feeling the type of buoyancy one feels while floating in the ocean. I had had a similar experience before, with Baba Muktananda. While receiving *shaktipat** he had tapped my third eye with a white peacock feather and I perceived the same expansive white light. Both experiences were equally unexpected as they were happening, but oddly both had ended in a tiny explosion, a pinpoint of blue light† that had left me feeling energized, yet calm.

As don Sebastian stepped back, I perceived a golden glow around his head, and his eyes captivated me—they were pitch black and aglow with the light of some kind of otherworldly knowing. I felt I was looking into the eyes of a puma. Despite the intensity of his eyes, his demeanor was humble, almost childlike. It was a stark contrast. Since it was late

---

*In its most basic explanation, shaktipat is a transmission of energy from one's guru to awaken the kundalini energy that sits at the base of the spine.

†In Siddha yoga this pinpoint of light is called the blue pearl. I had seen this light in Lakota Inipis, or sweat lodges, and it had been explained to me by Grandfather Wallace Black Elk as a confirmation of a spiritual blessing.

and don Sebastian was tired from his long walk, Americo introduced him to the group and told us we would work together the next day.

I could still feel don Sebastian's energy when I went to bed that night. I awoke in the wee hours of the morning with the vivid memory of a dream.

I am sitting with my back against the trunk of a huge, old, gnarled tree whose branches spread above me like an umbrella. There are cylinders of light—black, red, gold, and silver—spiraling around my throat. The wind picks up, and suddenly don Sebastian is sitting on my right. I can't tell whether it is the wind or him, but I hear one of them whispering, "Apus, Apus, Apus."* The wind blows more fiercely and black holes swirl in front of me that I intuit I can enter, but I am afraid to do so. I hear don Sebastian in my head say, "Don't be afraid. The dark leads to the light. You are meant to work with the dark side; it is not bad or evil but a place of great healing." In my own mind, I question if I need some form of protection if I enter them. Don Sebastian starts to brush my upper right arm with something coarse but I cannot see what it is. He says, "These four tattoos will allow you to enter and come back safely." I look down at my arm and see a spiral glyph tattoo there, and as he continues to draw the other three, I wake up.

Before breakfast, I sought out Americo, trusting he could explain the energy force I had felt coming from don Sebastian the day before and hoping he might shed light on the dream. He and I walked a short distance in silence up the hill behind the hacienda. Americo fingered a small, black crescent-shaped rock, and finally he handed it to me. He showed me how to hold it with my thumb in the depression of the crescent of one side of the stone and my pointer and middle finger supporting it on the

---

*In Quechua, *Apu* means "mountain" and Apus are the highest tutelary spirits. All paqos are in service to one or more Apus. (The proper Quechua plural for mountains is *Apukuna;* I have used an Americanized plural—Apus—in this book.)

other side. He instructed me to use only this rock in my work during the remainder of this trip, and not use any others that I had been collecting for my mesa. "You and this *khuya** need to get to know each other," he said. "Using other khuyas from your mesa will confuse the energies."

He motioned toward a grassy area, where we sat and talked. "I did not know when I first saw you," he said, "that we would also work together in the mystical domains of the right side of the mesa, but I see we will do work together in many dimensions. You have filaments coming from your qosqo† that nurture others, and although you do that with humility, you need to practice discernment. Nurturing is part of who you are and the work you have been called to do on this planet, in this lifetime. But you must be discerning about who you extend your filaments to. You have not learned that yet. Differentiating where and with whom you should share your filaments is not prejudice, it is an act of discrimination." Americo continued, saying that although he and I were becoming friends, and that brought him pleasure, most of the work we would eventually do together would not necessarily be in the waking world.

He then asked me to share my dream. When I finished telling him, he interpreted it. "The tubes you saw represent earth, air, fire, and water, but also signify the four bands of light, which represent the root chakra, sacral, heart, and throat. They designate your work as a *chunpi paqo*."‡ He said I would need a special set of five stones, called *mullu khuyas* or *chunpi khuyas,* before I was taught that body of work, but he saw a set would come to me.

---

*Khuyas are stones that carry a specific power within a paqo's mesa for healing or communicating with spirits.

†Qosqo means "navel" and is the primary energy center through which we interact with the world of living energy.

‡A chunpi paqo is one who works with the four major energy belts of the human body, representing the four elements, and the three *nawis*—the two physical eyes and the third eye—which together is considered the fifth belt. Weaving these energy belts helps one to develop one's perceptions when dealing with the unseen worlds. It would not be Americo who would instruct me in the chunpi belts and initiate me as a chunpi paqo; rather it would be Juan Nuñez del Prado.

He counseled me that when I felt confused or congested with energy, both from what may bubble up inside of me from my own emotions or from the work I did with others, I would need to learn to "eat" the filaments and release them to Pachamama. He stood up as he showed me one technique I could use if I felt confused, overwhelmed, or out of balance. In a dramatic flurry of gestures, he described how I should go out on the land barefooted with my uncertainty and open my qosqo—my spiritual stomach and power center—and my crown chakra, to receive the energy from the cosmos. I should then throw my arms wide while spiraling my body counterclockwise seven times to shift the energy and cast the discordant energy down into the earth's center. Pachamama would send up an answer through my feet as a stream of energy that would shoot up through my central tube or vibral core into my consciousness. I might perceive this stream of energy any number of ways, as a vibration of feeling, color or tone, or possibly a shift in the wind. "This is how one works with releasing dense energy and negotiates the salka energy," he said, "which has the ability to free us, while simultaneously bringing us back to a place of tranquility." It is an intentional interchange he suggested.

After the demonstration, I asked Americo specifically about don Sebastian showing himself in the dream. He said, "Nagual Julio is the nagual of the dream."* He explained that the Nagual Julio's filaments are attached to both him and don Sebastian. When don Sebastian works with me in my dreams, in some capacity Nagual Julio is working with me as well. Dreams, Americo said, exist in other dimensions. A dream is an access point to the *bardos,* the in-between worlds. These worlds are merely different realities. If I could stay lucid in my dreams, my soul could awaken in the luminosity of those realms and I could learn how to negotiate them. He told me that we were connected through our light-body filaments and had a shared destiny. "When you awaken in

---

*A nagual has many definitions but in this case Americo is referring to a dreamer-shaman.

the dream and see Nagual Julio on your right side and me on your left, you will know we are there to spiritually assist you."

I asked Americo what Nagual Julio looked like. He said he can take many forms, "maybe a man, maybe a jaguar, maybe as don Sebastian, maybe another form altogether." He explained that if in the dreamtime I see men in red clothing, Pachamama will have sent them to instruct or assist me. If the men in red took on a diamond shape while maintaining their color, they would be specific spirit helpers. He said he had about twelve of these red diamond spirit helpers himself, and perhaps some of them might start to work with me.

As we returned to the hacienda, I asked, "What was the light I saw when don Sebastian touched his third eye to mine?" Americo's response at first did not seem to be connected to my question. "A shaman's mirror is *Mama Quilla,* the moon. The moon takes the form of a wolf, or possibly a jaguar. Whichever form it takes, its energy will enter through your heart to work directly with you. That energy will help you to take on a new skin; it's important for paqos to move into new skin." I was about to repeat my question, but he held up his hand. "The black holes in your dream represent the dimensions of your own light and power. When you decide to travel within them, you will encounter your angelic self. You will not see wings, but you will see your own light, and that is what don Sebastian was reflecting back to you, your own light." Then, laughing, he hugged me and said that although he could support me with his energy body as I worked to strengthen my own light, only I could claim that part of myself. "And now," he said, lightheartedly, "it is time to feed these physical bodies." With that, we headed in for breakfast.

Later, in relating my experience when being greeted by don Sebastian to my friend Betty back in Boston, she clearly had her doubts about the reflection of light around his head and my seeing him as a puma when looking in his eyes. She teasingly asked, "So, do you think you stepped into the eye of the tiger on this journey?" This statement has become a friendly refrain between the two of us whenever something odd happens, but her question caused me to admit I truthfully didn't know what to make of the energy that had happened between me and Don Sebastian. I only knew I had felt it viscerally.

That I had made it to Peru was a dream come true, although the odd experiences during this trip were only a taste of things to come. I was still learning that the primary way to sense the energies of the *kawsay pacha*—the world of living energy—is through the physical body. I was beginning to understand that accumulating this energy—whether domesticated or undomesticated—was expanding the filaments of my current awareness and awakening me to a new potential of the infinite. One thing was quite clear after this trip: for me, everything in Peru—from the dreams I had while there, to rituals with the paqos, to the accumulated energy held within the ancient sacred stone sites, to the local village people at Mollomarka, to the salka energy of the Pachamama herself—oozed living energy.

11
Munay

Less than a year later, two dear friends gifted me with the means to return to Peru, this time with Mary, Joan, and another larger group. During this journey, I would both walk the Inca Trail into Machu Picchu and revisit Mollomarca. The Inca Trail follows the ancient sacred route the Inca royalty used to enter the citadel of Machu Picchu. I would be walking it, with the others, in a shamanic way, not as tourists. It was one of the most physically excruciating experiences of my life and one of my greatest physical accomplishments. There were points as we were cresting a fourteen-thousand-foot pass when I could barely breathe or muster the energy to take another step. There were mornings when the inside of my tent was iced, and no matter how deeply I burrowed into my sleeping bag I couldn't find warmth.

In contrast, there were exquisite moments—and many out-of-the-ordinary events. The night skies were amazing, thick with stars, and the Milky Way laid out her path before us. There was the glory of the Southern Cross. I and others witnessed lights that appeared like stars but were moving in unusual geometric formations across the heavens. Americo would just wink when we pointed them out and say, "Call them to you." And then there was that exceptional evening while participating in a night ceremony in the ruins of Machu Picchu when a

number of us witnessed blue orbs and tall willowy white forms waft-
ing between the stone structures. I had experienced magic here before,
and I would every time I returned to this sacred citadel.

When we got to Mollomarka, the villagers welcomed us with dancing, panpipes playing, and a barbeque of guinea pig, the traditional meal
for festivities. Many of us were grateful our teachers had also paid for a
lamb to be slaughtered, and there was plenty of corn, potatoes, bananas,
and passion fruit.

Once we had settled in, we concentrated on the shamanic teachings. On this visit Americo had arranged for us to work with don
Mariano Apasa Marchaqa, a Q'ero *kuraq akulleq,* which means "elder
chewer of the coca." This is the fourth, and currently the highest,
level on the path of a paqo. He arrived with don Juan Ordoñus, his
assistant and a *pampa mesayoq,* which is a healer and keeper of earth-
based ceremonies.

Both men were dressed similarly, in the traditional attire of the
region: sandals made from rubber tires, ponchos, and colorfully woven
caps with earflaps adorned with multicolored yarn tassels. Don Mariano
had a quality of authority everyone in the village recognized and honored, although he showed no semblance of ego about that. Like almost
all of the Q'ero, he was cryptically quiet and self-contained. He began
his work with us by making a *despacho,* which is an offering comprised
of natural items that is either buried to honor Pachamama or burned to
honor the Apus. After the despacho, we celebrated his and don Juan's
arrival with *pisco,* a strong local alcohol. Don Mariano imbibed generously, as we all did, for this was a time to celebrate the energetic connection of our coming together. Sometime into the night, during the
celebration, he disappeared.

The next morning, I heard a rumor don Mariano had been locked
in the chicken coop because it was suspected that with the influence of
the pisco, he might overstep boundaries with some of the women in our
group. I would learn later that wasn't true and was most likely a projection of one of our group leaders. However, this incident would later

become the kernel of a very powerful teaching for me about *munay,** the act of heart energy.

Several of us had scheduled private coca leaf readings with don Mariano. I was outside basking in the morning sun when Pepe, our cook, who speaks fluent English, Spanish, and Quechua and often served as translator, came to tell me it was my turn. He led me to the chicken coop. I looked at him questioningly, but he just motioned me inside and followed me in. Don Mariano was in the cramped hut, sitting on his manta cloth with his fluffy, white llama-fur coca bag on his lap. Don Juan prowled just inside the doorway like a jaguar protecting his cub, obviously agitated in stark contrast to don Mariano's profound composure. Don Mariano was definitely working from the place of balance, working the energies to release any heaviness.

In the Andean tradition, there is a single spectrum of energy, the two extremes of which are *hucha* and *sami.* Hucha is dense, disordered energy; sami is refined, ordered energy. Hucha can be shifted through an act of will and intention called *mikhuy,* which means literally to "digest" the dense energy through your own energy body, offering it to Pachamama to restore balance while simultaneously gathering refined energy from her to reestablish harmony. This is what I discerned don Mariano was doing.

Don Mariano motioned for me to sit opposite him, and with Pepe translating asked me what it was I wanted to know through the coca leaf reading. I asked what the Andean path held in store for me, how it might unfold if I honored the teachings and sincerely applied myself to the work. I explained briefly that although I was a novice in this tradition, I felt intimately connected to it and to Peru. Don Mariano was

---

*The Andean mystical tradition recognizes the existence of three aspects of the spiritual arts: the right side (paña), the left side (lloq'e), and the middle, called *chaupi,* which uses munay, or heart energy, as the catalyst or bridge to bring harmony between the right and left sides of the work. Along the path a student receives each of these as a series of teachings and through a ritual called a *karpay*—an exchange of energy and information from teacher to student.

chewing coca leaves,* which is common practice in Peru in both social and sacred gatherings, and he offered me a *k'intu*—three perfect leaves used as an offering—which I accepted. I held the k'intu between two fingers and my thumb, as I had been taught, and breathed my intention into them. I then offered them to the four directions to acknowledge the four sacred Apus of this region and then to the Spirit World for direction and gratitude. Then, as is customary, I chewed them.

Don Mariano buried his brown, weathered hands with their gnarled fingers in the coca leaf bag and extracted a large handful of leaves. With flicks of his wrist, he cast groups of coca leaves across his mesa cloth. He studied them closely, noting where they landed. Some had landed with their shiny side face up, others face down; some of the leaves were split and broken, others were unblemished. Some had landed off the old woven cloth entirely. Through Pepe, he read the leaves: my daughter would live a healthy life and be protected by the spirits. I would further merge my work with the work of an American woman and we would take our healing skills to a new level, not only for ourselves but for those who would come to us over the next seven years. There would be a time in the future when her path and mine would separate and I was not to take that personally, as each of us would need to grow individually in different directions. He pointed to my mesa, which I had only begun building earlier in the year, and predicted I would soon be the recipient of additional power objects, and he foretold that as the power of my mesa increased so would my abilities to see into the worlds beyond. I was meant to work in this tradition and to return to Peru many times. He counseled I should prepare myself to face further loss and grief in future years, but if I held to the teachings and was able to push the kawsay—the living energies—I would learn about my capacity for forgiveness. If I could stay in my heart, he said, and forgive those who would cause me sorrow, I will have learned the power of munay.

---

*Coca leaves have been used since pre-Inca times to overcome fatigue, hunger, and thirst. They are particularly effective against altitude sickness, to alleviate headaches, and to improve digestion.

With that he was finished. I thanked him and gifted him in the traditional way with coins. I was acutely aware both of his humility and the humble place in which he had decided to do his reading and offer me this teaching—the chicken coop. I speculated he was making a point to the person who had insisted that he be put there the previous night, but also to me about the strength of humility. And later that day, when he rejoined our group and showed nothing but kindness and respect to everyone, I realized don Mariano had provided me with my first lesson in the power of munay, heart energy based in forgiveness.*

Later that evening, after a full day of teachings, our group participated in a fire ceremony and then gathered once again in the main building to hear more of don Mariano's story about how he came to his spiritual path. He was going to share a teaching about working with the khuyas, the stones of power, and also would gift five of the students in the group with a khuya from his mesa. He conferred with the group leaders, indicating his choices, and each of the five was called forward, one at a time. Mary was first. Don Mariano handed her a brown and cream-colored stone and told her, through translation, that it represented the head and she would synthesize the Andean teachings with her clinical therapy to work with both individuals and groups. He called me next and gifted me a small, pitted white rock that looked like a little potato. Locking his eyes directly onto mine, he said this was a gift in recognition of my pure and gentle heart. I was moved by the simplicity of his statement, and I felt he was offering this rock as a reminder of the munay teachings earlier in the chicken coop. Joan also received a stone and was told she was destined to record the Q'ero tradition and share it through her writing.

I remember her wondering, later that night, how she was ever going to do that. As it would turn out, she and I would come to work with Juan Nuñez del Prado. Juan practically grew up among the Q'ero and

---

*In don Mariano's teachings, munay is not a set of karpays or multiple initiations, but rather is a way to personally acknowledge and release where one's ego limits the full expression of forgiveness.

is fully initiated into their tradition as a fourth-level kuraq akulleq. His father, anthropologist Oscar Nuñez del Prado, "discovered" the Q'ero Indians—direct descendants of the Inca—in 1949 at a festival in Paucartambo, leading the first expedition to their mountain villages in 1955. Juan is an anthropologist and speaks extensively on world religions and ancient cultures in addition to the Andean mystical tradition. He would become our primary teacher on the Andean path and the conduit through which Joan would years later interview six Q'ero, including don Mariano, to write her book in which the Q'ero speak for themselves.

In 1996, Joan invited me to join her in the private interviews, which were held at a small hacienda in the Sacred Valley. We spent a week alone with the Q'ero paqos, Juan Nuñez del Prado, and Dr. Ricardo Valderrama Fernandez, a Quechua interpreter from Cuzco's Universidad Nacional de San Antonio Adad, listening to the Q'ero's stories and discussing their sacred traditions. It was fortunate Joan recorded their words in the book now called *Masters of the Living Energy,* because within eight years' time, four of these paqos, including don Mariano, had died.

We left Mollomarka after five days of teachings and celebrations and returned to Cusco. The night before our departure to the United States, Americo invited Mary and me to his home. He had offered to bestow the Pachakuti rite to us, which we knew to be an honor. Pachacuti was a great and honored Inca leader who built Cuzco and was seen as a visionary. Pachakuti refers to a measure of time and, more specifically, to an upheaval or period of transformation: *pacha* means "Earth and time," and *kuti* means "turning or flipping." We are now in what is referred to as the Fifth Pachakuti, each of which comes in five-hundred-year intervals. Around 1982 we entered the Fifth Pachakuti, and prophecy said the thirty years leading up to 2012 would be a time of immense change for humanity.

Andean prophecy talks of a coming period of terrestrial transformation, when the Condor and the Eagle align, and of a cosmic overturning of time and space that will signal the end of time as we know it, ushering in the possibility of humans raising their consciousness and thus achieving a new way of being. There also will be a new relationship with the living Earth and an emergence into a golden age of peace. In a symbology similar to Tlakaelel's, the Eagle in the Andean tradition represents North America, material progress, and the physical body, whereas the Condor symbolizes South America, earth-based spirituality, and heart centeredness. In the early 1990s, tribal elders and shamans from the Andes began to share more openly with outsiders the traditional teachings and healing practices they had held closely since the Conquest.

The pure Q'ero teachings and practices I witnessed in the early 1990s maintained an essence of purity and pragmatic simplicity, without the detailed explanations or personal assessments that we in the West are often inclined to add or expand upon. They will not contradict our embellishments or cast judgment, because they see that as disrespectful. The practices they share even today teach about living humbly and with respect for each other and all that Pachamama offers, from a place of conscious intentionality while working within both the mundane and the mystical. That said, like many other indigenous cultures who have been enormously influenced by spiritual seekers, with the infusion of vast amounts of tourist money where before there was little and well-meaning efforts to upgrade their way of life for the better (clean water, health care, education), many paqos and village families are moving to the cities, abandoning their mountain villages for what they consider a better way of life. In many cases, what today are being shared as expanded Andean concepts, have become multilayered and in some cases take them far afield from the original teachings.

When Mary and I arrived at Americo's, his daughter was there and much to our delight and surprise don Mariano emerged from the shadows under the stairway. Americo said don Mariano would be the one performing the rite. Americo would translate Quechua to Spanish, and his daughter would ensure a full English translation. Americo opened an old cloth bundle to reveal two ancient puma statues. He handed them to don Mariano, who gently fingered them and then with great respect breathed his prayers into them, one after the other. He placed them back on the aged brown, cream, and gray Inca cloth and turned his attention to Mary and me. He studied us, head to foot, as if he were assessing our energy bodies. He lit a white candle, then picked up the pumas and handed each of us one. He blew into his llama coca leaf bag, calling to the energies of the four main sacred Apus that surround Cusco.

Then, with a marked expression in his eyes, he turned his attention back to us and performed a karpay, a transmission from his lineage. He was speaking in barely a whisper and his words at that point were not translated, but we didn't have to know what he was saying, for we felt the impact of the energy. He blew through his mesa first into the crowns of our heads and then into our hearts, linking logos and eros, which is one of the primary practices for becoming a conscious human being. He then pressed his mesa against our bellies, our qosqos, imparting the energy of his lineage to us.

Through translation, don Mariano explained that everything around us acts as a receptacle of light and that the puma statues represented the undomesticated, female energies, those of birthing and creation. He asked us now—as women, mothers, and healers—to set our prayers and intentions, and then to *camay*—animate through our breath—the puma figures with sami, refined energy, in support of humanity's ability to evolve during the coming transitional time. Although some part of our egos might have initially desired this initiation, we now humbly felt that through this karpay, in some small way, our prayers and intentions were helping to marshal the energy of the feminine forces to support the union of heart and intellect during this pachakuti period.

As I had come to understand them, karpays are transmissions that serve as energetic keys to unlock karmic seeds and awaken a student's potential. The form and structure of the teachings are very important as these create the container in which to experience the how and the why of the work one wishes to develop. However, the link to a teacher's lineage comes through the energetic exchange within the karpay rite.

By the end of the rite, my legs felt unsteady and the top of my head was exploding with light rays in a rainbow of colors. Mary was having similar sensations. We told Americo what we were experiencing and he shared it with don Mariano. This information seemed to make him happy as he smiled and in a knowing way nodded at us, although he did not say anything.

Americo briefly left the room. He returned carrying three stones— they were the oddest looking rocks I had ever seen, then and to this day. They were each about the size of a thumb, brown-black, and smooth in texture. They had face-like features and appeared to me as misshapen heads. For some strange reason I thought of them as siblings. Americo said they were from the cosmos and had been in his possession for a long time, although he did not feel comfortable sharing how he came to have them. I could tell simply by looking they weren't meteorites, which are sometimes found in Q'ero mesas and are particularly cherished because they are so rare. He gifted one to each of us, keeping the third for himself. He explained they would connect us across time and space, as brother and sisters, and help reinforce our connection to the cosmos.

As we prepared to leave, I shyly hugged don Mariano and wordlessly nodded my heartfelt thanks. We gathered our things so Americo could take us back to our hotel. I was vibrating and couldn't tell if that feeling was a result of the rite or the effect of the strange stone I still held tightly in my hand. The world outside felt electric and the stars seemed abnormally close, pulsating as if delivering a message in Morse code. There was no doubt the three of us felt high, giggling our way up the street toward Americo's VW Bug and babbling nonstop. Although we hadn't ingested anything but energy, it was like we were in hyperdrive.

The two khuyas I had received, which to this day I lovingly refer to as the potato and the little ET head, are two of the most precious gifts

I have received while walking the Andean path. I have often used the gentle energy of the potato to help clients open to their heart centers in the soul retrievals I continue to offer; the little ET head I have used more sparingly, as it seems to elicit in the few clients I have been moved to use it with, the same pulsating energy I had experienced.

As Mary and I continued offering the STAR Process, cleansed our own energy bodies, and participated in the work of the tradition, we became more aware of energies beyond the domains of the physical. Both we and our clients were capable of more effortlessly opening to the communication initiated by ascended masters, angelic beings, and those from other-dimensional realms. These forces exist beyond myth or mysticism, and are able to both unlock and transmit energies that can catapult humans into other dimensions of consciousness.

I worked with Americo one final time in Peru, along with four other women paqos, two of whom were Joan and Mary. We started our journey in the Cusco area doing ceremonies in the surrounding ruins and then traveled to Bolivia to work on the Islands of the Sun and Moon in Lake Titicaca. This trip was wild from start to finish, and I have a collection of memories that range from the endearing to the amusing to the transcendental. For instance, we worked for a full day on the Island of the Moon with the impressive khuyas or stones that blanketed the shoreline and stayed into the night for a fire ceremony. At that time, there was no lodging and only two or three fishing families who lived on the island. Later that evening, when our boat did not return, Americo arranged for us to stay overnight with one of the families. They were a family of eight, of meager means, living in a makeshift wooden house. The house had obviously been added to over the years, probably as the family had grown, resulting in additional rooms built at odd angles off the main structure. The mother offered the five of us the room her three daughters normally slept in, with Americo sleeping in another section of the house.

The bedroom sat above the main structure of their home and we had to climb a precarious, homemade ladder to get to it. There was a narrow ledge running along the outer wall we had to traverse to get to the door, which was merely an opening in the wall. There were two windows open to the night. One faced Lake Titicaca, pulling in the chilly night air, and the other opened to the backyard, where a llama and a couple of chickens wandered around the empty pails and containers that lay strewn about. The floor, where some of us needed to lay our sleeping bags, was dusty and splintered. Two narrow wooden bed platforms, each with a straw-filled mattress bound with rope, were pushed up against the walls under each of the windows. Despite the room's primitiveness, we were grateful for the family's hospitality and a place to rest.

In the morning, we heard soft giggles behind us and turned to see two of the sisters standing on the ledge and peering in the window watching us dress. It was apparent from their confused stares that they didn't understand what our bras were, but through gestures and more giggling they certainly made clear they were the silliest things they had ever seen. We were chuckling at the ridiculousness of it all, when their mom came up, swooshing them away and offering us coca tea as the sun broke through, finally offering us a bit of warmth.

In late morning, our boat showed up and we returned to the mainland to begin our journey back to the southern coastal section of Peru. As the trip continued to unfold, there occurred a situation in Paracas that was, paradoxically, both onerous and, only now in the retelling of it, amusing. On the way back from the Nazca lines, we had stopped in a small town, hoping to have a quiet lunch, but it was congested with revelers, for it happened to be the day of the Fisherman's Festival. We had to push our way into one of the mobbed local eating places, comically called the Topo Gigio. We were old enough to remember *The Ed Sullivan Show* and the funny little mouse puppet with the Italian accent that went by that name. There was no rhyme or reason for the name, as this was not an Italian restaurant. Sometime during that meal, the bag that contained all of our passports was stolen, although it was under the table and blocked in by our chairs. No passports left us in a very precarious situation. Even though we reported the theft to the police and they gave us a copy of the report, two weeks later it was hell being cleared to fly out of the country. We resorted to tears, pleading in our pidgin Spanish, and shelling out the last of our money to try to get through the process, until we realized we needed to do what we had been taught—to shift the energy through collectively *mikuying* or digesting the dense energy of our fear about getting back to our families and shifting the lack of cooperation from the police officials at the airport. It worked.

A more unexpected event that stands out from this same journey was of our time in Ica, where we worked with the psychoactive cactus San Pedro, which is considered a sacred plant medicine. The San Pedro cactus has been used for centuries throughout Peru as a visionary plant sacrament to gain information, such as in healing ceremonies to help resolve or bring understanding to physical, psychic, emotional, or spiritual issues. It is said one communicates directly with the plant itself within the ceremonial experience, which takes place at night because it is easier in the dark to connect with the vibrational allies and ancestors of the plant medicine in a fuller way. It is believed that everyone participating in this sacred ritual has his or her own destiny with the spirit essence of San Pedro. The initiation into the realm of any sacred plant medicine requires a respectful, serious attitude. It is not an opportunity for experimenting lightly or to be used recreationally. Typically, it is best to approach the plant spirit with a specific purpose in mind and a sense of openness toward seeking its guidance. San Pedro generally provides a powerful visionary experience inclusive of all of the senses, including the sixth sense of extrasensory perception whereby you can traverse the realms beyond matter and time.

My experience with San Pedro solidified my belief that there are times when one's past and present selves, or even one's multidimensional selves, cross paths and meet each other at the same point on the ribbon of time, space, and dimensionality. Time and space are an illusion we concretize for ourselves to physically experience this third-dimensional plane, and when we lift the veil through the use of San Pedro or in other ways, we can leap beyond the physical and meet "our other selves"; and it is then we realize that anything is possible. Although I believe we can have these experiences naturally, they come more easily when we bypass the ego and our logical minds, which is why they often happen during the dreamtime, during ceremonies such as sweat lodge, or through guided participation in sacred plant rituals.

Americo had made arrangements for us to stay outside of Ica, overnight in a bamboo hut at an isolated, ocean-side location that was deserted except for our group and the family who owned the cluster of huts. We were there specifically to participate in the San Pedro ceremony, and although inexplicable things happened to each of us during the ceremony, what happened for me personally was my first conscious introduction to one of my multidimensional selves. At one point during the evening, even while I was clearly with the group in the San Pedro ceremony, I was also far out in the cosmos with the galactic Legions of Light, participating in negotiations among the Golden-haired Ones with an aggressive force from another galaxy. However, in both locations I could clearly see, smell, hear, act, and react—but to two totally different realities that were occurring simultaneously. I actually felt physically bi-located and actively involved in both places, participating with an intentional, albeit different, purpose in each reality. Although I had experienced lucid moments of meeting other aspects of myself in the dreamtime work I had been doing for years, this was the first time I had experienced another "myself" while awake.

Each of us reported odd experiences that night, and the next morning we discovered that wildness had been witnessed by others. At first light the owners showed up our hut door appearing shaken and claiming that our hut had been glowing and vibrating throughout the night. They were so upset by what they had witnessed and heard that they insisted that we vacate their property immediately. We did.

The revelations of that night expanded my understanding that the light-encoded filaments we each are really composed of can be decoded, expanding the lens through which we can observe our very existence in a dynamic world. To me, this entire trip had been representative of how different realities can converge to form the single world of living energy. This journey was liberating both perceptually and physically because of everything we had encountered—the generosity of spirit from the family on the Island of the Moon, the San Pedro vision of penetrating the membrane of an alternate dimension and recognizing "another me," and the stealing of our identities in Paracas and how we had worked as one mind to negotiate our return home. Each had provided me a way to open to the world of living energy from a stance of gratitude, curiosity, and possibility, and to more easily accept my evolving understanding of the universal flow.

12

A Cloudy Observation

As I continued working with Grandmother Twylah and my Andean teachers, I also traveled with Mary around the United States conducting workshops on the Andean mystical tradition and offering STAR Process soul retrievals. In 1995 we had begun to train other psychotherapists, nurses, and bodyworkers in a three-year program so that they would feel confident using the STAR Process in their private practices. After six years of working together, Mary and I went on our first sojourn to Mexico in 1998, as a graduation journey for the dedicated group of therapists and healers we had trained. We introduced them to two teachers in particular, both from Mexico: Yaqui deer dancer* Gilberto Siqueiros and Vincenté Alfonso Rameriz Garcia of the Santería tradition. We worked with Vincenté only when we were in Veracruz; Gilberto was with us throughout the entire trip, sharing his teachings and serving as an interpreter. Mary and I taught energetic techniques to connect with the feminine and masculine sides of the self and practices to further align our filaments with the cosmos. Much of this work was done at the spectacular sacred site of

---

*The Yaqui of the northern Mexico states of Senora and Sinaloa perform the sacred Deer Dance, called La Danza del Venado. This dance re-enacts the struggle of the hunt, honoring the natural world and the white-tailed deer, who is a holy animal to the People because it gives everything of itself.

Teotihuacán, outside Mexico City, and the beautifully constructed mystical site of Palenque in the jungle of Chiapas.

At Veracruz, Vincenté conducted two rituals from the Santeria tradition. Santeria is a belief system that merged the Yoruba religion, which was brought to Cuban sugar plantations by African slaves, with Roman Catholic and Native Indian traditions. In the Yoruba philosophy, the destiny of all humans is to become one with the divine creator or Source of all energy. They believe our thoughts and actions on the physical plane affect the life-force of all living beings, including the Earth herself, by imprinting either ordered energy or disordered energy. As we refine our spiritual consciousness in this physical plane, transcendence becomes more possible. Thus, the Yoruba religion espouses the view that spiritual transcendence is only possible through cycles of existence in a physical body.

The first sacred ritual Vincenté led was one he did for many people seeking personal and family healing or to gather information concerning their future. He warned us it involved the sacrifice of a chicken to divine information in its entrails, a practice he said most Westerners found upsetting. That definitely proved true for our group. Although he was doing the ritual to cleanse the group's energy as we started our journey, the jury is still out on whether it ever accomplished that. I think it did more to traumatize the group than to cleanse us. Another ritual he used to divine information about an individual entailed running a fresh egg from head to toe through a person's energy field. He then cracked the egg into a glass of water and interpreted the signs he saw in the yolk according to its size, color, and how it floated in the water.

When Vincenté did the ritual for me, the egg had a double yoke, which he found of great interest. Through one of our interpreters, a Brit I will call Basil whom Mary and I had met during training in remote viewing and who remains a dear friend and brother to me to this day, I learned that Vincenté interpreted the double yolk as meaning I was living two lives simultaneously, one on the earth and one in the stars. Vincenté's interpretation of the yolk for Basil's egg topped that: "You *are* an extraterrestrial," he declared. We all got quite a chuckle out of that, even Basil, who seemed to accept that proclamation not only with a sense of delight, but also with an understanding that it answered some personal questions he had of himself.

After reading the yolks for all the others in group, Vincenté pulled out an odd-looking map and showed us a site, as yet unexcavated, he and his family called the Star Mounds. He told us that all of humanity was connected energetically to the stars, and he urged us to return one day to visit the three Star Mounds and feel the energies that lay below them for ourselves. Vincenté believed there were unexcavated temples beneath these mounds that would prove there had been contact between humans and star beings. He told us that the people who lived around the lake situated close to the mounds have reported many sightings of UFOs and visitations from "star brothers and sisters." Their community had witnessed these strange comings and goings for as long as they could remember. They insisted there were otherworldly beings living among them who traveled back and forth through time, monitoring human activity. He promised that if we returned he would take us to the Star Mounds himself.*

Many of my teachers—whether Native American, Peruvian, or Mesoamerican—had shared similar stories that extraterrestrial and interdimensional travelers had been visiting Earth from different star systems for millennia, observing, teaching, and sharing technological information at appropriate times. They believe ancient archeological sites had served as recharging stations for these travelers and their stellar crafts. They were also repositories of information, accessed by people with the "ears to hear" and the "eyes to see," and these sites are still believed to be centers of arcane information. In addition there is the

---

*In 2000, when I was leading a group of women back to this area, I felt lucky that Vincenté kept his promise, taking us to see the Star Mounds and to do rituals at the lake community whose members claimed a long history of contacts with the star beings. Unfortunately, during our visit he repeated the chicken ritual, which affected this group the same way it had the previous group.

belief that there is a series of tunnels that run under certain geographic areas that are causeways to enclaves where inter- and multidimensional beings exist. It is said Native People within those areas protect these tunnel openings, and if a person finds the doorway and enters into the labyrinth, he or she is seldom allowed to return, as it is imperative to protect the anonymity of these locations.

In the Peruvian tradition, the inhabitants of the Island of Taquile, in Lake Titicaca, say star beings have frequented their area from the beginning times. They report having seen the stellar crafts descending into and emerging from Lake Titicaca. In the larger Andean tradition, the god Viracocha, who is the "All-Knowing One," rose from Lake Titicaca following a time of great tribulation caused by a flood; his purpose was to bring light and knowledge to the people. He commanded the sun to move across the sky and carvings show him carrying thunderbolts in his hands. Viracocha breathed life into two stones to create the first two Inca, Manco Capac, whose name translates to "splendid foundation," and his female cohort, Mama Ocllo, whose name means "mother fertility." It is said they founded the great Inca empire.

Mesoamerican traditions, from the Teotihuacán to Aztec to Toltec, speak of a flying, feathered serpent, Quetzalcoatl, who traveled between Earth and sky, bringing learning and knowledge to the people. Quetzalcoatl is linked to the cycles of the planet Venus, and ceremonial rituals were timed with its appearance. This planet, which was seen as a deity with a dual or twin nature—the morning and evening star—and was thought of as the god of intelligence and self-reflection, is considered to be both "the lord of the dawn" and the "evening star." When the Teotihuacán site, whose name means "the place where the gods were born," was first established, the grand avenues and temples were not aligned with the solstices and equinoxes, as they are at many other sites around the world, but with the Pleiades. There are many ancient myths and stories that suggest places like Teotihuacán were constructed with the assistance of star-based civilizations, in particular a humanoid species from the Pleiades, who were said to have mingled their DNA with ours to advance our evolution after the close of the Third World or Fourth Sun. This might be why this site is also referred to as the place where "men were transformed into gods."

The great Mayan civilization says that Pacal Votan, the "Enlightened One," was a teacher who came to illuminate the people. He had initially traveled from the stars with his mother and young wife to impart his wisdom to an even more ancient civilization that eventually was destroyed by their misuse of power, the cataclysm causing their continent to sink into the sea and causing worldwide flooding. Pacal Votan came to Palenque, located in present day Chiapas, Mexico, with the mission of helping the Maya achieve their sacred destiny. His pictograph, carved onto the large stone that covers the sarcophagus crypt in the great Temple of Inscriptions, shows him with a spherical stone in one hand, representing the feminine, and a square stone in the other, representing the masculine. In this carving, similar to the ones depicting Viracocha and Quetzalcoatl, he looks like an ancient astronaut. Analogous to the Christian and Muslim beliefs of the return of Christ, and the Hindu belief of the return of Buddha, these Mesoamerican and South American civilizations prophesize the return of the "Shining One" at the end times.

Mary and I had purposely brought the STAR Process graduation group to Teotihuacán, to the grand Temple of the Sun, the third largest pyramid structure in the world, and to its complement the Temple of the Moon to weave the fabric of the two sides of the self. At both temples we worked with our Divine Masculine and Divine Feminine energies and interwove them through rituals that supported the sacred marriage of these aspects, the union of opposites. Once we completed the rites, with the purpose to merge these incarnate and discarnate aspects, we conducted a specific ritual to link our energies with the cosmic energy of Quetzalcoatl at the temple structure bearing his name. We then traveled to Palenque to intentionally work with the star energies and connect with the cosmos at a cellular level, thus weaving our cosmic energies with our terrestrial selves.

When we entered Palenque, the early morning haze had not yet lifted, making the mysterious force of the site even more palpable. The energies felt like electrical currents running under our feet and throughout the air around us. After taking in the grandeur of the site and exploring some of the smaller temples, we were drawn as a group to ascend the Temple of Inscriptions to meditate together. Locals and tourists climbed the steep stairway alongside us.

With little discussion among ourselves, we sat in a stone nook located on the top right-hand side of the temple across from another stairway that led down through a channel to Pacal Votan's burial chamber. We sat in a circle meditating, when, with little verbal instruction, we began to tone* in unison, our voices rising and falling melodically. The sounds of our song, as the tones rose and fell, seemed to go on forever. Although our physical bodies were sitting intoning in this physical temple, I felt we were transporting our consciousness and light bodies to an etheric imprint of this same temple in a higher nonphysical realm. I perceived as we toned that we were somehow connecting to this higher light temple and helping to manifest its energetic connection to the physical temple in which we sat; likewise I sensed the tones were awakening some molecule of memory in our physical selves as each of our unique sounds touched our higher vibratory selves.

Our group stopped toning in unison, as if by some shared command, and slowly we opened our eyes. There were people sitting quietly near us at the top of the staircase, and three uniformed guards stood between us and them. The guards previously had not been anywhere in sight. Now, they simply nodded to us and walked back down the long stairway. A young man from the nearby group said the guards had told those gathered there, mainly local teenagers on a school outing, not to disturb us during our "prayer."

We agreed it had indeed felt like a prayer. As we discussed our

---

*Toning and chanting are ancient techniques utilized to change vibrational frequencies for healing or divining information. In medieval times monks and nuns used chanting and toning to bring higher dimensions down to the earth plane.

shared experiences and impressions, two observations stood out as particularly significant to the shamanic work we had come to do at both Teotihuacán and Palenque. First, we concurred our physical bodies had been opened energetically in the ceremony we had performed at the top of the Pyramid of the Sun at Teotihuacán a few days prior to coming to Palenque. We had walked the Avenue of the Dead from the Pyramid of the Sun (to magnify our solar destiny) to the Temple of the Moon (to cleanse our unconscious) for the intentional rites of dying to who we had envisioned ourselves to be up until that point in our lives, and finished by reconnecting our energy filaments at the Temple of Quetzalcoatl to begin to open to our "other knowing." Now, at the Temple of Inscriptions in Palenque, our goal was to connect our own innate wisdom with the spiritual forces still palpable here, to the ancient Maya and their extraordinary connection to the earth and cosmic cycles.

Second, we agreed that here, at the Temple of Inscriptions, we had been worked on at a deep cellular level through the frequencies of the spontaneous sounds we had intoned separately and collectively. Each of our personal tones had combined to create a cohesive song in a process similar to how the creator and created give form to each other. We agreed that we needed to go deeper into the work of balancing our individual inner masculine and feminine. We also discussed how while traveling the shamanic realms, it is imperative to balance the right and left hemispheres of the brain, and how awakening to the inner Divine Feminine and Masculine can become a direct bridge to our higher spiritual selves. As we talked about being imprinted at a cellular level, other topics, including UFOlogy, quantum physics, and even genetics, came up.

As the conversation continued, I knew that the opinions being expressed were not unique to us, but were common to the larger esoteric community. In some metaphysical circles, there is a belief that humankind used to have a twelve-strand DNA structure, not our current two-strand double-helix DNA configuration. In fact, this was not theory to several of my mentors, as they believed and taught everything that exists on Mother Earth is composed not only of matter but also of spirit, which is light. They say we came from Spirit and when we embodied in the physical we forgot our prior form as universal essence and so have to reawaken to it. In our ancient past, they claim, we could communicate telepathically, use the power of our minds to create and maneuver matter, and communicate with Nature and beings of other realms. We are "of the light" and everything happens through light—not just the light of the sun, stars, and moon, but our inner light as well. Therefore, our terrestrial fabric is infused with our celestial essence. As we learn to raise our individual light vibrations, living with a balanced head and heart, we can awaken to those ancient memories and consciously become the true cosmic beings we are. When we do, our DNA has the potential to restructure itself into its original twelve-strand configuration.*

Many indigenous teachers and others in and out of the field of extraterrestrial phenomenon express the opinion that since primordial times beings from various galactic races have assisted us in our cultural and technological evolution, especially after cyclic global cataclysms. For example, some say that about 45,000 years ago, aberrant galactic beings who were on a lower end of the spectrum of consciousness manipulated our gene pool for their own ends, experimenting with cloning techniques and stripping our DNA structure down from twelve strands to two so that we would be a compliant workforce. Humans saw these deviant extraterrestrials as godlike because of their superior abilities and so bred with them. Many of the ancient Greek and Roman myths of gods and men, the Biblical stories of the fallen ones, and the creation legends of men and beasts, such as centaurs and the Minotaur, were

---

*The concept of twelve-strand DNA is metaphysical and does not yet have physical verification. However, in recent years genetic research is moving forward into areas that were once considered outside the realm of conventional biology. For example, see the work of Russian researchers Pjotr Garajajev, Ph.D., and Vladimir Poponin, Ph.D., who see DNA as a kind of biocomputer that is open to the influence of thoughts and environmental forces and fields. They also consider the field structure around DNA to be multidimensional.

the memories and oral stories passed down that relate to these possible unions and cloning experiment results. Those beings of a higher and finer consciousness denied humans access to the advanced cosmic technologies because we no longer had the moral consciousness to use them accountably. Still, the beings of higher consciousness helped us.

Ancient texts and oral traditions relate how over time, these advanced beings brought us mathematics, engineering, cultivation techniques, acoustical alchemy, sacred geometry, and special ceremonies to instruct and uplift us. The munificent races have watched over us, protecting us and apportioning knowledge according to our ability to handle it well. The more malevolent beings schemed to manipulate us, offering advanced technology even though our use of it could endanger even their existence. Still there is a difference, barriers if you will, between advanced beings and divine beings. Advanced galactic beings, just like conscious human beings, are working towards the same goal, which is to discover and recognize our expression in divinity and to move toward the ultimate unification with Source.

After a few hours of discussing such theories, our group left Palenque, buzzing with ideas and the energy we had accumulated. A massive thunderstorm was approaching, and we wanted to get back to the hotel before it broke. As we gathered on a room balcony for the final ceremony of the day, the sky was still an angry black mass of clouds. After we had completed our ritual, we were amazed when the storm clouds suddenly dissipated, revealing a deepening blue sky in which four huge, billowy white clouds materialized and held stationary. As we watched, discussing what it was we were seeing, small lightning bolts flashed from the clouds each time we directed our collective energy at them, as if in response.

For more than an hour this back and forth went on, creating such a spectacular light show that other guests at the hotel were drawn onto their balconies to observe this strange display. During that time they neither moved nor changed in shape as clouds normally would. Gilberto marveled at the interplay between us and these cloud formations, expressing aloud what we all felt: that these anomalous clouds were some form of cloaked otherworldly presence, possibly communicating with us because of the cellular energy we had activated as a group at the Temple of Inscriptions.

Unlike the incident that sent me racing to Gram Twylah's years prior, this time I was not alone; our group of thirteen, and others at the hotel, witnessed this event. Although we didn't know exactly what we had seen, because whatever they were had not fully revealed themselves, when these atypical cloud formations vanished, as spontaneously as they had appeared, we all agreed the interchange was nothing short of supranatural.

13

It Gets Complex Sometimes

In May 1998, I came across a conference called the Star Wisdom Conference that drew my interest. Fortunately, it was being held in the Boston area, which would save on expenses, and since it was close to my birthday, I decided to gift myself. Since my encounter with the little gray dude years before, I had not experienced any direct contact with the beings. However, everywhere I was to travel over the years for study or to teach—from Peru to Mexico to England to Italy—I ran into people who believed in, had witnessed, or whose cultural history spoke of contacts with galactic beings. It was a topic that was discussed, and argued about, by professionals in many fields—astrophysics, biomedicine, psychiatry, the military—and by people of many cultural and religious traditions.

For anyone interested in the topic, there was no shortage of information: extensive Native traditional legends and prophecies; the famous Roswell incident of the late 1940s; the 1952 UFO flap witnessed by so many people over Washington, D.C.; the Majestic project; Area 51; reported sightings from commercial airline pilots, astronauts, and military intelligence; the spontaneous shutdown of missile silos in Montana during the Cold War; the Betty and Barney Hill controversy; the increasing number of accounts from abductees; and physical UFO sightings by people of all colors and creeds from around the globe, even direct comments on personal sightings by four of our previous presidents. The subject was also given a public voice by scholars such as J. J. Hurtak, Jim Marrs, John Mack, and Stan Freidman; journalists, authors, and researchers such as Jaime Maussan, Budd Hopkins, and Colin Andrews; and military or NASA officials such as Colonel Donald Ware, Dr. J. Allen Hyneck, Colonel Wendelle Stevens, and Maurice Chatelain, who was the former Chief of NASA Communications Systems.

A November 1996 Newsweek poll and a September 1997 US Gallup Poll revealed that 48 percent of the U.S. population believe that UFOs are real. Further, 72 percent believe that life exists beyond Earth, and increasing from 48 percent in 1996, to 71 percent in 1997, citizens believe the United States government knows more about the UFO phenomenon than it is sharing. In 2010 when I was collecting information for this book, another Gallup poll revealed that over 100 million people worldwide have reported on the UFO phenomenon. The growing number of believers and the detailed accounts of encounters by witnesses through the years cannot be ignored, despite the efforts to dismiss them by high-ranking officials, detractors, and disbelievers. For example, former CIA director Admiral Roscoe H. Hillenkoeter publicly voiced in a *New York Times* article on February 28, 1960, that he was concerned about major UFO cover-ups. Excerpts from the article quote him as saying, "Behind the scenes, high-ranking Air Force officers are soberly concerned about the UFOs. But through official secrecy and ridicule, many citizens are led to believe the unknown flying objects are nonsense . . . to hide the facts, the Air Force has silenced its personnel."* That was in 1960, and over these past fifty-plus years detailed information and corroboration from many qualified eyewitnesses is still being suppressed today. In September 2010 six former USAF officers and one former enlisted man broke their silence at a press conference held at Washington D.C.'s National Press Club and told how they had

---

*"Air Forge [*sic*] Order on 'Saucers' Cited; Pamphlet by the Inspector General Called Objects a 'Serious Business,'" *New York Times,* February 28, 1960, Sunday, p. 30.

observed UFOs hovering over, and even disarming, nuclear missiles at various Air Force bases from the 60s through the 80s.*

However, as the number of reported sightings rises, so too has the openness of many governments. In January 1992, the Spanish Air Force began declassifying UFO files, and in 2007 the French government was the first to declassify official records on sightings and contacts. Over the next few years, other governments—Greece, Canada, Denmark, Finland, Mexico, Peru, Brazil, Italy, Russia, Australia, New Zealand, India, China, and Ireland—released previously classified information on the subject. In 2011, the Ministry of Defense (MoD) of the United Kingdom followed suit.† It is clear there is a massive cross-cultural belief in the reality of "visitors" that is not going to go away.‡

The 1998 Star Wisdom Conference was being organized by Dr. John Mack, a Pulitzer Prize–winning author, tenured professor of

---

*"US Nuclear Weapons Have Been Compromised by Unidentified Aerial Objects" by Robert Salas and Robert Hastings (Press Release), Washington, D.C. (September 15, 2010) and "National Press Club: UFOs Tampering with Nukes," Part 1/7 on YouTube.

†On August 17, 2011, the *Huffington Post* ran an article quoting Nick Pope, who was the project chief of MoD for UFO investigations from 1991–1994 and who openly admitted the government had engaged in tactics to keep the UFO phenomena under wraps. He said of those efforts, "We were trying to do two things: either to kill any media story on the subject, or if a media story ran, insure that it ran in such a way that it would make the subject seem ridiculous and that it would make the people who were interested in this seem ridiculous." "As U.K. Releases UFO Project Chief Apologizes for 'Spin and Dirty Tricks,'" *Huffington Post,* August 17, 2011, updated October 17, 2011. http://www.huffingtonpost.com/2011/08/17/uk-releases-ufo-files_n_927351.html.

‡In January 2011, the Global Competitiveness Forum took place in Riyadh, Saudi Arabia. One of the panel discussions, called *Contact: Learning from Outer Space,* sought "to introduce, perhaps for the first time, many world business leaders to key issues concerning UFOs and extraterrestrial life, and how these impact on economic competitiveness." Speakers at the event included well-known scientists, journalists, physicists, venture capitalists, and past heads of state such as Tony Blair and President Clinton. To quote Richard O'Connor, M.D., about the seriousness of the intent: "Big companies, big money, big ideas. There is one characteristic about such a group as this of which we can be certain: they would not have their time wasted on nonsense." From "Global Competitiveness Forum and UFOs," Exopolotics Institute News Service, Riyadh, Saudi Arabia (January 26, 2011).

psychiatry at Harvard Medical School, and founder of the Center for Psychology and Social Change. Despite his interest in anomalous experiences, he was well-credentialed in conventional academia: he graduated *cum laude* from Harvard Medical School, was a graduate of the Boston Psychoanalytic Society, and was certified in child and adult psychoanalysis, with more than forty years of clinical psychiatric experience.

In 1994, he wrote his first book on the contact phenomenon, *Abduction: Human Encounters with Aliens.* He was soon recognized as an authoritative expert on the abduction phenomenon. He initiated and directed the Program for Extraordinary Experience Research (PEER) and conducted extensive research with hundreds of people who exhibited the physical and traumatic emotional effects of contact experiences, which could not be explained by the conventional psychiatric model. His willingness to accept that life might exist elsewhere and his support of the ontological veracity of encounters by contactees stunned many of his colleagues, but probably none more so than the Harvard academic community, some of whom worked to have him dismissed. Interestingly, although his investigations caused controversy, they introduced him to like-minded scientific, medical, and indigenous groups from around the world. Harvard had to deal with this odd prestige, while at the same time cope with the subject's controversial aspects.

The Star Wisdom Conference was an invitation for individuals, therapists, doctors, and scientists to be exposed to the findings of an array of professionals from diverse backgrounds and disciplines who were researching this extra- and interdimensional phenomenon—some from their own experiences, others from their cultural traditions, and still others from a purely intellectual view. They included the Native teachers Dhyani Ywahoo and Sequoyah Trueblood; Peyxoto-Uru, a healer from the Amazon basin; Dr. Edgar Mitchell, former astronaut and founder of the Institute of Noetic Sciences (IONS); David Pritchard, physics professor at MIT; Rudy Schild, astrophysicist and cosmologist from the Harvard-Smithsonian Center; Budd Hopkins, a well-known author on ET phenomena; and Dr. Mack. One of the more interesting offerings during the weekend was a workshop for counselors, nurses, and therapists who might be bumping up against the subject with clients or patients who had no context in which to put their anomalous experiences. I was looking forward to this panel as this had been a topic of conversation with participants during the STAR Process training sessions and in my workshops. It had also arisen during a few soul retrievals and, more recently, with two clients in my private practice.

After the general introductions that first morning of the conference, there were a variety of break-out sessions, and I made my way to the "contactee room." To my surprise, the room was already packed, so I settled myself in one of the few empty chairs in the back. I readied my notebook to take what I was sure would be copious notes. On the raised platform was Dr. Mack's assistant, Roberta Colasanti, who was the clinical director for the Center for Psychology and Social Change and had helped Dr. Mack organize this conference. It was she who had gathered the experiencers for this panel, thinking that the clinical community would benefit from hearing their accounts of contact.

Four experiencers she and Dr. Mack had been working with for a few years had volunteered to share their anomalous stories. As I had entered the room late, I had missed their personal introductions. Each of the four recounted their abduction or contactee stories—they referenced themselves as *experiencers*. Although they displayed levels of anger or fear due to lack of personal control during their contact episodes, all were educated people speaking rationally about what some in society would consider an irrational subject. I was struck by how centered they were, even though emotional, while relating their charged stories and changed realities. When they were finished Roberta conducted a question-and-answer session.

There was one experiencer in particular who drew my attention. He repeatedly brushed back his hair with his hand as he spoke. That action provoked an awareness of something hidden in the recesses of my memory and made me extremely uncomfortable. It appeared to me that one of his arms was broken and in a sling. I stared at him hard, trying to figure out where on earth I had seen him before. As he repositioned himself in the chair, his pinned arm faced me directly and I realized he had no arm. I felt an intense, unexplained confusion. I was losing my breath and my head begin to swim with detailed images. I found myself both experiencing and observing a scene definitely not of this world.

I am on a metal gurney or table. I see what appears to be a thin Mylar-type blanket covering my body. The table I am on is positioned in front of a series of small round windows through which I look out at the stars. I know "they" have put me here because watching the stars seems to calm me. Somehow, I also know that five of us are frequently brought to this room to have information imparted to us, and worse, samples taken from us. In the scene unfolding before me, I and one of the boys are the oldest—maybe fourteen or fifteen—although I know we have been meeting them since we were much younger. The other three kids are younger. I can't see them in the room now. I am concerned because I don't always know where they are taken and so I can't stay watchful for their safety; not that I could keep them safe even if I wanted to. I don't like being here; I don't like when they take me without my permission; and I really don't like that I have no control over any of this.

I hear a commotion, and I know Billy is probably acting up again, trying to get off his gurney. It pisses me off; if he would just stay calm this would be over quickly and we could all go back to our homes. I turn to look at Billy and reach my arm over towards him. I know they are examining him and he hates it. This has become a routine: he acts up, I reach out my hand to him, and he quiets down. I have had to do this many times in the past when they come for us, because he always tries to fight them off, thinking he can get up and get away. To my horror, he cannot reach his arm to me this time. He has no arm anymore! I begin screaming, sure they are about to take one of my limbs, too. Where was the "man in the blue hat"? He would help me. Large penetrating dark eyes look into mine.

I snapped to—scared, disoriented, and needing desperately to get away. I rushed blindly out of the room into the large auditorium looking for an escape, any escape. I saw a sign leading to an emergency exit door and rushed out. I didn't care where it took me. I just wanted fresh air, to see the sky and trees, and to hear the noise of traffic—to know I was in the here and now. As I stumbled outside onto a landing, I almost crashed into a lone figure having a cigarette.

Damn, I wanted to be alone!

I thought for sure I must look like the mad woman in the attic as I tried to catch my breath, eyes darting, looking for some type of what . . . I didn't know, maybe a protective sanctuary. But protection from what? I focused on the man, trying to regain my composure, and was about to offer my apologies for bumping into him when I recognized him as Dr. Edgar Mitchell.

He just smiled and offered me his cigarette pack. "You look like you could use one of these."

I grabbed a cigarette, grateful for something to do with my hands and the reality of the burn in my throat from the smoke when I inhaled deeply.

"Something in there upset you?" he asked, nonchalantly.

I wanted to yell, "You bet your ass it did." But jeez, this is Edgar Mitchell for Christ's sake, a little decorum please. "Yeah," I responded slowly, gathering my wits, "I wasn't expecting something that just happened." We talked in generalities for a few minutes, smoking our cigarettes. I was not going to tell this distinguished man I may have just slipped through the cracks in my own mind. Putting out his cigarette, he said offhandedly, "It gets complex sometimes, but whatever just happened for you, I think you should stay." With that, he headed back inside.

Gets complex sometimes? Now there was an understatement if I'd ever heard one.

I finished the conference that day, as Dr. Mitchell had suggested, grateful for having no other upsetting experiences, although still trying to shake a memory that would not "go back in the box." In the days that followed the conference, other memories flooded in and I could not stop them. Unable to overcome my distress, I called Roberta at PEER about a week later. I asked cautiously if she had heard from anyone else at the conference. "In what regard?" she wanted to know. I hesitantly responded that I had bolted from the contactee room because I thought I might have recognized someone on the panel. "That was bothersome," I said. "No, it was downright scary," I corrected myself.

Roberta asked what had upset me so that I had fled from the room. I explained about being triggered by the one-armed man and how I had thought initially his arm was in a sling before realizing he was an amputee. I asked her, "Was he born that way or did he lose his arm, like around fourteen or something?" Roberta answered, "I think you already know the answer to that question." I burst into tears, as her response shattered the last of the resolve that was allowing me to pretend I might have made up the memory. When I could speak again, I asked if she had a private practice and if I could see her as soon as there was an opening in her schedule. She said she did, but then asked me instead if I wanted to be seen by PEER and participate in their research. I emphatically responded, "No!"

The next day I visited her at her home office and spilled the whole story about my reaction to the one-armed man and the vision I had of being on the "ship." She told me she had seen me leave the panel room and had sent her assistant to find me to make sure I was all right, but he hadn't been able to locate me. I told her I had stayed at the conference but had tried to hide out as much as possible. During our session, I related the vision I had at the break-out session and the memories that had been flooding back since. She asked me to draw a picture of "the man in the blue hat." I felt weird doing so, first because it seemed to concretize something by giving him form, and secondly because I couldn't understand why I always felt both happy and anxious to connect with him. Roberta put the picture aside, though I was sure it would find its way into my file, and we continued to discuss the feelings that some of the memories of him elicited. It wasn't until months later that I learned she had already been introduced to the man in the blue hat.

For the next couple of months I worked with Roberta at uncovering more memories—of many nights as a child being encircled in a blue light, moving through the glass pane of my bedroom window without shattering it and up into a huge, spinning, circular craft with rotating lights; walking in the woods as a kid and being approached by Greys, which I had unconsciously camouflaged as huge black-eyed chipmunks. I uncovered the times they would take me onto the ship and place me, and others, in what looked like a huge screening room. Projected on the screen were scenes of Earth's history, from its earliest formation to the current time. Many were beatific images revealing how everything on Earth—from a tree to an insect to water—and the planet itself is a living being. But others were horrendous, showing the destruction of our ecosystem through greed and stupidity, the chaos that ensues when we permanently ruin our water sources, pollution so damaging to trees that they start to die from the tops down, and trails of chemicals in the sky that compromise our immune systems and eventually our genetics. They showed that the forces of nature—the nature beings themselves— at one point will turn against us, as our thoughtlessness and lack of respect cause our own difficult reality. We were shown wars, ethnic genocide, and the use of nuclear and biological weapons that devastated nature and led to the destruction of civilization, as it had on other planets, such as Mars. I felt the images were meant not so much to scare us, but rather to warn us about what might happen if we refused to take responsibility for our own future.

At other times while on the ship we were given what I can only describe as educational sessions. Telepathically, they told us the Earth was shifting her frequency, as could humanity, from a third-dimensional vibration to fourth- and fifth-dimensional awareness. New life-forms would appear which would be a sign that significant Earth changes were likely, and if we survived those changes and were able to shift to a higher vibration we would be able to see a golden corona around the planet. I knew, somehow, that Earth herself would not perish, although clearly not everyone would make the transition. We were told that each planet goes through a purification period before a great leap forward in its inhabitants' evolution, and at this point in history, not only Earth but all the planets in our solar system are evolving simultaneously. And further, they indicated that we will be assisted after the changes by the galactic brotherhood, who have assisted other civilizations throughout Earth's history, but who, according to the laws of the universe, will not and cannot prevent us from freely making our own choices. The degree of difficulty we encounter during the shift depends on our ability to understand our part in the greater whole and to accept responsibility for our own ascension to a higher state of conscious being.

As the memories continued to tumble back to conscious awareness, I remembered that there are sanctuaries on Earth where members of off-planet civilizations exist in underground and underwater communities. And there are also off-planet species of questionable intentions who are housed on some of our military bases, instructing high-level military personnel and representatives from multinational corporations about how to construct technologically advanced machines. I remembered being taken to one of the underwater bases when I was about six or eight years old, and how amazing it had been to be able to breathe in these structures under water with no apparatus, how beautiful the color of the lighting that diffused the area was, and how peacefully the beings interacted in this underwater world. As a child I had thought these were dreams, and now, as I recovered these memories with Roberta, I knew they were not. I could not talk about any of this with my family or close friends, but I was retrieving information just like the Golden-haired Ones had predicted years before. I was grateful there were people, such as Roberta, who listened and believed me, and that I was meeting others who had experienced similar wonderments.

So many things were beginning to finally make sense to me at a time when family and friends would have assessed I was making no sense at all. I felt these experiences, contacts, and memories had pushed me to the brink of my known logical reality, but in leaving that definition of reality behind, I had exchanged that worldview for a larger concept of what reality can potentially be. The encounters challenged me to confront my abject fear of the beings because I knew they could find me wherever I was, but simultaneously I gained a new sense of calm that grew with the spiritual awareness of the more expansive perceptions these beings were offering me. I came to realize that on some level, conscious or unconscious, prebirth or at birth, I had agreed to take this journey and quite possibly whatever was happening was not being done *to* me, but *for* me.

In my work with Roberta, two things in particular kept drawing me back to wanting to know more about Billy, the boy in my vision, who was the one-armed man from the conference and whose real name I had been told was Will Maney. He was an experiencer who had been working for some time with Roberta and John through the study at PEER. I had remembered times we were taken together to a huge machine at the center of the craft. It was covered with dials and buttons that looked as if they had hieroglyphic writing on them. In some capacity we were instructed or tested at this machine by entities taller, thinner, more pale-skinned, and with even more penetrating black eyes than the shorter Greys. The other memory, that for years I had simply thought was a dream but that had come back that day during the Star Conference, concerned the man in the blue hat. He would show up when Will and I were together on the ship. I was always so excited to see him, although he was not human. In some fashion he had become a link to my believing in my experiences, helping me both to feel safer during them and to learn new things from them. I was always so sad to see him go.

After I had worked with Roberta for about six months, she told me that Will had a story similar to mine, and she asked me if I wanted to meet him. I felt anxiety, but also curiosity, so I agreed. She said she would also have to get his permission to meet me, and at our next meeting she told me he had agreed, although he was nervous about how verifying his story would affect his view of reality. He had also given her permission to share some of his story with me before that meeting.*

She told me that Will had spoken often of "the blonde girl" from the ship in his session with her and John. He had continually expressed anxiety that the "blonde girl was getting closer." He was afraid that one day he would encounter her on the street and of what that would mean for his sense of reality if he did. He had been hesitant to speak at the Star Wisdom Conference because he felt the blonde girl would find him. It turned out that during the months I was working with Roberta, Will often came in for his session only hours after I had had mine. As he approached the chair I had previously occupied, he expressed agitation, saying "the blonde girl is getting much closer." His story was indeed similar to mine. He spoke about an entity he fondly referred to as Big Blue, like me feeling safety and calm in his presence and loss in his absence. He had drawn almost the same image I had of the man in the blue hat months before I had drawn mine during my first session with Roberta. Will also had given a description of a big machine inscribed with hieroglyphic-type symbols where he remembered being tested.

During that first meeting, Will and I found we had many other things in common. He recounted an episode where he was able to free his upper body from where he was restrained on the table to fight off the beings. Will had not lost his arm until his teens in an electrical accident, and in his memory of his efforts to escape he had tried to choke the being who was examining him. In his recall, during his attempted getaway, the blonde girl was on another table to his side and was pleading to him with her eyes not to cause trouble, even though in his mind he was trying to protect them both.

---

*As I was to learn much later, because Will and I were disclosing the same information, Roberta and John had taken our case to the Human Subject Committee at the Harvard Medical School for their advice, since it was the committee who had given them the permission required to do their study. The committee advised John and Roberta that they could disclose to me only that information that Will had already shared publicly, but if I thought it was in my best interest, they could, with my permission, disclose my existence to Will.

Besides discussing our shared memories in greater detail, we also spoke about what we thought the beings wanted us to understand from these encounters. We likewise had similar beliefs, such as the veracity of the predictions about Earth events. We both could communicate at times with those who had crossed over, and we both had strong and often prophetic dreams. We were highly sensitive to injustices and became agitated when we encountered situations in our lives where we had no control or, worse still, in which we felt controlled. We were both divorced and both had one child (he a son and I a daughter). Ironically, we even read the same Thoth tarot deck.

During the meeting, John queried us about the details of our contact memories. "You saw a purple light engulf you as you floated through your bedroom window?" he asked me. "No," I corrected, "a blue light." He would do the same with Will. We thought he was simply not listening well, but it soon became clear that he was probing to see if we would tell our individual stories the same way every time. I was surprised, and frankly unnerved, when Will erupted in rage at my answer to one of the questions John asked me: what did I feel about the man in the blue hat. I had answered in an even tone that although, for some odd reason, I trusted the man in the blue hat and I was always happy to see him, if he really was protecting me then I shouldn't have had to go through some of the procedures the entities had put me through. Will leapt to his feet screaming obscenities at John. They let him rant, and when things had calmed down I learned that over their past few sessions John had been trying gently to ask Will to consider that Big Blue might not be totally altruistic. Will had always resisted that possibility, and now, at this meeting, they agreed to revisit it privately at their next session.

I was clear I was done with this meeting and just wanted to get out of there. Sitting so close to Will, in the flesh, and recounting these shared events made them all the more real. How could I discount my memories or ignore all the odd occurrences when we both remembered the same incidents? As agitated as we both were by confirming each other's memories, we agreed with John and Roberta to meet again in another month or so.

Two weeks later I had a private session with John and Roberta. I reiterated how these encounters had shattered my secular worldview, even as they had opened a much larger view of the "possible." I felt infused with new information, the reality of which felt paradoxically both elusive and unequivocal. My memories had given me another level of concern for our environment and the future of our children, a feeling of profound oneness with the Whole, and a new appreciation of the pervasiveness of consciousness. I could never go back to a simpler view of the world. And I wanted to meet the entities with a feeling that I had some measure of control. "It would be exhilarating to meet them in the light of day. Maybe we could even have tea in my living room with friends to prove their existence and then I could ask them about their intentions." I had said this jokingly, although part of me held out the expectation that this would be fabulous if it could one day happen. John cautioned me that I might never have firm proof of their existence, saying that although he and Roberta believed me and the other experiencers they'd worked with over the years, I would have to get comfortable with the fact that many people might never believe me. That truth was both sad and frustrating to me. John went on to say that even though there is a wealth of information from all corners of the globe supporting contact phenomena, ultimately I would have to come to my own acceptance of what was true for me.

The evening after that session, as I prepared for bed, I made an inner request that the entities visit me again in a tangible way. I had a dream in which . . .

I am sitting on a rocky outcropping above an ocean that stretches as far and as wide as I can see. Waves are crashing up the face of the rocks. There is a fine golden-pink haze permeating the atmosphere and two suns rise at different angles in the sky. The entire scene is beyond beautiful and I know this planet exists somewhere.

I awakened suddenly and sensed something close by. I saw a bulbous-shaped "head" float through my bedroom door about three feet off the floor. I panicked, thinking *Oh my God, this is it!* And, realizing instantly that I was in no way ready for what I had petitioned, I dove for the bedside lamp, throwing light into the room. There in the doorway was the green helium-filled balloon Nyssa had gotten at a fair we had attended a few days before. Obviously, it had broken loose from where it had been tied to her bedroom chair and had floated into my room.

Okay, I thought, *maybe I talk a good story, but middle-of-the-night visits offer no tangible proof I can share with anyone.* I tried rationalizing, as if it would really make any difference, that visits in the light of day, instead of the dark of night, would make that reality more tolerable. Still, rather wistfully, I thought it would be a whole lot easier if I could just have tea with the entities and my friends. In an odd synchronicity, at dawn Nyssa came into my room and shared a dream she had just had about a beautiful planet she used to live on that had two suns. She asked me if I knew the name of that planet and why Earth has only one sun. Confirmations come in the strangest of ways sometimes, although it appeared there would be lots of things I couldn't prove or answer.

It wasn't just the contact experiences that were adding new twists to my life. During this time in the fall of 1998, while offering separate workshops, Mary and I met the men whom we would each marry the following year. We would both be called to new places, she to Phoenix and me to Winston-Salem. Further, when Will and I met at our next session, he revealed he had met a woman and was moving with her to North Carolina. Bizarre as it was, the new man in my life, whom I will call Frank, was living in North Carolina.

Frank had appeared when I had least expected it and when I certainly was not looking for anyone. I met him while visiting my friend Joan, who herself had just moved to North Carolina and who had invited me down to conduct STAR Process soul retrievals and offer tarot readings. Frank had come for a tarot reading concerning his business, and in the week following my return to Massachusetts, he sent me a surprisingly personal letter and phoned more than a few times. I was resistant at first, but our talks were frequent and there arose a fast and deep acknowledgment of each other.

There were sticky aspects for each of us in our burgeoning relationship, and mine was how to honestly reveal the odder aspects of my life. John and Roberta, knowing Will and I were each developing serious personal relationships, expressed the opinion that we should not only tell our prospective partners about our contact experiences, but also that we should all meet. At the prospect of such a meeting, I thought to myself, *Now how in the hell can I bring up this anomalous, uncomfortable topic with Frank when I hadn't even discussed it with close friends and trusted family members?*

Frank and I spoke nightly for hours by phone, sharing intimacies, and one night I saw my window of opportunity to bring up the experiencer subject. Frank had asked me if I had ever taken a cruise or if I liked to sail. He had once owned a boat and loved to travel the seas. He shared a dream that someday, after he sold his company, we would move to the Mediterranean and live on a ship, enjoying the latter years of our lives together. Here was my chance—lame as it was. I told him in fact I had been on ships but not the ocean-going kind. There was silence on the other end of the line. Frank knew I was involved in a lot of edgy things, and I knew Frank too had experienced his own fair share of unusual life circumstances, but I considered opening this odd topic would be stretching his boundaries for sure. Rather hesitantly, Frank asked what kind of "ships" I was referring to. I took a breath and let him have it. Without missing a beat, although he must have certainly been chewing on a mass of new information, Frank said, "If that is what you have experienced and what you believe, then who am I to doubt you?" I suppose it was at that exact moment when I fell completely for him.

A month later Frank came to see me in Massachusetts. Roberta and John had arranged for Frank and me and Will and his lady to meet. We all felt extremely self-conscious as we sat outside John's office saying little to each other. Neither Will nor I felt anything of a romantic nature toward each other, but we were intimately connected through our shared experiences. Here we were two people who had grown up without knowing each other and yet we shared memories of being together in an entirely different reality. Our prospective partners were opening themselves to a new world view through their relationships with us. It would have been unfair not to have such a meeting so they could know some of what we had been through and ask the questions they might need to in order to feel more comfortable with the idea. The feeling of discomfort in the waiting room increased when we learned John had inadvertently double booked another meeting at this same time and it took precedence. After a few minutes of small talk and then awkward goodbyes, there was a palpable sense of relief the meeting hadn't actually happened.

Within months, Will and his fiancée had moved, and by May 1999, I was packing up the new townhouse I had recently moved into just prior to meeting Frank and closing my ten-year practice in Massachusetts. I was flying back and forth to North Carolina to arrange for a new school for Nyssa, while looking with Frank for a home where we could begin as a new family. It was a huge, exciting adventure, a huge although calculated loss of my counseling practice and the life Nyssa and I had known, and a huge promise of new love. Those things felt tangible and I felt liberated from some of the odder aspects of my life as I looked forward to this new reality.

14

Belief Is Enough

The years from 1998 to 2001 continued to create enormous transitions in my work and personal life. In 1999 Mary and I scheduled one last journey to Mexico. Our work as teachers and co-creators in the STAR Process over the past seven years was coming to an end, just as had been predicted during my first coca leaf reading. Though ours was a poignant separation after working so closely for so many years, as don Mariano had predicted, seven years into working together, we each had separate destinies calling us. Thirty metaphysically diverse, well-studied men and women joined us on our last journey to work the energies at the sacred Mayan sites of Uxmal and Dzibilchaltun, and to have personal healing sessions with Mayan elder Señor Manuel.

Uxmal is an impressive site of multiple intricately carved stone structures. Here the ancient ones were said to have used sound and sacred geometry for spiritual, scientific, and consciousness-raising purposes. The name of the massive Magician's Pyramid, also known as the Pyramid of the Dwarf, arises from a legend about a magical dwarf who came to Earth, hatched from an egg, grew to adulthood overnight, and built the pyramid in a single day with his magic wand. When hearing this story, it didn't escape me the ancient people of this land may have been trying to explain something they were witnessing and didn't fully understand. Seen in the context of the long history of extraterrestrial visitations, could not the magical dwarf be a small being from another galaxy who came out of an egg-shaped capsule and appeared to grow in stature and awe because he was able to construct the colossal temple in one day, a feat which was beyond the comprehension of the people of that time? Might he have assembled this huge pyramid using sound or laser energy of some sort from his "wand" to transport the rocks into formation? Does one story sound any more outrageous than the other?

Early on during this journey, Mary and I had split the larger group into smaller groups of six. Each group represented a certain star or cluster, such as the Pleiades, Sirius, Regal in Orion's belt, Arcturus, and so forth. Each group would be open to receiving information energetically, intuitively, and symbolically that was relevant to their star or cluster, through group meditation at various structures in the temple complex of Uxmal. Each person would filter the information through their own *Merkaba*. In its simplest translation, *mer* means "light," *ka* means "spirit," and *ba* means "soul." The Merkaba is a geometric energy field of living light in the form of a three-dimensional tetrahedron (see p. 172) that surrounds the human body, radiating outward in all directions and accessed through a specific series of breaths and visualizations. When infused with unconditional love, the Merkaba becomes a vehicle that can take one to higher dimensions of consciousness and helps one move through these realities. Everything on Earth, including the planet itself, has a Merkaba.

Mary and I used the merkaba meditation in our personal work as an initial breathing technique to open the client's field in the Star Process soul retrievals, and as an experiential exercise in our workshops or on our journeys to sacred sites. Most of the information being circulated about the Merkaba at that time had been channeled through three different people: Alton Kadmon, whom Mary had worked with, and Dr. J. J. Hurtak and Drunvalo Melchizedek, both of whom I had worked with. These men had similar and varying opinions on instruction to access the Merkaba, and they were just a few of

Merkaba

the teachers who were training others in the meditative techniques to access and expand the Merkaba field and educate them on the concept of the Flower of Life.

The study of the Merkaba teaches that our light body is alive, that through love we can access higher realms of consciousness, and that our light body, and thus our physical body, responds to consciousness on a cellular level. In its simplest explanation, the Flower of Life is said to contain the patterns of creation. In *The Ancient Secret of the Flower of Life, Volume 1,* Drunvalo Melchizedek writes, "Within its proportions the Flower of Life contains every single mathematical formula, every law of physics, every harmony in music, every biological life form right down to your specific body." Its complex concentric holographic form emerges from a simple shape that is

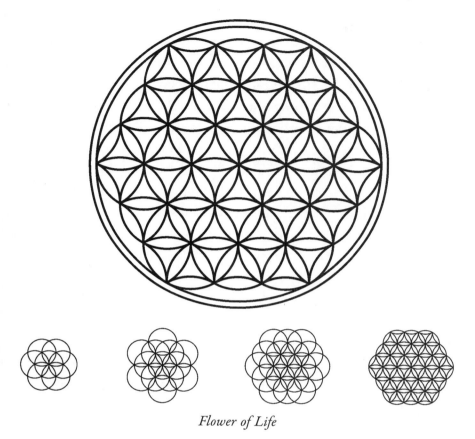

Flower of Life

initially formed by two overlapping spheres, representing the Divine Masculine and Feminine principles, and forming the *vesica piscis,* symbolizing the unmanifest made manifest and whose form is a predominate feature in sacred geometry. It holds within its structure all of the platonic solids, geometrical forms that serve as models on which all life is patterned.

These overlapping spheres of the vesica piscis are then repeated symmetrically to create the intricate, expanded flowerlike pattern from which the Flower of Life takes its name. The spheres repeat in a series of seven harmonic octaves, with a new form created every eighth octave. This geometric and harmonic pattern suffuses all of nature and is imprinted into every living form so that metaphorically the Flower of Life symbolizes the interconnectedness of all life and spirit within the universe. The pattern that forms the basic cube foundation of the Flower of Life is identical to the third division of the zygote—which is a cluster of eight cells—that is formed during human embryonic development. It is said that the imprint of who we really are—our immortal consciousness—is contained within these initial eight cells. Unlike all the other cells in our body, which are replaced regularly, the eight foundational cells of the zygote formation never change, from conception until death. It is my opinion that this group of eight cells, which can be thought of as the container for our eternal awareness, is what we tap into when we ignite our kundalini energy.

The Flower of Life is depicted in ancient and modern cultures around the world. For instance, in the Egyptian Mystery schools, as described in the Emerald Tablets of Thoth, the Flower of Life was seen as the "life source code." Carved in the Temple of Osiris at Abydos is one of the oldest examples of this design. Within Kabbalistic studies, the Tree of Life* can be seen contained in the Flower of Life pattern and the Tree consists of ten Sephiroth,† which share commonalities to wisdom paths contained in the Flower of Life, where each Sephiroth or sphere acts as a divine emanation or seed of information. The Flower of Life shows up as a medieval motif in churches throughout Europe, such as Chartres, and synagogues in Galilee and Masada. It was of symbolic importance to the ancient societies of the Cathars and the Knights Templar, and is still used in Freemasonry today.

In our trips to Mexican sacred sites over these two years, Mary and I, and those who joined us, utilized the merkaba meditation, in conjunction with sacred sound and toning, to help expand our levels of con-

---

*At its simplest definition, the Tree of Life in esoteric Judaism is used to describe the path to God and illustrates how the universe came into being and man's place in it.
†The Sephiroth exist as energy centers, spheres, or emanations on the Tree of Life. They are interconnected by twenty-two paths that teach different attributes of these specific energies.

scious awareness. We were experimenting on this particular journey with three ends in mind. First, we wanted to see if through toning we could access ancient information imprinted within these sacred stone sites and restore memories held in our cellular structure. Second, we sought to connect with the ancients and possibly the Star Nations who may have influenced these sites, and with the avatars who visited them. And lastly, as a collective, we had intuited in preliminary work that Uxmal was an energetic vortex where master magicians had created a schism in the spiritual balance of male and female energies, helping to foster some form of discord or misalignment in the physical realm.

This last topic was discussed during a merkaba meditation meeting, where the group was feeling the energy of disconnection. Our group cohesiveness had collapsed; both the men and the women had stopped being supportive of each other, engaging in petty arguments, some not talking to each other and causing hurt feelings. Mary and I were also falling out of sync with each other. During this trip, we had come to realize our time working together was complete, but the way that parting was unfolding was regrettable given all the years we'd worked together.

As we brought the group back for a more in-depth discussion of the issues, a common theme arose. Given all the work of balancing the male and female aspects within ourselves that we were engaging in both individually and as a collective, we agreed on two points: for humans to truly understand unconditional love and bring it fully into existence, we needed to value how the feminine energy feeds the masculine to enrich and nurture without sacrifice or depletion, and how the masculine energy's greatest gifts are to protect and act while cherishing the sanctity of the feminine source, including Mother Earth.

It is my belief that these are not gender-based roles, but rather they are an understanding of what each of us has to find within ourselves for inner balance. Though the energies are not synonymous with men and women per se, they do describe two different types of psychic energy and fundamental ways of being. Once men and women stop acquiring their complementary energy in distorted ways—rather, in ways that are not so needy or emotionally adolescent—we have the potential to live in the fullness of union, initially within our self and ultimately with each other. It is my sense that when we know that we each can project out to the world our heart energy, and direct our attention or actions to what needs to be resolved within ourselves individually to authentically do that, then we can bring the best of our nurturing and leadership qualities through to others.

If everyone in the group could refocus on balancing their male and female energies during the rest of this journey, it would help us to regain our cohesion, cultivating respect for the struggle of our emerging "new selves" as they informed our changing "current" selves. I believed if we each stayed accountable for our actions, then we could more easily and productively face the challenges this trip was bringing up. As most spiritual adventurers will no doubt agree, any journey out of our comfort zone—both in terms of being in a foreign land and delving into unexpected territory of the Self—can be difficult. Some journeys prove more difficult than others because our experiences, even while shining a light on our divine selves, usually bring illumination to the dark corners of our distinctly human selves. Still, if the intent of a metaphysical journey includes repairing the frayed threads of the soul, as we merge our wakeful humanness with our divine consciousness, then there can be no judgment about how insight, revelation, and healing unfold. Staying open to "what is" within ourselves *is* the journey.

At Uxmal, the group dispersed throughout the temple complex to meditate within their personal Merkaba and then each group came back together to merge into a collective Merkaba to attract the energies as cosmic connectors through the star clusters they had been assigned. When we regrouped to share the information, none of us could have envisioned what was about to occur. Anyone observing the group might have thought we were doing a bizarre ritual, and even we were in disbelief at what spontaneously unfolded. Some of the groups felt they had connected to star energies that they sensed were trying to birth themselves into our plane of existence; others felt as humans we were being pulled into a different "program" that required us to open to an understanding that our genetics are directly linked to the genetics of otherworldly beings.

While we were discussing this, one of the men suddenly collapsed to the ground covering his lower abdomen area with his hands and writhing in pain. He was not kidding, and he was both scared and confused. What we witnessed over the next hour, metaphorically, was the birthing of a new energetic being from a male virgin. All of us, especially the men, had expressions on our faces that said, *What the fuck?* But without missing a beat and seemingly each knowing our parts—which confused us even more—we collectively stepped in as midwives: many of the women encircled him, supporting his body physically and energetically; others moved into their merkaba meditations to hold the energies on another level; and a few of the men actually stepped in to catch the energetic being as it was born. One of the men offered the being to the cosmos and then the earth, and then everyone walked in a procession to a different section of the complex where the "father-mother" had been intuitively called to release the invisible yet energetically perceived being to the Earth plane.

We were mystified by the whole birthing episode. It seemed making any logical sense of, or giving any definition to, this complexity was impossible, except for knowing that there are unseen aspects to energy and that essentially it is energy that gives the physical its form. However, it is not that some other material existed separately in those unseen domains as much as it is that what we create in the physical is the experience of that unseen energy. The group had localized their experience into a given form. In exhaustion and still not knowing what to think, we each went off in different directions to ground ourselves and to shift the energy of the confusing space in which we all found ourselves.

You might dismiss this event as a collective play of persuasion from some energy outside of ourselves, or succumbing to the midday heat of the Mexican sun, or perhaps even as the overactive imagination of a group of spiritual seekers desiring change who had localized their energies to create this unseen form. However, if today you asked anyone who was there I think we would all be hard pressed to tell you exactly what happened and why. But of this I am sure—we were acting within a unified field, a morphic field,* in what felt like a transmission of energy from beyond ourselves to which we had responded.

I honestly had, and still have, a hard time knowing if I should have included this incident in the book. Despite all of the out-of-the-ordinary experiences I have had, especially the contactee experiences, this one was almost too much for even me to believe, and I cannot fathom how this must sound to some readers who are less steeped in the anomalous. However, the only way I can bring credence to this episode is through my knowledge that contact experiencers sometimes feel one of their purposes or aims is to integrate both the human and alien aspects of themselves. We feel, as embodied third-dimensional beings, that we have forgotten our alien dimension, which is one part of who we are on a multidimensional level and important for our soul's growth. By understanding the larger dimensionality of who we are, we can perhaps more fully occupy the enlightened state of all our possible selves. At its most basic level, this incident had introduced a different dimensional possibility.

Nonetheless, the group was deeply shaken by the bizarre situation, and after it was over they once again splintered off from each other both emotionally and physically. It took us a full day to regroup and continue our trip. We traveled next to Dzibilchaltun to balance the

---

*The term *morphic field* was introduced by biologist Rupert Sheldrake in the early 1990s to describe the invisible fields that organize matter and can be imprinted with information from nature, human activity and thought, and other influences. All of nature is formed from organized fields, and matter is bound within these fields. According to Sheldrake, the transmission of shared informational patterns arising from the morphic field might provide an explanation for Jung's theory of the collective unconscious.

light and dense awareness of what had been stirred in us at Uxmal in a more personal way. Dzibilchaltun is the oldest Mayan worship center of the almost two thousand sites that have been uncovered throughout the Yucatan and Central America; its name means "the place where there is writing on stones." It was once a major Mayan city, with a population estimated at fifty thousand at its height, and was still inhabited when the Spaniards arrived in the 1500s.

At the center of Dzibilchaltun is one of its most famous buildings—the Temple of the Seven Dolls, which is also called the Temple of the Sun or the Observatory. The square temple sits on a platform with four staircases, one on each side, leading to its vaulted central room. As is true of many other temple structures and stone circle sites around the world, it was constructed based on astronomical alignments and certain of its features mark seasonal cycles. For example, during the spring and fall equinoxes, the sun's light climbs the east stairway at dawn, projects through the east window and across the temple to the west window, and for a fleeting moment the ball of the sun appears perfectly balanced at the center of the main inner platform. This intricate alignment is yet another tribute to the astronomical and architectural genius of the Maya.

The Temple of the Seven Dolls is named after the seven small primitive clay figures that were discovered buried under the structure's floor. Each exhibits a deformity, such as a hunchback, a shortened limb, or a swollen belly. These effigies may have served as spiritual "messengers" during ceremonies to cure illness, but they have never been explained definitively. Some Native tribes saw certain deformities and even forms of mental illness as evidence of a soul imbalance. I think it is not unreasonable to speculate that these figures might have been used by the Mayan in ceremony to contact the "essence" of a soul imbalance in order to help individuals reframe their perception of their disability, regain strength, or renew health.

Our group gathered at the back of the temple, and one by one, we climbed the steps to the main platform to declare one distorted belief we held about ourselves that we were willing to release. We each then claimed an aspect of our extraordinary selves we were willing to birth into manifestation during the coming year. Just as the ancients witnessed the balancing of light and dark during the equinoxes, we were bearing witness for each other to the potential integration of the luminous and dark within ourselves. This was a testament to the level of both the personal and spiritual work this group had already brought of themselves to this journey. Even so, it took a tremendous act of trust in each other—to be present to each other's vulnerabilities without judgment and to celebrate what we each sought to become—regardless of everything that had already transpired up to this point.

The next day we were looking forward to continuing to grow the seed of our realized selves through spiritual cleansing rituals with Mayan elder Señor Manuel, who lived outside the city of Merida. The meeting had been arranged by Gilberto Siqueiros, who had traveled with Mary, Basil, and me on each of our previous journeys to Mexico, and by José Luis, a friend of Gilberto's. In his everyday life Gilberto is an elementary school principal in his local pueblo, but on his spiritual path he is a Yaqui Deer Dancer. José Luis worked in Merida as a fourth-grade teacher, but was trained in the Aztec traditions.

Our group arrived by bus to the outskirts of Merida looking forward to the work we had planned to do with Señor Manuel. However, it wasn't a given we would be able to do so. It is a gesture of respect to ask an elder if he or she is still willing to work with you once you actually arrive at the village. The three translators, Mary, and I made our way through the scrub brush to have this discussion with Señor Manuel. He and his wife, Señora Maria, were already waiting for us outside their small home. They warmly greeted us, individually each grasped our hands within theirs, while looking us sincerely in the eyes.

Señor Manuel was a small man, at that time easily in his late seventies, with a full head of gray hair and a lopsided grin. He wore a simple cotton shirt, gray pants, and navy sneakers. Señora Maria was about the same height as her husband and wore a white cotton dress with an embroidered bodice. She wore her hair in a salt-and-pepper braid that hung down her back and the gaze of her black eyes was direct and frank.

They announced with pride, tinged with humility, that this was their new home, recently built by their community. It was a simple one-story, cinder-block house, with red and white cloth curtains covering the two visible windows that faced us in the front yard, and an open front doorway. From where we stood, it was too dark within the interior to see anything specifically, but there was light coming from another doorway on the opposite side of the house, showing it to be wide open too.

They spoke softly in Spanish to Gilberto and José. The four of them would occasionally look over at Mary, Basil, and me, where we waited respectfully off to the side. Basil said they were making introductions and asking Señor Manuel if he would work with our group. I was grateful to have Gilberto and José with us, as I knew our being welcomed was in part because these men shared similar traditions and a common language. It would have been difficult for Mary, me, and our group to have access to Señor Manuel without Gilberto and José. Shortly, Gilberto led Señor Manuel over to us.

Through translation, Señor Manuel told us the work he did involved both birthing and healing. However, before he could work with anyone requesting healing from him, he first had to petition his spirit helpers. He emphatically explained his spirit guides had been his "doctors for the past forty-three years." Manuel told us he would put a glass of water next to his bed, and his answer to our request would come from the stars, through the ethers, and into the water. When he tapped the water glass at dawn's first light, the message from his spirit guides would be clear to him. This process was similar to the one Tlakaelel had shared with me years back about dream contact.

Señor Manuel further explained that he had eighteen ancient Mayan gods who protected him in his work, and although many people came to him for healing, some also came to ask him "to do bad things to others." He wanted us to be clear he was a spiritual healer and not a sorcerer. He would do no harm. He promised he would send word the next day about the answer he received from his spirit guides. In the meantime, he said, in preparation for that work, should his guides grant permission, our group should eat lightly for the remainder of the day.

We understood and respected Señor Manuel's need to consult with his guides, but we also knew the group had anticipated working with him right away, so the wait would disappoint them. Still, he was going to consult his guides that night—to "see our hearts" and to determine if it was right he work with us—so one way or another, the wait wouldn't be long. When we explained everything to the group they were, as expected, disappointed, but soon rallied, deciding to spend the afternoon buying food staples and fresh produce for Señor Manuel and his community at the local mercado, which was close to our hotel back in Merida. The group also had time to relax and commune around the hotel pool.

That evening we went into the plaza for a light meal, to dance to the local street musicians, and just have fun. An important part of any spiritual work is fun. Expectations, spiritual aha moments, the rigor of the work, and the constant release of pent-up energies can be both exhilarating and exhausting. The work we had done at the temple sites thus far had been intense and there were many emotions floating around. Our evening out in the plaza for laughter and dancing created more lightness of being, an essential element for a balanced heart. I knew it would be important for Señor Manuel and his guides to feel the group's balanced heart energy if he was to agree to work with us the following day.

Early the next morning we were summoned to Señor Manuel's, where he informed us his spirit guides had told him we were a sincere group of travelers and that each of us was developing a strong spiritual path. "This is good," he said. Mary was to go back to the open field where the group was waiting at the bus and coordinate sending each of the star cluster groups down one at a time. While they awaited their rotation, the other groups would center themselves within their individual merkaba meditation and review within their groups the information they had gathered thus far. Manuel indicated that I was to stay with Gilberto and Basil, who would serve as translators. I would greet each of the groups as they came down for their individual healings and be present for each, in case of any problems. José had left, as he needed to return to his classroom.

With the logistics arranged, Señor Manuel welcomed Gilberto, Basil, and me into his home. As we stooped through the low doorway, I took in everything around me. The interior had an open floor plan, consisting of three sections that appeared to include shared sleeping quarters, an eating area, and a healing space. Directly in front of us on the floor were the bags of flour, rice, and cornmeal our group had provided. We were told the food stuff would be distributed to the rest of the community later that day. Scurrying out of nowhere came at least six kittens, who commenced jumping all over the bags and tripping over our feet. I saw a young girl of about five or six, who was introduced as Manuel's and Maria's granddaughter. She was sitting on a coffee sack, leaning against the wall, and quietly observing us with huge brown eyes. She smiled shyly as we took seats on three folding chairs that had been positioned for us in the cross ventilation created by the open front and back doors. I could partially see out the back door, beyond which was a courtyard. The doorway was lit by the sun, which was rising quickly and was already making the air inside the house feel hot and sultry. To the left of the back doorway was a small area that was sectioned off with an old blue shower curtain with a flower pattern. To the right of the doorway was a small, rustic, wood table stacked with a few cooking pots.

It was what was inside the room adjacent to the front entrance that seized my attention and held it: an altar set up with all kinds of icons, statues both religious and otherwise, many candles in various stages of being burned down, and bottles containing what appeared to be different colored oils or perfumes. Strung from the ceiling along several thick cords were bundles of dried and fresh herbs. Though there were pictures and some religious objects hung on the wall behind the altar space, what hung directly above it was the most astounding object I had ever seen—a huge black doll, positioned as if on a cross with its arms outstretched and its head flopped to one side. It stood out from everything else in the house, and although it appeared more than a little strange to me, bordering on grotesque almost, I knew it must hold some very special significance for Señor Manuel.

In front of the altar, Señor Manuel had set a wooden chair with carved arms. He spoke in Spanish to Gilberto, who translated, explaining that as each person came in, he or she was to sit in the chair with feet flat on the floor. Through the instruction or intervention of one of his spirit guides, Manuel would determine what would help each person physically, mentally, emotionally, psychically, or spiritually. By reading the person's energy body and listening to his guides, he would know which of the herbs and oils to use.

After further discussion between Señor Manuel and Gilberto, Gilberto explained what had transpired the night before when Señor Manuel had asked permission of his spirit guides to work with us and the information they had communicated back to him via the water glass. Manuel had mixed rose water and holy water into a glass along with specific flower blossoms. He had stood out under the stars, beseeching his spirit guides to grant him permission to work with our group. Almost immediately, he said he had felt the presence of one of his greatest spirit helpers, whom he called Emilio Campos, as a pressure that moved up and down his spine. This spirit guide said he would work with us, and would indicate to Manuel what was going on energetically for each person and in what capacity to work with him or her. Manuel also had been advised during his dreams the night before by a "spiritual sister" what foods he should eat so he would be in spiritual resonance with his guides for the healing sessions. It was unclear to us whether she was a living person or in the spirit world. I also could not discern if what he spoke of eating was energetic in nature or actual food he had to ingest. He did not explain those details, and we did not interrupt him to ask.

Señor Manuel continued his explanation by telling us the most important protective guides for him were two he referred to as the Guardian Angel IX* (the Mayan glyph *IX* is pronounced "eesh") and Maximo Kin. Three other spirit guides who he respectfully named as Marachita Mai, Isidra Chuc, and Barbarita Chuc had indicated they too would be working with him during the healings. He told us the Christ was very important in his work and sometimes he came directly to instruct Señor Manuel how to work with particular patients. Manuel also thinks of the Christ as Adoni, the sun, and this celestial energy had always helped him during difficult births or healings. He said, modestly, "One has to have a good relationship with God to be able to work with the spirit guides in this way."

Finished with his explanation, Señor Manuel lit some of the candles on his altar. He pointed out three herb bundles and indicated these were the ones he tended to use the most. I recognized them as spearmint, basil, and rue. I knew from my herbal work that spearmint was energetically uplifting and its smell can sharpen mental powers; basil is more fiery in nature and is said to draw away evil; and rue has been used since ancient times to relieve headaches and is added to mixtures to break hexes or clear negativity. Señor Manuel next pointed to the bottles on his altar containing oils and perfumes, explaining he used many kinds of flower infusions and different scents to attract the spirits during a healing. Concerning a set of seven vials of liquid set off to the side, he said, "These seven essences protect you from the bad spirits. They are used on the seven power centers of the human body when there is an energy blockage." (The seven power centers he was referring to were what are commonly referenced as the chakras.) According to

---

*I was able to discover three meanings for who or what *IX* is in the Mayan pantheon of gods. IX is said to live in the realms of emotions, integrity, and heart-knowing and is linked to magic, timelessness, receptivity, and global consciousness. In Yucatec Mayan, IX is the name of the fourteenth Tzolkin day sign, depicted by the jaguar. According to the 2008 Mayan Aid and Education Project by Mark Pitts, *IX* is the prefix that designates the feminine in general or a specific female, whereas the prefix *AJ* in Mayan usually designates the masculine.

his beliefs, "Bad spirits and bad ideas are one and the same. If you constantly direct bad thoughts or ideas at people or situations, even unconsciously, it will attract bad spirits." He counseled, "You must always be awake, always conscious in your mind to turn that energy around."

Manuel indicated he was now ready to begin the sessions, so I invited in the first person from the first group. With each person, he would explain what he was doing through Gilberto's translation. Generally, with each person he followed the same pattern. He would run his hands around and over the person's physical body, mainly around the head. I could sense he was discerning that person's level of both positive and discordant energy in their subtle body fields. Sometimes he would speak in a whisper and sometimes he would virtually command an unseen something or someone to assist him while using one of the herb bundles to brush, gently pat, or vigorously strike specific areas of the person's body. Sometimes he could detect "holes" in the person's energetic field where past physical injuries had occurred or where old, unresolved emotional stagnation was creating energetic blockages that might later affect their physical health. He had some people inhale one or more of the scented oils; with others, he sprinkled flower infusions or holy water on them.

After the first small group had been administered to individually, Señor Manuel clearly appeared to be agitated about something. I inconspicuously leaned toward Basil, asking what was happening. Gilberto heard my question and replied, "He is getting upset with my translations. He says most of the words I am using are correct, but I am not always getting the emotional impact right." I had no idea how Manuel could object to Gilberto's English translation when Manuel didn't speak English, but I didn't pursue that question. I simply looked at Señor Manuel questioningly. He said clear as a bell, "You will do the translating." I turned to Gilberto confused. "I didn't know he could speak English!" I also thought to myself I wouldn't be very good at translating as I knew very little Spanish. And, if it was the case that Gilberto, whose native tongue was Spanish, was having a hard time conveying the emotional content of Manuel's messages, then how could I? Gilberto said, "He doesn't speak English. He just spoke to you in Mayan and I don't understand Mayan." I was dumbfounded. I had heard him as if he were speaking English. I looked from Gilberto to Basil and back to Señor Manuel, who simply nodded at me. There was nothing more he wished to discuss. I was mystified at this turn of events, but it seemed I would be translating. The second group arrived, and the next person was called in.

As with the elder in Tulum years back, I understood everything Manuel said. He seemed happy with how the translations were going and did not stop or correct me. He even had me write down what he was telling each person, including which of his guides was working with them or protecting them. He also instructed me to tell each of them where he was sensing an energetic hole in their field and how it was affecting their subtle or physical bodies. I found it all intriguing, to say the very least.

While he was working on one man, a clinical psychologist whom I will call Dan, who I knew well because he had taken the three-year STAR Process training, Manual had me explain that because of an accident Dan had when he was younger, "bad spirits had entered him and were limiting his potential." Manuel relayed that Dan would have to take specific preparatory steps before he could complete the healing on him. He directed Señora Maria, who had been present throughout the healings ready to assist with whatever Señor Manuel might request of her, to prepare a particular concoction. He rattled off the names of herbs and flowers as Maria moved deftly around the kitchen collecting them. She filled a large bowl with water, sprinkled some liquid into it from a bottle Manuel handed her (one of the seven special essences he had showed us earlier), and then added a handful each of the different herbs and fresh yellow and white flower blossoms. She then drew aside the shower curtain that partitioned off an area at the back entrance and placed the bowl of water on a stool that was just inside the alcove.

I was instructed to tell Dan to go there, draw the curtain for privacy, and disrobe. Once Dan was behind the curtain, Señor Manuel instructed me to tell him that once he was naked, he was to pee into his hands and wash his entire body down with his urine, and then to thoroughly wash himself again with the flower-infused water. I hesitated and looked skeptically at Señor Manuel, thinking for sure I must have misunderstood him. He simply nodded at me as he motioned Gilberto to call in the next person. Still dubious, I looked at Basil and told him in English what Manuel was requesting of Dan. He shrugged his shoulders, obviously not knowing what to say. Not knowing what else to do, I translated the rest of the instructions to Dan. He whipped his head out from behind the shower curtain, staring wide-eyed at me in disbelief. Señora Maria, standing in front of the curtain and knowing Manuel's instruction, simply nodded in acknowledgment.

Trying to show respect for the scene unfolding before me, it took every ounce of control not to laugh out loud at the expression on Dan's face. Like Maria, I simply nodded, as Dan disappeared behind the curtain, although I could tell he was definitely feeling distress. As Manuel worked on the next person, he asked me to relay to Dan, "If you don't want to be healed, that's up to you. If you wish to get better I can work with you. This ritual will expel the dark energy, and not let it back in, but you must do what the spirit guides are instructing you to do." I conveyed this back to Dan, and heard him sigh deeply.

When Dan returned, he sat back in the chair and Señor Manuel resumed working on him, striking him repeatedly with the basil and rue herbal bundles. He placed a simple, white plastic rosary around Dan's neck, like a necklace, and told him to wear it until the string broke on its own. He then instructed him to go to the mercado when we returned to Merida, look up a specific woman vendor whose stall was near the post office, and purchase a special scent called Black Narcissus, which was the essence Señora Maria had added to the bowl of water and flowers. He was to use this very powerful protective essence as an energetic shield until he felt totally cleared and the rosary string had broken.

It was late afternoon when all of the healings for the group were completed, and now it was my turn. I could not take my eyes off of the large black doll hanging on the wall above the altar. She was almost repulsive as she hung there, yet at the same time exuded an energy I felt was highly protective. Señor Manuel seemed to know what I was feeling and told me the doll had once belonged to Emilia Virajones, a woman who had been a great healer in the area. When she had crossed over, her sons had refused to care for the icon, even though it carried an extremely powerful healing energy. Now it was up to Manuel to make peace between the mother, the spirit energy of the black doll, and the sons, otherwise there would be no tranquility in their homes. Señor Manuel also shared that Emilia had been protected by the Virgin of Guadalupe, and now because he cared for the black icon, he too was protected by the Virgin. He said the Lady of Guadalupe had been watching me throughout these healing sessions because she was also one of my spiritual protectors. That was why he felt I could interpret the essence or spirit of his words when the others could only translate the words. He told me if I ever fell physically ill, I was to put my fingers in a bowl of water and concentrate on the energy of the Lady. She would eat the dense energy and I would be well again. He ended simply by saying, "Belief is enough."

After my session, as we were taking our leave, Manuel reverted back to Spanish and I completely fell out of sync with understanding him. The day was over, and he was obviously tired from the effort of working on such a large group. As I said my goodbyes, nodding my thanks and hugging Manuel and Señora Maria, I could see women already lining up in the courtyard to receive some of the food staples we had provided and possibly blessings or healings. In all likelihood Señor Manuel's day was not yet done. He was after all the healer of his community, and I surmised some of those lining up were probably looking for a type of nourishment totally different from flour and rice.

When the bus dropped us off at our hotel, I walked to the nearby plaza to pay my respects at the central church. It had been a good day and I wanted to say a prayer of thanks to the Virgin of Guadalupe, in the way I had been raised in my youth in the Catholic Church. Somehow, doing so just felt right. As I approached the church, an old mestizo woman with a deeply wrinkled face was sitting alone on the steps in front of the large, ornately carved wooden doors. When she saw me she hurried over, as if she had been waiting for me, and wordlessly pressed something into my hand. As she hobbled away down the street, I opened my hand to find a bracelet-sized rosary with a medal of the Lady of Guadalupe connecting the loop of beads to the string from which the crucifix hung. The rosary represented the first Station of the Cross.* I silently thanked the old woman, as well as the Lady.

My teacher Maya Perez had observed the Stations of the Cross from a unique metaphysical perspective, and I identified now with her teaching about the first station. She had told me that when she was visiting the Holy Sepulchre, Saint Anne's Church in Jerusalem, she was taken through the fourteen stations and given information about their meanings from "a voice beyond" herself. According to her, at the first station, where Jesus is condemned to the cross, "the crucifixion symbolizes the death of man's lower self, making possible the transition back to God consciousness." I thought this bracelet symbolized a similar message about shifting from my lower self to a higher understanding: Spirit was reminding me that the shifts I was experiencing were purposefully meant to stretch the bounds of my reality—this trip had certainly done that—and that for my own self-development to continue I must concretize nothing as absolute fact.

Since that journey, the Virgin of Guadalupe has been one of my constant protective guides. When I am confused she makes herself

---

*The Stations of the Cross, or the Way of the Cross, is a symbolic spiritual pilgrimage of prayer one undertakes by meditating upon the scenes leading up to and encompassing Christ's death, and specific prayers are generally done using rosary beads. It is largely a Roman Catholic ceremony, although it is found in other Christian denominations, such as Lutheran.

known and brings clarity, and she has symbolically appeared to me like a beacon of protection above every home I have moved to during these past thirteen years. She has been present, too, in my ceremonial work, in some soul retrieval sessions, and in dreams when I need to find forgiveness with people who have caused me pain. Yes, just as Señor Manuel had said, belief *is* enough.

15

Are You Kidding Me?

Frank and I married in October of 1999, a year to the day after we had met. I was unaware then of how important that October date would be, as over the coming years that day would many times signal change in my life. We lived in North Carolina for almost two years, during which time I opened a new counseling practice, continued offering Star Process soul retrievals, and conducted local-area workshops. I also traveled back and forth to Massachusetts, where I maintained a limited client base, and traveled internationally leading metaphysical journeys. Meaning no criticism and no judgment, there is a sense of gentility and a different pace in the South along with an unspoken understanding that you don't put certain things in someone's face, even if everyone knows clearly what's going on behind the scenes. What I considered my snappy, sometimes sarcastic, Boston "wit" didn't have a place there with most folks. That said, my practice grew, we made many dear friends, and life for me for those first few years was basically one of contentment.

However, the anomalous experiences continued. Since I was young, I have had the ability to communicate and see the spectral images of people who have crossed over. I have never sought them out, nor have they ever been people I have known in my current life. They have appeared to me as they want, mostly just passing through. In our new home, every time I passed our laundry room I caught a glimpse of an older man in a fedora-type hat out of the corner of my eye. I knew he was not connected with the previous owner because we had gotten to know him and his wife well and we knew their personal history. To me, the man in the laundry room seemed lost, and although I could see him spectrally, I couldn't get his attention and he never tried to get mine.

In addition, over many months, I was overwhelmed by almost nightly visits by Confederate soldiers in my dreams; depending on their personalities, I would talk to them in my sleep, petitioning, cajoling, or praying for them to enter the Light. The nightly conversations were making Frank a tad nuts. He would awaken me and ask who I was talking with. I would murmur, "Dead people," then fall back into a deep sleep.

I had two previous experiences with Civil War soldiers. For whatever the reason I seemed to connect to men from this particular war. One incident was when I was in college. I lived with a few roommates on the second floor of an old house. At the top of the house and adjacent to our living quarters was an attic; the first floor was occupied by the landlords and their daughter. I would often hear what sounded like metal rattling or dragging across the attic floor. The odd sounds unnerved me as they only seemed to happen when I was there alone, but they didn't scare me as much as when occasionally I caught a glimpse of a young man in a blue uniform in the living room. He would follow me around and try to engage me; I would ignore him, pretending he wasn't there. One day he "spoke to me" and communicated that his name was Joe; he said he had died in the Civil War. Joe said simply enough that he didn't want anything from me except to be acknowledged. But I didn't want to see him much less acknowledge him.

My curiosity, however, was piqued, so one day I asked the landlord's daughter if they had any relatives who had fought in the Civil War. She said she thought her father's grandfather had fought for the Union and she remembered that there might be an old trunk in the attic containing memorabilia. Upon investigation we found the trunk tucked deep in the eaves. A brass plate on its side was inscribed with the name of

Sgt. Joseph _____.* The trunk contained his uniform, sword and scabbard, and a tin-type picture of him in uniform. Apparently this was enough of an acknowledgment for Joe, because true to his word, his spirit never appeared to me again.

I remember the ruckus I caused by relating this story to my mother and two grandmothers while we were out to dinner one evening. My mother and maternal grandmother thought the incident was quite funny and simply laughed it off. However, my paternal grandmother was furious with me, thinking it outrageous that I would believe in ghosts and, if that was the case, we should all just "let Joe pick up the check." I never mentioned these types of experiences to family members again; they simply had no frame of reference for things of this nature. Although I knew they loved me, I also knew discussions of this nature frightened them on some level and that their emotional reactions were coming from a place of discomfort.

While offering a workshop with Mary and Dan, the psychologist from our STAR Process training, outside of Atlanta, I had had another experience with Confederate soldiers. We couldn't teach the workshop in the space we had rented because it felt dense with sad energy and filled with what we sensed were many disincarnate souls. We explained to the owner what we were picking up and asked her what had happened in this area. She told us there had been a uniform factory about a quarter of a mile up the road that had been turned into an army hospital during the Civil War. Thousands of Confederate soldiers had come there, wounded and dying. She reluctantly admitted other groups had not been able to use this workshop space either, although they had never been as specific as we were about why.

At the Winston-Salem house, two friends, visiting separately, had become startled while walking past the laundry room doorway by a man they thought they saw standing there. Confirmation is always a comforting thing. One afternoon, a few months after we had moved

---

*For reasons of privacy I am withholding the family name.

in, I was out in the front yard planting when one of the neighbors came over. We introduced ourselves and got to talking. He appeared both agitated and somewhat angry, and he soon told me why. He had intended to go on a hunting trip that day, but his mother, a convalescent whom he now lived with, needed his help. He was upset he couldn't go hunting, or do many other things a thirty-year-old would like to do, because he had become his mom's sole caretaker. One of the reasons he lived with his mother was because his dad, an oncologist, had committed suicide in the family basement two years previously. He felt his father had copped out and had left him to deal with his mother. I asked him to describe his dad. He described him as having been in his late sixties, always dressed in a suit and wearing a fedora hat when he went out. He had been diagnosed with cancer and had shot himself.

I now knew who my laundry visitor was. And although I didn't tell my neighbor this, I resolved to pray for his father and do a release ceremony to help him cross over, as I had been taught by one of my Native teachers. By the end of that summer, our house was free of specters and so were my dreams.

In October 2000—on our first wedding anniversary—Frank and I traveled to Boston for a health care convention where he would be showing his hospital-related product line. He had started a fledgling company a few years before and had been revamping its structure when he moved to North Carolina. The company brought large, backlit panoramic nature scenes into high-stress hospital settings to help alleviate patient stress and uplift the clinical environment. At that time, evidence-based design—redesigning hospitals and other medical venues to be more of a healing sanctuary for patients—was still somewhat in its infancy in the medical model, but the concept was catching on quickly with patients, architects, and eventually hospital administrators.

This October conference introduced a new element to our world. During the convention we were approached in our sales booth by a large, barrel-chested, silver-haired man wearing fancy cowboy boots. He and his wife, who both hailed from Houston, Texas, were starting a new company. As we later learned, he had been involved in the oil and gas industry and had reinvented himself any number of times after the oil crash in the late 1970s. He was a "good talker." His new business was to use mobile coaches for CT and MRI exams as outreach stations for Houston-area hospitals, and he wanted to incorporate our backlit products into these mobile units to help with patient comfort. Frank had been looking for someone to expand the market presence of his products, so the two of them had any number of discussions at the conference and after we had returned home. Frank invited them to come for the Thanksgiving holiday, and during that long weekend Frank and "Mr. Houston," as I privately referred to him, solidified a deal based on a number of legitimate contracts Mr. Houston said he had with Houston-area hospitals.

Frank had been selling the product throughout the United States and we weren't limited by where the company needed to be located. We were landlocked in North Carolina, and since we both preferred to live closer to the ocean, we began exploring the idea of moving to the Maryland coast. We had actively engaged this vision as a family in the months following the verbal deal with Mr. Houston by house-hunting along the Maryland shore. However, as the months unfolded, the business contracts weren't moving as rapidly as had been discussed and Mr. Houston suggested maybe things would move faster if we relocated to Texas. This would allow for daily interactions, more frequent presentations to local hospitals and architectural firms, and a more hands-on approach toward developing their alliance.

I offer my apologies straight out for what I am about to say, both to all those creative, intelligent, kind, and funny couples and individuals we befriended in Texas and to the many more good people who make their lives there. At that time there were only four states in this terrific country I never had any intention or desire to move to—and Texas was first on the list. To compound my feelings, this was the state from which we had just elected a president and vice-president whose policies I vehemently disagreed with. Be that as it may, this could be a good opportunity for us, and so we found ourselves packing up our North Carolina home in June 2001 and heading for a house we had put a good-faith deposit on outside of Houston.

Sending the moving van ahead of us, we said our goodbyes to friends, hitched a small U-Haul to our car to transport our numerous plants and a few special items, and headed off. During our three-day drive, Nyssa lamented, "We were headed back north to Maryland, don't either of you see we're driving deeper south?" I told her everything would be all right, and let's just see this as a new adventure. Frank was obviously happy we believed in him enough to make this trek to the Great State of Texas.

To me, it was never about disbelief in Frank, his company, or his dreams. However, silently I had begun to worry about this new partner, as he foisted his fresh belief in Jesus into every discussion and insisted on ending every conversation with a group prayer. These prayers always leaned towards something he wanted but hadn't directly asked of us, or seemed timed as a distraction from something he didn't wish to address. To be clear, it is not that I do not believe in and honor the Christ, nor is it that I am at all opposed to prayer—prayers of gratitude are a big part of my life. Perhaps it is overly judgmental, and I recognize we all come to our beliefs as we need to, but I assessed that Mr. Houston's religious fervor arose more as a means to camouflage all the wily and selfish things he had done in his life, which he had unabashedly shared with us, than from any kind of genuine devotion.

Again, despite my years of training, I ignored my metaphysical teachings on extending filaments, discerning energy, and creating boundaries, thinking I was being narrow-minded, and instead tried to be open and courteous. I wanted this move to work.

We reached Houston the day tropical storm Allison hit. Our moving van was one of the last vehicles to make it through I-10 and into Houston before the roads flooded. The house we had secured weeks earlier partially flooded, so we let our good-faith payment go and backed out of the deal. We thought that after the storm passed we would quickly find somewhere else to call home. After all, Allison wasn't a full blown hurricane, merely a tropical depression. We were lucky enough to find lodging at a La Quinta just outside the Houston international airport, figuring we would ride out the storm and then resume life on our new adventure.

It turns out we were wrong. As the news programs soon made clear, the storm had wreaked havoc in the area: all the main highways were closed; downtown hospitals, theaters, and businesses were flooded; and many people within the city limits had water up to their rooftops. As the pictures came across the television screen those first few days, it was clear we were in the middle of a disaster. To make matters worse, as the waters began to recede, it was evident the hospitals would not be able to honor any of their proposed contracts, as they were desperately trying to attend to the damage they had experienced. In addition, the Houston housing market was thriving; each house we put an offer on was scooped up by others before our paperwork even reached the seller.

Stuck in the hotel, Frank began to sell his products at the desk in the sitting area and I did my counseling work with clients on the phone in the bedroom, while Nyssa watched television in between reading and crying. Our money was disappearing quickly. Our furniture, hidden in some downtown warehouse, was collecting daily storage fees. The hotel room was costly, even though as the days dragged by the hotel management kindly offered us a deal. Our staples were frozen pizzas or foods that we heated in the only thing we had to cook in—the room's microwave. We had brought all our plants into the room to get them out of the U-Haul and the heat and oppressive humidity, which neither the plants nor we were used to. Our one daily respite between working in the room and looking at houses with our realtor was going down to the pool's gazebo in the cooler, late afternoon air, with a cold bottle of chardonnay, where the three of us would play gin rummy. We were confined to that hotel room for a full ten weeks.

It was clear Mr. Houston could not help us. He was not as connected in the medical world as he had made himself out to be and, frankly, he didn't have the finances to help himself much less to lend us a hand in the circumstances in which we found ourselves. It was in our best interest to sever ties. Frank was more miserable than Nyssa and I, and that was saying a lot because we were pretty miserable; it was a rough start for a fairly new marriage and family. On top of that, I felt guilty, as I knew we had asked a lot of Nyssa, disrupting her with two big moves in her teenage years. This was not easy for her emotionally, yet she never lashed out or gave us any attitude in the way fifteen-year-olds easily can. Frank and I should have gotten just how very blessed we were on so many different levels, despite the turmoil, but in that moment we often forgot to feel gratitude and just tried to make it through, day to day.

We had been in the hotel almost nine weeks at this point. Adding to everyone's anxiety, school was starting the following week but we were not allowed to register Nyssa until we had secured a residence. Also, Frank couldn't look for office space until we were first settled as a family. One afternoon in mid-August the hotel's assistant manager asked if we would meet her in the gazebo after work. We had no idea what she wanted. We had gotten to know the staff well over those two and a half months. We had paid our bill weekly with credit cards and borrowed money, and I was eventually forced to cash stocks that had been put aside for Nyssa's college fund. We thought we were prepared for anything, given how things had been going.

Once we were in the gazebo, sans Nyssa, the assistant manager explained she felt she had gotten to know and respect us, and she didn't know who else to turn to now—she was pregnant. She wanted our opinion on what she should do. I thought, *Are you kidding me?* We didn't know what to tell her, and once she had left, Frank and I decided this was it—we needed a break, any break. To make a truly awful situation even more untenable, I received a call from one of my sisters that evening telling me Mom had been diagnosed with a brain tumor. Could we come home for Labor Day to see her and be together as a family before her scheduled surgery?

They say God doesn't give you more than you can handle, but quite frankly God was really pushing the far outside reaches of my envelope. As if knowing we had to be rescued from the abyss, our prayers were heard and literally that next day we found a house. Frank would need to do some fancy footwork with the loan officer because of the seller's conditions, and we would need to pay a grotesque amount of money to get our furniture out of storage. Even so, we had a home.

As I silently said a prayer of gratitude, there she was—what I had come to equate as the symbolic energy representative of the Virgin of Guadalupe—above the house, guaranteeing in my mind it would all go through favorably. It did, and the day after school started, Nyssa was officially registered. The three of us had made it this far. By overcoming all of these challenges, I was confident we had the capacity as a family to make it through anything.

With things settled as well as they could be for the moment, Frank stayed and secured the remainder of things with the house, while Nyssa and I went to be with my family on Cape Cod for Labor Day weekend. Being home was balm to my soul. It was the first time in five years all of us were at the same place at the same time. Even my brother, who traveled the world as a merchant marine, found his rotation allowed him to be home. Although the circumstances were bittersweet because of my mother's diagnosis, there was an air of camaraderie, laughter, and hopefulness. We spent the weekend at the beach, picnicking, playing volleyball, sharing political opinions, commiserating while watching our now mainly grown kids playing together, and assuring Mom everything would be all right.

I found that here with my family I could unburden myself of some of the tension that had been building in married life because of everything we had just come through. Thankfully, because my family has always been there for each other, by the time I left I was laughing about some of the circumstances that had been "my summer of 2001." On a more serious note, Mom's surgery was scheduled for two weeks out. Regrettably, most of us needed to make our way back to our prospective homes or jobs after the weekend. None of us could have known that weekend the extent to which our world—everyone's world—would soon never be the same.

Nyssa and I headed back home to begin our new life, "Texas-Style." And, yet, there was about to be another twist.

Our family, I guess, is not all that different from many current modern families across the country in that it is a blended family. With divorce rates, blended families—all manner of alternative family configurations—have become common. Nyssa's dad, who lived in Massachusetts, had lost his job during the time we lived at the La Quinta. In a scenario that was not totally comfortable for me, but on its merits seemed to make some semblance of sense, Frank, who needed another salesperson to help reform the company, asked Ben if he wanted to come to Texas to work for him. Part of the attractiveness of the offer for Ben, beyond a new job, was that he could participate in Nyssa's life.

Friends and family cautioned loudly against such a scenario. I guess *cautioned* is a kind characterization of folks' reactions; the reality was everyone thought we were lunatics. Nyssa was preoccupied by the pressing concern of finding a like-minded group of classmates after moving to yet another state and another new school for the second time in three years. I needed to put my energies into opening an office and restarting my shamanic counseling practice. Frank needed to secure a sales office and bring down Nyssa's dad. Good, bad, or ugly, everyone had their own agendas. There we were, almost at the two-year marriage mark and having surmounted what already seemed like years and years of challenges and yet as shaky as it had gotten sometimes, Frank and I were still holding hands.

16

Pretend

September 9, 1999, Dream Journal Entry

I am standing across a river looking at the skyline of a large city. It is a clear blue-skied day. I see three ICBM missiles go over my head. One has a red tail and one has a gray tail, the third one seems to go beyond the city skyline. I feel great concern because they are so close to the buildings. From where I stand I can see little mushroom clouds form side by side as the red-tailed and gray-tailed missiles seem to hit their marks. There are great clouds of billowing smoke, and debris fills the air. I fear for the people over there. Something awful is happening.

Less than two weeks after Nyssa and I returned from the family reunion, Frank and I turned on *Good Morning America* to watch the news and have our coffee as was our morning routine. There was breaking news by Charles and Diane about a tragedy unfolding concerning a plane that had hit the North Tower of the World Trade Center. It was September 11, 2001.

To our horror, minutes later we witnessed another plane, this time hitting the South Tower. I felt a horrible twist in my heart and turned to Frank, saying in disbelief, "I think I know someone on that plane."

I continued to speak almost in spite of myself, not knowing where the information was coming from. "Both towers are going to collapse completely." Frank tried to reassure me. "I'm sure there is no one you know on that plane. Those towers will never collapse. They've been constructed to withstand any kind of disaster."

I feared for my many friends and acquaintances who lived in New York City and for their family members or friends who I knew worked in the World Trade Center. I hoped none of them had been hurt. No one seemed to know what was going on. Even most of what was being reported as "news" was really just speculation. It was clear, however, our country was being attacked on more than one front, as the news came in that another plane had crashed into the Pentagon and still another had either crashed or been shot down in Pennsylvania. Worse still, although there were no details released yet about the second plane, the newscasters had reported the first plane to hit the Twin Towers was American Flight 11, which had originated in Boston. I felt an awful foreboding because of all the friends and family I had there.

I called my mom to check on her, as she lived alone and I knew this news would unnerve her. She was frantic: she was convinced my brother was on one of the planes but she couldn't get through to my sister-in-law to check. "He can't be," I said trying to calm her. "He is scheduled to leave tomorrow." Jay, my brother, was supposed to fly out on September 12 so he could ship out on a tanker leaving San Francisco for Asia the next day. "No!" she insisted, then explained he had told her he was leaving a day earlier to help his best friend secure a position on his tanker. "*No,*" I now insisted, "that can't be true." But with a sinking heart, I already knew, for even as I protested I felt an intuitive knowing. I "saw" my brother's hand take my father's hand in the "ethers," and I had not felt such emptiness in my heart since Callie's death. Still, my human self held out some hope that we would hear at any moment Jay was safe, already home with his family, and as upset as the rest of us by what was happening to our country.

We stayed glued to the television watching the devastation and following the continual special broadcasts. We were sickened as the Twin Towers erupted in fire from the jet fuel and other explosions that seemed to be coming from the base of the towers. We watched with hope as brave firemen, policemen, and civilians entered the towers to find the living and do their best to deal with an impossible situation. We could barely look as the television cameras turned on those trapped inside who had no recourse other than to jump from their offices, which were engulfed by fire. Within two hours, the Twin Towers had collapsed.

Our family called each other back and forth throughout the day, hoping someone had received word about Jay. My mother had finally been able to get hold of my sister-in-law, who told her he had flown on a United flight, not on American Flight 11. I held to that information as good news. There was total confusion on the news loops, with reporters contradicting each other as to what had happened with these flights.

It had been reported that some of the passengers had been able to make cellular phone calls. We all agreed if our brother had indeed been an able passenger on any of those flights he would have done everything possible to get word to his wife. Planes were being grounded all over the country, so we optimistically rationalized that maybe his plane had landed in another city and in the chaos he hadn't been able to contact us yet. My sister-in-law had told us he had been very late and, in fact, when she had dropped him off he had taken off running to try to make the flight. Maybe he had missed it, was still at the airport, and his cell phone, like so many others that day, couldn't get a signal. We were holding out for any possibility, as you do when the truth might be too painful to wrap your head around.

To compound the emotional turmoil, I was worried about my friend Renny, who now lived in New York and whose brother-in-law worked in the World Trade Center. Despite repeated efforts, I couldn't reach her, so I called one of our mutual friends, Betty, to see if she had any news. The word was not good. The plane that hit the North Tower had made a direct hit on the offices of Cantor Fitzgerald Investments, where Renny's brother-in-law worked. When I later got through to Renny, she revealed the overwhelming news that her brother-in-law had perished, as did, we would later learn, more than 650 other employees of that firm. Among them were the brothers of other old friends.

Finally, late in the day, we got the call no one in our family wanted to receive. Friends who were with my sister-in-law revealed the devastating news that the plane that had hit the South Tower was United Flight 175 out of Boston, headed to San Francisco—Jay had been confirmed as a passenger. There could be no more pretending.

The losses of that day were, and still are, incomprehensible. The following days and months were equally mind-numbing. It's almost impossible to process loss, never mind to begin making the agonizingly slow journey toward resolution, when there is no body to bury, no clear-cut ability to say goodbye in the ways that bring solace. Add to that, a loss that continues to remain so public, for despite how personal it is for the individual families, by its very nature it is a national loss as well. Almost everyone in our family gave DNA samples in the hope something, anything, might be found to bring us some measure of closure. It wasn't until well over a year later that the forensic investigators provided some small remains that could be brought home to lay to rest. That in itself was miraculous, and we realized we were luckier, if I can even use that term, than many.

A few months after that infamous event, I went to stand at ground zero and offer prayers on behalf of my family. No one else could or wanted to make the trip. Renny's husband, Rob, one of my best friends since I was in my early twenties, accompanied me. The sidewalks along the streets leading to the devastatingly deep crater were covered with posters of missing persons, remembrances left by family members, prayer cards, flowers, and candles. Access to ground zero was cordoned off, and only the workers who sifted through the debris, many of whom in the years following this disaster would suffer from illnesses caused by working at the impact zone, were allowed in. An acrid smell still hung in the air in that part of the city, and the area was suffused with what I can only describe as a quiet numbness.

People from more than ninety countries had been lost here and on the flights: 2,670 from the United States and 375 foreign nationals, the youngest age two and the oldest eighty-nine. Too many, including my brother, had left children without one of their parents.

Despite the War on Terror that would eventually be directed at Iraq for unsubstantiated weapons of mass destruction, fifteen of the nineteen jihadist al-Qaeda-trained terrorists had come from Saudi Arabia. I imagine that's why, when the rest of our country was prohibited from flying in the days following the attack, the Bush administration allowed three planes filled with Saudi nationals, some from the bin Laden family, out of the country under secret cover.

I did not then, nor do I to this day, over a decade later, hold the people of any country in the Middle East, or Muslims in particular, responsible for 9/11. As a global community, we have witnessed too much death, and we all bury our children with pain in our hearts. No religion, at its core, promotes death, although many people throughout countless centuries have died in the name of someone's god. It is not God who kills; it is people who do—those who cannot conceive of a better way to relate to each other without the useless act of killing as a means to an end. I believe every country and every religion has its crazies and its zealots. I do still wonder, though, what certain government agencies, from the United States and abroad, knew or didn't know.

In spite of the 9/11 Commission report, I wonder what evidence was lost or buried or covered up as "secrets" from government agencies that ignored or disregarded the reporting of field agents because of a sense of superiority or interagency jealousy. In fact, in the ten years since 9/11, there has been compelling evidence that U.S. intelligence agencies knew something had been brewing as early as 1998, when our embassies in Kenya and Tanzania were bombed.*

---

*Although Osama bin Laden was the leader behind the African embassy bombing plot, it was Khalid Sheikh Mohammed and his nephew Ramzi Yousef who were the actual masterminds of the 9/11 attacks. Osama bin Laden was killed by U.S. Navy SEALs on May 1, 2011.

For something as big as the 9/11 plot to have succeeded, there had to have been rumblings somewhere. I compare this attack to Pearl Harbor, for it was only a secret to those on the ground and on the ships. There were high-ranking officials at that time who ignored the signs, and I staunchly believe that although absolutely no one wanted something of that nature to occur in 1942—or on September 11, 2001—there had to have been officials who had their suspicions in the months and years leading up to that awful day.

I want to make it clear that, while I believe governments knew more than they have let on and could perhaps have averted the massive scale of these tragedies, I am not suggesting complicity by any U.S. president in office during either of those time periods. I cannot imagine what President Roosevelt or President Bush had to deal with on those fateful days or during the aftermath of the attacks. Nor am I making accusations about any political party. Grief knows no boundaries, including party affiliations.

I also am not suggesting there was a government conspiracy. I think conspiracy theories make it easy for people to ridicule and dismiss legitimate questions. However, I do have to ask, "Who benefited from this incident?" Maybe it is safer not to ask this question, although it certainly is not saner.

In retrospect, I see that I spun myself into an emotional cocoon for a number of years after the loss of my brother. Death has a way of doing that, even as we manage to go through our daily routines, appearing as if we are seemingly doing okay. I thought I had risen above the loss in the months following his death, as I convinced myself nothing would ever feel as devastating as losing my daughter, and I had, after all, survived that loss, had I not? And there was a blessing to be thankful for as, gratefully, my mom had come through her brain surgery with no ill side effects.

However, I was not all right. I seethed internally at the comments from strong Bush supporters, who seemed to be everywhere around me, about the wonderful job his administration was doing in their "war on terror." I was watching our country lose more and more of its respect around the world, as 9/11 was used for other agendas. I was dismayed at the erosion of our civil rights while we were told we were being protected by Homeland Security and at the people who blindly accepted the reasons given for the loss of our privacy as citizens. Maybe I was naïve, or maybe questioning has its place. It doesn't matter, the Bill of Rights promises us as American citizens that we are entitled to our personal beliefs and opinions—and I was entitled to mine.

Moreover, we disagreed about these issues in our own home, as discussions often led to political polarization and angry arguments, which certainly wasn't helping me at all. I know we are responsible for how we walk upon the earth, and I admit I was getting angrier and more defensive for reasons I wasn't always clear about, despite what I knew I *was* clear about. What I needed, especially at home, was gentle understanding for my grief and not callous political comments or mean-spirited partisan opinions. Suffice it to say, I was neither in a good place emotionally nor was I in balance in my spiritual center. So, I did what all good Americans do—I distracted myself by throwing myself completely into my work.

I opened an office just weeks after 9/11, and created a small sanctuary; it felt good to be there. Even if local clientele was slow at first, I still had my phone sessions with clients on the East Coast. However, over the next year, hard as I tried, I couldn't seem to grow the local practice. In an effort to expand, I had new business cards printed, as well as advertising flyers that briefly explained my work. I posted them at places where potential clients might see them, such as natural herb centers, massage offices, and chiropractic offices. I also attended a few local seminars, where I met some great folks, and was asked to write a monthly column for a New Age magazine. There was no doubt, a large and active community of alternative practitioners existed in Houston.

Whether it was my attitude, the astrological alignment of the stars, or life just trying to push me in a new direction, I wasn't attracting clients and my plans for expanding my practice were unraveling. At the first place I took my business cards, the owner ordered me out of her store, declaring she did not allow "satanic practitioners" to advertise. Sure that there had been a misprint on the cards I hadn't caught, I explained I was a *shamanic* practitioner not a *satanic* practitioner. As I looked at the card on my way to the door, it was clear that there was no print mistake. I judged her next comment—that they were "one and the same"—which followed me out the door, as totally unevolved.

Further, in what was the utter collapse of my ability to cope, I had my own "unevolved" encounter with a new client. She had phoned saying that she had heard I was good at helping people identify, confront, and move past their limitations. She booked a session, during which I learned her limitation was the inability to lose weight. She was quite heavy and although she told me she sincerely wanted to lose weight, there was a caveat—she drank a six pack of Pepsi and ate a fair number of Mallomars every day and she made it clear she would not change that routine, as it brought her comfort in her stressed-out world. Without censoring myself, and responding in a way totally counter to my years of professional training, I blurted out, "What do you think, I'm the good fairy? I can go poof with my magic wand and you will lose fifty pounds?" What in heaven's name was I doing? What an unkind, thoughtless statement. Understandably, she promptly walked out.

I consulted with a counselor friend of mine back in Massachusetts about my behavior. He cautioned that perhaps I needed a break from my practice, and maybe the past few years had emotionally been too much; perhaps I needed to do something else in the short term. Kindly, he told me he knew I was good at what I did, and he knew I would come back to a full practice eventually, but in the "now" I needed to take care of myself. Taking his advice, I decided to close up shop, shutting down my Texas office in October of 2002.

When I told Frank what had happened, and of my resulting decision, he suggested I come to work for him, as he needed additional sales staff. I couldn't imagine working daily with him and with my ex-husband; those odds just seemed too unfair. Plus, I had never done cold-call sales before and I didn't think I would be good at it. However, I believed in the concept of nature as visual art in hospital settings, so I gave it a try. To my surprise, once I got comfortable with the sales lingo, I actually excelled at it. As the months passed and I became passionate about the company and its products, I also began writing articles for medical and architectural magazines and continued to write the monthly column for the New Age magazine. At the same time, I maintained a scaled-down version of my other practice in Massachusetts and continued to take spiritual seekers on yearly journeys internationally to sacred sites or esoteric communities.

In late 2001 and again in spring 2002, I had taken the first of many groups to Italy to the metaphysical, and controversial, community of the Federation of Damanhur.* Damanhur proved to be an excellent place to quiet myself and turn my attention inward to regain some balance. Although I questioned some of the dictates of Damanhur's founder,† I had no doubt about the sincerity of its citizens. Despite their detractors, Damanhurians are devoted to their spiritual practices, artistic expression, and a belief in expanding their consciousness outside the proverbial box. Simply put, what they have created is amazing. Here I found I could be a student as well as a teacher.

One of the places we did energetic and meditative work was the spectacular underground Temples of Humankind, which is dedicated to the divine nature of humanity; it is a place to open up, or tap into one's insights, creativity, or dreams. The temple consists of nine beautiful rooms on five levels and has been constructed like a three-dimensional book. Each room and passageway is magnificently decorated with stunning murals, mosaics, sculptures, and intricate stained

---

*Damanhur is an eco-society founded in 1975 whose members share spiritual, ethical, ecological, and artistic values. In 2005 it was recognized as a model for a sustainable future by the United Nations and awarded their Global Human Settlements award.
†Oberto Airaudi, Damanhur's founder, officially called Falco by everyone who lives in or has visited the community, passed away on June 23, 2013, at the age of sixty-three.

glass images. Halls dedicated to earth, water, metal, and to spheres filled with alchemical liquids* are accessed through secret doorways and tunnels that lead through the underground labyrinth.

In one of the nine rooms, the Hall of Mirrors, I meditated and worked with the Andean energetic art of mikhuy, allowing the mirrors to reflect back to me my own sadness and frustration. By "digesting" the hucha, the heavy aspects of my sadness and frustration, I took the first steps toward addressing what I needed to change in myself in order to regain my center. If only for that reason, and there were certainly many others over the ensuing years and visits, I am grateful for the people and community of Damanhur for what it offers.

The truth was I was overjoyed just to be back in Italy. Frank and I had honeymooned there in conjunction with an invitation I had received to conduct an Andean workshop for a large group of Italians and Germans at Lago d'Orta in the Dolomites. Italy has always been one of my favorite countries, full of beauty, art, and never a bad meal. Over the ensuing years, Frank and I tried to get to Italy and other European countries whenever we could, although those trips were contingent on one of us having work there, after which we'd take some downtime to enjoy ourselves.

We traveled well together when it was only the two of us, for our interests and passions mirrored each other's—everything from viewing art to exploring ruins, from trying new wines to checking out local restaurants. The important part of traveling for us as a couple was that we each found renewal in foreign travel and delighted in those we met along the way in the many countries we were privileged to visit. Travel took us out of the stresses of working the daily needs of the company, which we attended to as if it were a growing child. We both still held

---

*Located in the Hall of Spheres are nine large spheres that contain alchemically prepared liquids of various colors, each with a chalice above filled with special metals. According to Damanhurian philosophy, these are linked to different planets and constellations, as well as lunar cycles, emotions, and feelings, so connecting to these energies during meditative states helps to recall the human soul structure.

fast to the vision of that reward of the "ship on the Mediterranean" once we had sold the company and could realize our larger dream of days at sea where we would not be pushed or pulled by the company's needs.

Sadly, as the years went by, and as my professional world in Texas continued to shrink, working with my husband in the day to day of the business was creating stresses beyond the norm of what couples usually experience. Building a company together changed the nature of our relationship, even as we saw it as an end goal for our future. We had little time apart and the office and the needs of the office always followed us home and took precedence. Foolishly, we allowed the boundaries between our work life and personal life to blur, and there was no separation of "church and state." It was easier to blame the tension between us on the financial constraints of the company, his work, my work, Texas, and other people than to admit the real truth—that we were doing this to ourselves.

The conflict in my professional shamanic practice increased when in 2003 the state authorities threatened to fine me if I kept writing my column for the local New Age paper under the heading of "Shamanic Psychology." I had aroused someone's ire, and that person had reported me to the Texas State Board of Examiners of Psychologists in Austin, who called me and said I needed to stop writing the column as I was not a licensed psychologist in the state of Texas. I was shocked, as in the column I merely gave techniques and meditative examples or stories from my Native and metaphysical teachings on how to confront life's vagaries and how to release or reframe emotions. I couldn't believe someone would take offense at that or misconstrue it as conventional psychology.

I asked the administrator, "Can I know my accuser? Maybe if I can speak with them, they will tell me what is offending or challenging them and I can explain it." The official said, "No. In the state of Texas, we can't share the name of your accuser. But if you don't cease and desist writing your column, you will be heavily fined." The following day an official letter arrived stating the same thing.

I was pissed beyond measure, and in defiance I simply changed the column title, not its content. With the consent of the editor, the column was changed to "Shamanic Counseling." However, with the steam of anger dissipating and feeling Texas simply wasn't my place, I reduced the frequency of the column to bimonthly. Valuing my contribution, the editor asked if I would write a major article about how I had come to be trained as a shamanic practitioner, so those less familiar with the term would have more of a sense of what I did. I was so disheartened at that point that I felt I had nothing to write so I told her I would think it over, while wondering what if anything it would accomplish.*

In a show of support, some of my friends who had been observing my free fall into depression and who had been on my last two journeys to Damanhur suggested I take another group to Peru. Being in Peru had always lifted my heart, expanded my awareness, and helped me to ground. Perhaps that was a possibility.

Within a week, I had contacted my long-time Andean mentor, Juan Nuñez del Prado. He knew about the loss of my brother, and I spoke with him honestly about my lack of an internal compass. I asked if we could arrange a trip. The friends who had encouraged the trip all had agreed to go, no matter what Juan and I planned, and before long there were twelve people committed to going. Juan asked me how I wanted to design the trip, and in the weeks that followed, with his input, I finalized the itinerary—Cusco and its surrounding ruins, Machu Picchu, Tambomachay, Raqchi, Sillustani, and Lake Titicaca to explore the Island of Taquile and Uros, the floating reed islands. As the trip came together, my spirits begin to lift.

During one of our final discussions about logistics, Juan told me he

---

*In 2004 I did write the article, called "A Journey through the Stones & Bones of the Andes: Sifting through Personal Terrain." It was printed in that magazine, the *Indigo Sun Magazine*, and later picked up by two other New Age papers, one in North Carolina and the other in Massachusetts.

had secured a good *ayahuasquero** and had arranged for our group to go into the Amazon jungle for the final six days of our two-and-a-half-week journey to experience the "medicine plant," ayahuasca, also called the vine of the soul or the death vine. I had not specifically asked to work with the sacred vine, so I thought Juan had either misinterpreted something in my itinerary request or had inserted something of his own. I didn't question him at that time, thinking maybe he was moving me beyond my comfort level and providing an opportunity for a new teaching. However, when we were finally together in Peru, I asked what had motivated him to include the vine as part of the trip. It wasn't until then that he realized I had never requested it as part of the itinerary. Ultimately, we agreed maybe it was the essence of ayahuasca herself who was directing us. And, who knows, maybe because of all the issues of death and dying that I was dealing with, working with the death vine was exactly what I needed.

---

*An ayahuasquero is a person who has been trained in the ritual use of the ayahuasca plant, its ceremonial songs, and how to guide its energies with seekers who wish to use the medicine for accessing alternative states of awareness.

17

Pico de Flores, the Hummingbird

Our journey with Juan was scheduled for October 2003, and Frank accompanied me, as he would when I returned with other groups to Peru for the next three consecutive years. Besides the work with the death vine in the Amazon, our program included two rituals I had never participated in before. The first was with the Niño Compadrito and the second was a more detailed extension of a ritual Juan had initiated me in during 1993, the purpose of which is to energetically "witness our own death."

The Niño Compadrito is the skeleton of a male child, rumored to be a mummy from one of the Incan royal families. It sits in a domestic shrine at the home of the Cusco family that has been its caretaker for five generations. Although in future visits I would see it dressed in different outfits, at this first visit it was dressed in an ornate green and gold garment, similar to how the Christ is sometimes dressed on Catholic altars. The Niño is not worshipped as the Christ nor is it thought to mirror the sacredness of the Christ, although those devoted to him say he grants miracles. First displayed in the 1950s, the Niño was put into hiding in 1976 after a local bishop declared the icon heretical, only to resurface for public visits in 1982.

There is a long history within the Catholic church of worshipping relics, such as the bones of saints and martyrs, and the Indian-Spanish-Catholic culture in Peru has a similar reverence for the bones of ancestors. I once heard a story in Cusco that the Inca used to parade twelve of their respected ancestors, as mummy bundles, around the main square during certain rituals and festivals. They were honored for cultural reasons and used to petition unseen forces for help or miracles.

When the Catholic priests started converting the populace, they misinterpreted this reverence as worship, declared it blasphemous, and ordered that it cease. They declared that only saints could be accorded such reverence. The Natives complied, carrying plaster statues of the recommended saints in their processions. During one of these processions, a statue fell off its pallet, cracking its plaster and revealing a mummy bundle within. The Indians didn't care what or who you called the energy; they simply knew their ancestors provided a link to the past and would bring light to the future.

The Niño Compadrito is said to reveal his wishes to people through their dreams or in visions. It had been reported that in response to those who have petitioned for his help, he has performed healings and granted personal requests such as a long-desired pregnancy or financial help. Although some disbelievers and conventional religionists believe only magicians and *brujas* (witches) visit the Niño, it was clear to me, when our group arrived, that people from every walk of life visited. At that time, people entered the small room one at a time to privately petition the Niño.

When it was our turn, we were instructed to each take a candle from the wooden bin that was set just outside the door and to sit for a few minutes to carefully consider how we wanted to phrase our petition or prayer. When we entered the sanctuary room where the Niño was "watching" behind a glass enclosure, we were to light our candle from one on the altar that was already lit, placing our candle on the altar as we offered our petition, and then quietly exit so the next person could go in.

I loved the fact that one prayer candle was lit from another, symbolically extending the other person's prayer and eventually having our own prayers continued by the people who would follow us and ignite their candle from our flame. This circle of prayer made me once again feel we are in some small but significant way all connected in this life. Although I didn't experience anything other than a minor energetic tug as I placed my candle in front of the Niño Compadrito, my fervent prayer was that I would find the strength within myself to be all I was capable of being in this lifetime. I knew I would need to find a level of internal peace by letting go of "my story" since moving to Texas and by fully resuming my shamanic practice, wherever that led me. Further, I fervently prayed that the tensions that seemed to continuously search out and find Frank and me would cease.

The visit to the Niño was one of several significant rituals to touch the three energetically diverse but linked worlds of the Andean mystical tradition. Work within these three worlds—*ukhu pacha, kay pacha,* and *hanaq pacha*—provided the substance of Juan's teachings. We started that work at Lake Wakarpay outside Cusco, which had been the location for one of the summer palaces for the Inca royalty and is associated on the mystical path with the lower world, the ukhu pacha. Here Juan related the story of Atahualpa, his half-brother, Huáscar, and their father, Huayna Capac, who had been one of the last free Inca before the Spanish conquest by Pizzaro.

As Juan told the story, the half-brothers were fighting over who would become the successor to their father, who had died of small pox while on a military campaign. Although Huayna Capac had not fathered any children with his sister-wife,* he had many children with his other wives. Huáscar, being the oldest son, brought his father's body to Cusco and declared himself the ruler. Meanwhile, Atahualpa

---

*Modern societies have placed restrictions on intermarriage among relatives, with marriage between brothers and sisters forbidden. However in some ancient dynasties, such as the Egyptian, Hawaiian, and Incan, marriage with siblings in royal families was the norm, although the male sovereigns were allowed to take more than one wife.

had claimed he was the true ruler. Although the half-brothers served as co-rulers for a time, a civil war finally broke out over the issue. On a journey to Cusco to confront his brother, Atahualpa was captured by Pizzaro. In an effort to save his own life, Atahualpa made a pact with Pizzaro that should Pizzaro's soldiers kill Huáscar, the Spanish would have safe passage throughout the Inca Empire. Pizzaro agreed and arranged for Huáscar's death, whose body it is said was thrown into Lake Wakarpay. Ultimately, Pizarro betrayed Atahualpa at Cajamarca, as he was making his way south to Cusco, and ordered his death by garroting.

According to mystical lore, both brothers descended into the lower world. Because the brothers' act of jealousy had left the people of the empire with no leadership, they had broken the rule of *ayni* (reciprocity and service for the communal good). For that transgression they are now living in the lower world and will remain there until they learn ayni and teach it to all those who occupy the lower world with them.

As already indicated, in the Andean cosmology of the kawsay pacha—the world of living energy—there are three levels or worlds: the ukhu pacha, kay pacha, and hanaq pacha. Each relates to a plane of existence and has specific energies.

The ukhu pacha is the underworld, which exists within both the earth and an individual's psyche. The least refined energies are found in the underworld, and there are those, such as the Niño Compadrito, who can traverse that plane to bring information to a quester. Others in the shamanic traditions who are trained to delve into the dense planes, such as the ukhu pacha, include medicine men and women, Andean paqos, soul retrievalists, and exorcists. The totem of the unconscious or lower plane is the snake.

The second plane, or middle world, is the kay pacha, which consists of everything in the material universe—including Pachamama and the Cosmic Mother, or creatrix energy—and encompasses our everyday reality. The energies of this plane can be both refined and dense because we humans are sometimes in ayni and sometimes we simply are not. The earth plane is a school where we make mistakes and gain knowledge by which we can correct our mistakes, thus experiencing growth and achieving more balance in our lives. The totem of this world or sphere of consciousness is the jaguar.

The third Andean world is called the hanaq pacha, which is the upper or superior world of the most refined energies, or sami. It is inhabited by those spiritual beings we may perceive, given our spiritual persuasion, as saints, angels, high Inca, avatars, or sacred beings. The totem for this level, equated with the superconsciousness, is the condor and, depending on the teaching, the hummingbird.

The three worlds are connected in an energetic exchange. Those in the lower world, like Huáscar and Atahualpa, need to learn ayni to rise again, and by learning it themselves and teaching ayni to all those who also inhabit the underworld, they can bring those souls with them out of the ukhu pacha at the end times. We on the kay pacha help encourage the evolution of the lower-world beings by cleansing our own dense energy, such as through the practice of mikhuy, and by sending them our refined energy. This is an act of ayni, or reciprocity.

Juan said, "Perfect ayni comes from the heart, but the longest road for humans is from their head to their heart. This is a journey of experiencing the Self." I understood this to mean that munay, heart energy, is the bridge between our human selves and divine selves. By using our heart energy, by directing the light of our inner, divine self to matter—our earthly, human selves—we can radically shift our perceptions to gain a multidimensional understanding of life.

Practicing ayni, therefore, teaches us the gratitude and humility to embrace life as sacred. Service to others, which is a primary teaching on the Andean path, unites those concerned with the future, because it influences both personal and collective spiritual growth. For service to be authentic, however, it must be altruistic, with no expectations attached. This is easier said than done. It is thought that when you do service for someone, or even speak well of someone, the energetic effect goes out into the world as vibrations of pure colors. Each color vibration attracts more of the same, increasing the intensity of that stream of energy and empowering both the giver and receiver. Part of the work is being aware of whether our thoughts and actions are nourishing or poisonous, for human consciousness can only evolve through individual effort.

The next day we worked at Tambomachay, another sacred site just outside of Cusco. It has three levels of Incan walls with channels—called fountains—through which water continuously runs. It is speculated that Tambomachay was a place of rest for Inca royalty and that the fountains were used for rejuvenation. Niches cut into the walls above the fountains represent the four winds and carry female energy. To the right of the fountains is a stone throne, which Juan called the "chair of life," that is carved out of a single boulder. A dirt road—which is seen in this ritual as an energetic *seque* or passage between this world and the next—runs parallel to a river along the front of the small complex. On the other side of the road and river is a massive flat stone that Juan called the "rock of life after life."

The ritual we would be performing here was to project ourselves forward in time to see our own death and what may happen beyond that death. This was not to induce fear of our death; rather it was meant to connect us more fully to our personal power while here on the earth plane. The ritual would assist us to awaken the potential of, and to connect us to, our Absolute Self. This would serve two purposes: by living from a balanced place of personal power, we would walk more consciously on the earth plane, remembering that acts of love and service are primary to elevating consciousness; and by connecting through our death to the realization that we have an immortal soul—the Absolute Self—we might better live this life as an expression of our highest selves, which would mirror sacredness back into our everyday world.

During the ritual of death, we were to use the water from the first, and highest, channel or fountain, which had a single flow of water, to anoint our third eye and our heart, symbolically creating a *japu,* or uni-fication, of two perfectly aligned energies. At the second level, the single fountain separated into two channels, where we were to intend the sep-aration of our physical body from our spirit body. In this case the spirit body represents the continuity of our soul's essence, and the physical body represents the template and personality we inhabit within each Earthwalk. We were to then go to the chair of life, where we would sit and cast our filaments across the seque to the river, symbolically cross-ing into death. We were to visualize ourselves at the river, where we would disrobe and wash our clothes, leaving them on the bank of the river as we crossed to the rock of life after life. We were to note what occurred during this meditation, especially the details of how we died and what manifested at the rock of life after life.

In the Andean tradition, when someone dies, the family washes that person's clothes at a river, symbolically washing the deceased's spirit of any remaining hucha. In that way, the person enters death with the most sami possible. Another Andean belief is that while in the pro-cess of dying, if you feel lost as you cross, a dog will appear who will lead you across the river between life and death, because the dog always knows the way.

When it was my turn, as instructed, at the first fountain I anointed my third eye and heart, and at the second, I intended the separation of my body and spirit. I then made my way to the stone chair of life. Once seated, I centered myself and allowed my mind to detach from my internal chatter. I intuited this ritual had yet another purpose for me, besides seeing my death. Although no ritual or ceremony alone would change me, if I was willing to name and work with my imperfections, and was determined to make changes within myself, then I could "die to all I thought I was" and all I had brought with me on this journey to Peru. To fully take personal responsibility for my life was a continua-tion of the prayer I had offered in front of the Niño Compadrito.

Energetically in my mind, I went to the river, washed my clothes, and mikhuyed my *poq'po*—my light body—of the dense energies I had been holding these past couple of years. I wondered if anything different would happen now than it had from the first time I had done this ritual less formally in 1993, when I had only briefly been shown how I might die. A lot had happened since then, and this ritual included many more elements and steps than that first one had, such as crossing the river, symbolically washing, and going to the rock of life after life.

As I visualized my way across the river towards the rock of life after life, a scene flashed in my mind of how and where and when I would die. This vision was more specific than the glimpse I had gotten ten years ago: I could see what I was doing, what I was wearing, I knew how old I was, and I could see death approach. My death felt real, but it was not frightening. In fact, I felt a great peace. In my visualization . . .

I approached the rock of life after life, where there appeared an etheric young lady clothed in a white gossamer dress and bathed in light; she was dancing hypnotically and beckoning to me. An enormous hummingbird appeared from my left and lifted me—as I shape-shifted, taking the form of a huge white lily—and carried me toward her. As I approached her outstretched arms, something energetically shifted . . .

And I was aware of myself once again physically sitting on the chair of life, with the next person waiting his turn.

Once the ceremony had been completed by everyone, Juan and I walked together back down the road to the bus and he asked me if I wanted to share my experience. He said he had been watching my face while I was sitting on the chair of life, and at one point I had been suffused with tranquility, something he hadn't seen in me since I had arrived. He knew I had touched something in those moments.

I shared what had happened. He suggested the lady, whom he called a *nust'a*, was both energy unto herself and a reflection of my divine female energy, and as we are all multidimensional, some aspect of her being would be there to greet me when it was my time to cross over. He knew from discussions we'd shared over the years that I had done a lot of personal energy work and rituals with the feminine energies, so the image of the lily he felt really fit, because lilies are one of the flowers that represent the Great Mother. The *pico de flores* (picker of flowers), the hummingbird was associated with access to the hanaq pacha, the upper world, and was connected to the citadel of Machu Picchu.

We discussed the energetic connection I had always felt with the mountain Putu Cusi, the female Apu that stands before the citadel and that legend says is an access point for the refined frequencies of the "higher city of light," whose vortex is within Machu Picchu. Juan told me, "Apus won't generally appear to you, but their spirit can. I see the hummingbird as that spirit, and it is possible the spirit of Machu Picchu and Putu Cusi will guide you when you cross." That sparked something I had recently been told—that the hummingbird is symbolically associated with rebirth because they appear to become lifeless on very cold nights and revive again the following morning with the warmth of the sun. My vision in the life after life exercise suggested again that at death there is the potential for a rebirth into the "light of a new day." These teachings were making possible what I had sought when I undertook this trip, the desire for personal revival.

I had learned over the years while working with Juan that the service an Apu offers a paqo is determined by the command of personal energy a paqo has within their environment. As such, realizing the energetic connection with the hummingbird, or the spirit of the Apu as a guide during my death, was akin to what Oh Shinnah had suggested about utilizing your death chant as you cross back into the Light. It isn't necessarily the song, the Apu, or the hummingbird that will guide you, although when the curtain is raised at death that may well be. Rather, I think it is the intentional accumulation of personal energy—through knowing your death chant, knowing your connection to the Apus, knowing the cosmos resides in the Self at all levels—that will empower how you consciously move through death. Juan and I spoke briefly about intention, perception, experience, and the potential of the "Inca seed" within each of our hearts as we continued to walk.

In 1992, Juan had begun training me in the work of the Inca seed and I knew that according to the Andean mystical tradition developing our potential and growing our Inca seed are two of the reasons we are on this Earth. I had purposefully undertaken this current journey because, still hurting from the discouragements and losses of the last two years, I felt my Inca seed had stopped growing. And if my Inca seed had stopped growing, then so had my command of the energy within my daily environment. Feeling re-empowered could happen only if I continued to work the energies, including how I allowed them to affect me. Years prior when I first started working with Juan he told me the sacred path takes effort and will challenge you. Although the karpays have the capacity to open your energy body, personal development and your ability to navigate the kawsay pacha daily are what expand and fertilize your Inca seed.

Juan teaches two karpays, or initiations, both passed down to him by his teachers. He had taught them to me, and eventually I had brought others to Peru to participate in them. The right-side teachings, called the Hatun Karpay Paña, which Juan has offered since 1992, belong to the lineage of don Benito Qoriwaman and provide participants the opportunity to be prepared through privilege, not through blood, for the crowning ritual of the Inca emperor.

Within the Inca Empire there were twelve royal lines, called *panacas,* and a son from each of those families was chosen to represent their panaca's lineage. This coronation ceremony was done at Raqchi, which was the first temple, according to Juan, "to be dedicated to the metaphysical God." Each of the twelve young men was escorted by a *mamacuna*, or a matron of the sun, through the six upper temples and the six lower temples before being brought to the central court, which was laid out in the shape of a *tawantin*,* a four-sided stepped cross that represented the four quarters of the Inca Empire. In that central plaza, the candidates formed two lines, six to the right of the plaza and six to the left. Each would then get his turn to speak to the people, presenting himself as an aspirant to the Inca throne.

However, it wasn't what they said that determined who was crowned. The chosen one was revealed to the people and chosen in an act of unity when they saw him literally glow. This aura of light indicated the candidate had achieved the fifth level of consciousness, for only one who was powerful and pure enough to contain their energy, and have it be perceived as a visible manifestation to others, was worthy of leading the people. The rites of the Hatun Karpay Paña mirror this coronation process, with the ultimate aim of nurturing your Inca seed so you can cultivate the fifth level of consciousness. Clearly the karpay does not give you the fifth level of consciousness, but the work offers you the capacity to reach your potential.

The rituals of this karpay take place at various sacred sites throughout Peru. At Machu Picchu, initiates align their consciousness with the upper world, which is represented by the hummingbird. Here we also performed two specific rituals to connect the Divine Masculine and Divine Feminine aspects of the self, whose potential for integration is held within the Inca seed. The flowering of our Inca seed allows us to mediate the living energies through the power of our personal energetic field. The male rites are performed at the top of Huayna Picchu, the larger mountain of the citadel, and their purpose is to align with the spirit of the Apus, or mountain protectors.

---

*Tawantinsuyu was the word used to describe the Inca Empire. In Quechua, the native language of the Q'ero, *tawantin* is a group of four things and *suyu* means "province." The Inca Empire was divided into four regions, whose corners met at the empire's capital, Cusco.

Down a steep trail just beyond one side of the citadel is the Cave of the Moon; it is here where the female rites are performed to incorporate the seven powers of the underworld.

The other major karpay, the Hatun Karpay Lloq'e, concerns the left-side teachings, from the lineages of two of Juan's other teachers, don Melchor Desa, of the Cusco region, and Tata Lorenza, keeper of the knowledge of the Lake Titicaca basin. These rites assist us to awaken the feminine principles of compassion and flexibility. The ritual sites are different in this initiation and take us to Cusco, which was considered the "navel" of the Inca Empire and represents the power of the puma. The puma links to the kay pacha, this manifest world, and symbolically spreads its length along the Cusco valley, encompassing seven eyes, called *nawis,* which were power centers in the city of Cusco. We worked at these seven power centers, pulling sami, refined energy, down into the ukhu pacha, the lower world, which in this karpay is symbolically related to the anaconda of the Lake Titicaca region. A major aspect of this karpay is to blend the energies of the three worlds to awaken the Willka power, which is related to the black light or the Black Ñust'a—an energy necessary to master the craft of working at the fifth level of consciousness.

In Peru, Machu Picchu is the primary holder of male energy and Lake Titicaca of female energy, although we work at integrating both energies at just about every site included in the karpays. For example, one ritual is to awaken the Willka Ñust'a, or sacred princess of the Vilconota River, which runs through the town of Aguas Calientes at the base of Machu Picchu. Juan explained that through this ritual we could touch the roots of the Inca lineage. To begin the rite, we meditated on the banks of the Vilconota on the spirit of the Willka Ñust'a, which is also called the Black Ñust'a because of the black energy related to the fifth level of consciousness.

Here we used our intention to integrate our filaments with the Black Ñust'a, the surrounding Apus, and a stone we had selected from the river to serve as an *apacheta,* a doorway or gate, to the underworld. We were instructed to put the stone to our qosqo—our belly area—and release our hucha—our heavy, dense energy—into it. We then were to throw the stone into the river, offering our hucha as a gift to the Black Ñust'a. Because of her powers, she would mikhuy the hucha, digesting it like food and returning sami to us in exchange for our gift.

During the second part of the rite we were to meditate directly on the Black Ñust'a, connecting our filaments with her fundamental nature. Once we had established that connection we were to choose another stone from the river bank, which we would add to our mesas, representing her connective energy back to us. As I have said, khuyas are one of the major healing tools of a paqo's bundle and are used to cleanse hucha from the energy body. Because the color black is associated with the lloq'e—the left side of both the Andean path and the mesa—this stone would add to the healing capacity of our mesa. Finally, once we had selected that second stone, we were to make our way one by one to where Juan was waiting for us to bestow a blessing from the lineage of don Benito.

We each went off to do the rite, and I walked along the river until I found the stone I wanted to use as a gateway to the lower world into which I would release my dense, pent-up feelings and energy. As I settled by the river, I took my time reviewing the frustrations, disappointments, and losses I had been accumulating over the preceding two years. I also recapitulated other aspects of my personal story, not wanting to drag that tale like a burden bundle along behind me any longer. I wanted to leave it all here. I held the stone to my belly and went deep within, practicing the art of mikhuy to release what I intentionally wanted to let go of. When I felt complete, I cast the stone into the Vilconota. Then I sat in a meditative state as Juan had instructed, waiting to see if the Black Ñust'a would have any message for me. I could feel my energy body being pulled by the river's current and . . .

I see a huge, black female snake arise from the depths of the raging river. She unhinges her jaws wide and swallows me whole. As she plunges back to the river's bottom, I tumble within her belly, spinning within threads of silver and gold until I am held in the center of a tiny galaxy of light.

I see a brilliant cobalt-blue star with a purple corona. It is resting alone on a black background that looks exactly like the scales of the snake's skin. Suddenly, with a great force, she spits me out and I am caught by a large dark-skinned woman who dances me back up to the bank of the river.

As I emerge from the meditation, I find I somehow already have a rock—egg-sized and black—in my hand. I'm a little confused as I do not remember picking it up, but as Juan had instructed once we had the second stone, I went over to him so he could bestow the blessing. As I did I was pushed backwards, losing my balance, and saw in my mind's eye a short, wild-eyed man with unruly, coarse black hair. He pushed his thumb forcefully into my third eye. Juan grabbed my arm to steady me, and then asked me what had just happened. After I briefly told him about the man who had energetically pushed me, I related what had happened during my meditation.

He explained the black serpent represents the first level of consciousness and the dark-skinned woman represents the second level. He seemed pleased as he told me, "You are making progress in the work." He continued with his interpretation of my meditation, saying the cobalt star was "my star," my connection to the cosmos; and my emerging from the meditation with a stone already in my hand meant the Willka, or Black Ñust'a, was offering me a new connection to help continue to grow my Inca seed. He chuckled at my description of the wild-haired man and said it was a perfect description of don Benito, whom I had never seen a picture of. Continuing to smile he said, "It appears don Benito gave you a personal karpay."

As the karpay rites came to a close, we prepared for the final stage of our journey. The following day we would return by train to Cusco to board a flight back to Lima and continue our travels that would take us both physically and metaphysically into the Amazon jungle, where we would meet the sacred vine. We were all full from the energetic work, both the *yachay*—the intellectual and spiritual knowledge grounded in experiences—and *llank'ay*—the physical labor and effort of participating in our many ritual experiences. And now we were about to undertake what could be the most challenging leg of the trip from both of these perspectives.

18

You Only Bargain
with Yourself

We arrived in late afternoon at the Lima airport to take our flight to Iquitos, which would be our entry point to go down the Amazon and into the jungle. As we collected our luggage we ran into a small group of European travelers working with a teacher that Juan knew. They had all just returned from the jungle where they had spent time working with Mother Ayahuasca.* They looked completely exhausted. I suddenly had trepidation about this work for myself personally, as I had not worked with this potently visionary plant mixture before. It is called the death vine for a reason, and I although I certainly had experienced my share of death, this healing plant is said to help you confront your soul. Although I wanted that, I also knew I might not like what I was shown. Because the visionary experiences facilitated by ayahuasca can be extremely intense, breaking down ego structures and revealing the shadow self, I wasn't all that sure what hidden aspects of myself it would reveal. In addition, although almost everyone in the group had agreed to journey with the death vine, as the group's organizer, I felt

---

*While the vine itself is called ayahuasca, the visionary brew is a mixture of the ayahuasca plant and other plants that contain DMT.

the weight of responsibility for their well-being, wondering if they too would be able to handle it.

When we landed in Iquitos, we were met by Pio, the psychologist and ayahuasquero who would be leading the ceremonies. We got into tiny two- and three-seater motorized vehicles that would take us to our bus. They were decorated with pictures of saints, little plastic statues of the Madonna, banners, and multicolored ribbons, looking similar to rickshaws hooked to old motorbikes. We hung tightly to the side bars as our drivers recklessly zoomed past each other down the road paying little heed to the congestion of people or cars.

Instead of taking us directly to the boats that would take us down the Amazon River and to the jungle village where we would stay for the next six days, Pio had the bus driver take us on a tour of Iquitos, which we thought was a complete waste of our time. In fact, it was not. It turned out Pio was using this time to assess our energy fields. He perceived we were both tired and anxious, and he was trying to lighten our moods and shift the group energy.

At one point, we were taken to a small city zoo, but because we were weary and short-tempered, we refused to get off the bus. We weren't trying to be rude, but we just did not know at the time why Pio had insisted on taking us on this sightseeing tour. We were driven from the zoo to an ice cream parlor, where Juan basically ordered us all off the bus. Everyone got off but me—I had a massive headache and was not about to move. Juan had a different idea. When I told him why I didn't want an ice cream, he said, "You have a headache because you have taken on the hucha of the group's anxiety. You've known for years how to mikhuy. Do it, and go get an ice cream." Feeling berated, I harrumphed my way to the door. It became obvious once I had joined the group that Pio and Juan had known exactly what they were doing, for the group's energy had shifted. We all were acting like little kids, licking our cones and tasting each other's flavors.

Finally, Pio felt we were ready to go. Once at the shore of the Amazon River, we boarded a thatched-roofed dugout canoe and set off.

Our first stop was a sanctuary for abandoned or recovering animals—turtles, monkeys, anteaters, baby jaguars, boa constrictors, parrots, and coati. Unlike the other concrete zoo, here was a "zoo" we all could relate to and we spent over an hour holding, petting, and communing with the animals. Where Pio couldn't get us off the bus at the first zoo, he had to insist we leave this one, shooing us back into the canoe. When we finally got to the sandy inlet that was the jumping off point into the jungle, we unloaded and sorted our gear, and walked a path through the jungle growth to a small village of simple huts. A large thatched-roofed building on the edge of the village, facing the dense jungle, was set aside for us.

Once we had settled into the various small rustic rooms, we were informed we had been invited to a communal building where the villagers would dance and sing, for in their tradition doing so was an exchange of energies that welcomed us to their community. Another reason for this tradition, I would later learn, was so the villagers could mingle their energies with ours, not only to ensure that we were bringing good energy into their village, but also so that later during the ayahuasca ceremonies they could spiritually watch over us.

When I first saw the dancers, I felt as if I were seeing a picture from a *National Geographic* magazine. Both men and women were bare breasted, dressed in traditional grass skirts, and adorned with macaw feathers and shell necklaces. The chief of the village opened the gathering with the beating of a huge bamboo-like drum. Then his wife and the women began the dances. The men, women, and children who had gathered to welcome us were open and lighthearted as they performed a variety of ritual dances. During one of the dances, they gathered around Juan. Pio explained to us that this was a gesture of honor and a communal blessing. They then came over and took Pio out to the center of their circle to do the same to him. Finally, in a spirit of friendship they invited all of us to join in their dance. Everyone laughed as we fumbled at the steps they so effortlessly danced, but it was all good-natured.

The next day, however, we saw them in their everyday or work attire: jeans and T-shirts or skirts. Their traditional dress during the welcoming ceremony had not been for show; it was a way of linking to and honoring their spiritual and cultural ancestors, and of introducing us to their heritage.

Upon our arrival in the village, we had been instructed we would be following the ayahuasca diet, which is a cleansing preparation for the ceremonies. It involved eating no salt, sugar, spices, dairy, meat, or fermented foods; and abstaining from sex. Pio informed us we would be following the diet and eating very lightly for the next few days. He also told us that when we did the ceremonies, they would be at night, after full dark, for better communication with the ancestors and spirits of the jungle.

On the day of the first ceremony, in early afternoon, as preparation we drank a concoction called *lobos,* which is a purgative. We drank it until we vomited, energetically releasing the hurts that were held in our hearts and the hucha held in our energetic bodies. Not purging might mean that tonight, when we would actually drink the brew made from the vine of the soul, we would not be open to our fullest extent. My intent during this purge was to release the pain at the loss of loved ones, the hurt in my heart from the growing disrespect I felt coming from my husband, and the lack of personal direction I felt in my work. It turned out that for me, the purging was the grossest part of the six days. And after listening to the others vomit, I knew it had been no picnic for them either. I sure hoped Mother Ayahuasca showed herself to us so this would all be worth it.

Once we had purged, we cleansed our bodies with a water-flower-herb infusion that held the scent of a light perfume and then dressed in fresh clothes. The flower infusion was to help us cleanse and close our energy field from taking in any further negative influences such as those we had just expelled through vomiting. Both the aromatic wash and dressing in clean clothes prepared us externally, showing our respect for the vine and its teachings. Pio explained he would guide us through three ayahuasca ceremonies, one every other night. The dose would increase, as would the strength of the brew, over each ceremony. On the morning after each journey with the vine, he and Juan would sit with us individually to help clarify our visions and explain anything we might not understand.

As I went into the first ayahuasca ceremony, Pio sprayed each of us with Florida Water and passed tobacco smoke around our heads. I had expectations of receiving insight and answers to the three concerns I had worked at purging. However, as I was about to learn, there is no point having expectations because Mother Ayahuasca decides what will be revealed to you, as she is the master arbiter of what is necessary and timely. Although the reports in the ayahuasca literature are of intense visions and drastic emotional swings, my first encounter with the vine was more perceptual than emotional. My sensory perceptions were indeed heightened: colors and sounds were intensified, geometric patterns and esoteric symbols came and went.

What struck me most about that first journey was my connection with the jungle: it seemed to breathe as it glowed in the most beautiful golden-green haze. The sounds of nature were amplified and each was utterly distinct—that was a bug crawling, that was a leaf unfurling, that was a root growing. I could even hear what I sensed were the whispers of the villagers. When I detected the strong smell of sweat, I thought it was my own, and then realized it was the pungent odor of the jungle herself. Above, the thatched roof gave way to the night sky, where I saw the Milky Way stretched out beyond the canopy of trees, stars shining brightly.

The others sitting on mats around me glowed in the night, a diffused aura around each. As Pio sang the *icaros*—the sacred songs— he alternated between sitting and standing. At times his body slowly spun in circles and he extended his arms, seemingly beckoning something or someone with his hands. As he did, the energy rose and fell accordingly. I had the sense his movements were in sync with the rise and fall of our energies, guiding us through the experience. I felt calm and "at-one-ment" with everything around me. The journey didn't seem to last long, although I knew it had been hours. Pio brought the ceremony to a close at dawn with a final song, and then told us it was time for us to sleep.

I remember only a snippet of a dream I had that night. In it, I am pulled deep into the jungle, following a blue star that leads down a path through the undergrowth. Normally, I wake up frequently during the night, but after that first ceremony I slept deeply for the first time in years. The next morning, when I consulted with Juan and Pio, neither had much to say about my experience. Pio suggested simply, "You have a light you must follow, and *Sachamama*—the Spirit Mother of the jungle—and the sacred vine will guide you."

During the second ceremony, the dose was larger and the brew was stronger, so it was harder to swallow and tasted even more revolting. As I sat on my mat waiting for the ayahuasca to take effect, my heart suddenly felt tight and my chest full of pressure. I was scared, and in an effort to calm myself, I breathed into my heart. A vision erupted.

A window opens in front of me and I hear a bell ringing. A huge black snake thrusts itself out of my heart. It slithers up to the top of a tree at the perimeter of the jungle. Both the snake and the tree start to glow. I watch as their separate energies respond to one another. They exude filaments of light that create intricate geometric patterns through which they share some kind of primal communication. As the snake slowly makes its way back down a large, thick branch, enormous pink dogwood flowers blossom along its trail as it wends its way back down the tree. My attention is pulled from the snake by an eruption of intense colors and dewdrop-laden spider webs that connect everything in the environment around me. A stream of male faces appears, connected in some kind of sequential order going back through time: a more youthful Juan, the wild-eyed don Benito, and a host of unrecognizable men.

The next day, during the review of my experience, Pio said the bell was a warning for me to pay attention. The pink dogwood flowers symbolized the durability of the healing energy of the heart and the black anaconda is considered by the Natives of the area as "the most healing snake of all." As Pio explained, "The people use its fat to heal bones or wounds, and one knows the healing is complete when the oil flows out the opposite side of the body from where the wound was." He felt the snake coming out of my heart represented the healing of losses and relationship wounds, and he said that the more I worked with the energy of the black anaconda, as a sort of totem reptile, the more ability I would have in my healing practice. "The snake has healed your heart," he said, "but you have to know that, and not slip back into your melancholy. Now you can go back out into the world more balanced because with one hand you have healed yourself by opening to Mother Ayahuasca and by extending your other hand you can share the work for healing with others."

Both he and Juan agreed the parade of faces was Juan's mystical lineage, moving back from Juan to his teachers and to their teachers, extending back to the Inca. This vision indicated, in their opinion, that the Incan mystical tradition was my path as well. They encouraged me to teach this work more, saying that doing so would help me gain greater self-respect and release any disrespect I had felt directed toward me over these past couple of years.

At this point, having known about some of the dynamics in my marriage, Juan also offered the unsolicited opinion that getting back into my work would enhance the opportunity for a more balanced partnership between Frank and me. "You and Frank carry strong forces between you," he said. "In part that's what attracted you to each other. Frank's instincts are strong and your intuition is strong, but you need to blend them in a noncompetitive dance using respect and munay inside your private circle, and then bring your combined power to the outside in dealings with others, life, and work."

He went on to say we had made an agreement to come together to learn these things from each other in this lifetime. In Juan's words, I was in this relationship with Frank so he could help me to listen better to needs different from my own, and Frank was with me to learn how to soften his heart with love. "You need to learn not to hold the hucha directed at you in your heart, but to bring it down to your qosqo for release and to stabilize your power," he counseled, "and Frank needs to learn to bring his energy up from his qosqo to his heart and risk feeling the true power of love."

Pio interjected that I needed to call on the power of my feminine again, because it was through the feminine I could nurture myself and others. As the balanced feminine, I could learn to walk in harmony with my inner male and my "outer man," meaning my husband. I would not have to walk behind him or in front of him, or have to direct him or be subservient to him, but could walk next to him. If I achieved this harmony, I would experience personal growth and regain my self-respect, although I had to have no expectations of how such behavior on my part would or should be received by my husband or anyone else. Both Juan and Pio agreed I should ask Mother Ayahuasca and the feminine forces of the jungle to reenergize and rebalance my spirit during the final ceremony.

By that final ceremony we were all emotionally and physically spent. Maybe this was a good thing, as we had no more resistance to the teachings of the vine of the soul. I felt I had dropped all my resistances: I wanted to really hear from my soul, and as if in response, this final ceremony was extremely intense for me. I no sooner felt the brew working in me when . . .

The thatched roof above me completely disappears. A huge spider comes toward my face, and not knowing if it is real or of spirit, I attempt to block it out by forcing my attention to the edge of the jungle, where I can see thousands of filaments of light weaving themselves into intricate patterns. Suddenly, I am in the jungle. It is buzzing with a cacophony of sound and ablaze with tiny twinkling lights. As I walk through the dense jungle growth, I am astonished to realize I am a jaguar. I see through the eyes of the jaguar, smell through the nostrils of the jaguar, taste the jungle air on the tongue of the jaguar, and feel the jungle through the pads of the jaguar's feet and along the length of the jaguar's tail. Suddenly, in front of me is the Niño, and grinning slyly he tells me he has a bargain he wants to make.

At that moment, I was pulled out of the experience. The woman sitting next to me, Tina, who is a good friend and had once been a client of mine, was retching in dry heaves and obviously frightened. As Pio leaned in close, whispering in her ear, Juan brought her a bucket in case she got sick. Most of the others were unaffected, deep in their own experiences, and I could again see auras of light around them. Pio firmly placed Tina's hand in mine and told me not to let go and to stay present for her. There was no going back to my experience, as I totally attuned to her needs, but the incredible perceptual clarity the vine imparts remained. As Tina implored me not to leave her side, I could not only feel the blood, in rivulets, flowing through her hand, I could see dense blobs of energy running out of her. Her fear and resistance were palpable, as she anxiously narrated her inner experience. Pio had resumed singing the sacred songs, only now much louder and with more intensity. I knew he was seeing the dark blobs, too. By the time dawn broke, Tina was exhausted and had calmed down.

Ironically, even though I thought I had not had much time for my own experience during this ceremony, Pio and Juan had a lot to say during our review. Pio said emphatically, "Sandy, wake up!" Then he explained it was time to "become" my totem, and to use the work of the sacred plant to do what I had come here to do, heal my own wounds, move past my old story, and continue to help people through their healing processes. He told me the jaguar can sit calmly and be watchful, and so can taste, see, and smell everything in its territory before it acts.

I had to do the same in my own inner landscape; only in this way could I act from a place of power and not react in a way that gave away my power.

He explained, "There is a difference between power and force. Power, in its highest form, has the ability to bring transformation and comes from a place of center; whereas force is a reaction to resistance, our own or others, and is not centered." He felt a lot of people misinterpret what it means to attain personal power, confusing it with personal force, which is more akin to control or coercion. Force, he counseled, is essentially born out of fear or from choosing not to be accountable for our actions, and as such it is a symptom of our inner resistance to grow. When we are mindful of this dynamic, we can act from awareness rather than react from our projections.

Pio said the vine had pulled me out of my own visions in order to be a grounding rod for my friend's healing process. Although that process ultimately was her own, she needed my presence in order to feel safe. He said, "She surrendered in trust to you because she knew you were there for her and so it was safe to have her inner experience. You have been given an important opportunity to practice shifting out of your personal energy to be fully present for another person."

Juan interjected at this point that the Niño had been teaching me a lesson about personal power, too. In my ayahuasca journey, the Niño was testing me. If I had bargained with him, it would have shown the Niño I had not been sincere about my prayer back in Cusco at the beginning of the journey, to be all I was capable of, which ultimately, Juan said, is to stand in my power. If I had moved into negotiations with the Niño it would have been an act of giving my power away. He felt I had done enough of that in my life already. He advised me that if the Niño ever appeared again in my dreams or visions, I should interact with him as an equal. No matter what was discussed, any agreements or decisions had to be fully mine. "This," he said, "is how one stands in their power—by knowing who they are."

Needless to say, this journey had given me a variety of insights to help me continue learning how not to be undermined by the happenstances of life. The Nino had offered a connection to the ukhu pacha within me, so I could see how I bargained with myself, often to the detriment of claiming my personal power. Previously, my experience with the rock of life after life had shown me how universally we each need to attend to life, but that our existence includes far more than these life experiences. By connecting to other more refined realms, such as the Andean hanaq pacha, I could confront the illusions separating me from the fullness of myself. Now, my visionary journeys with Mother Ayahuasca had shown me how to move forward in life—in the kay pacha—with greater resilience and compassion for myself. It was up to me to see how I would take all of this back home and integrate it into daily living. Doing so would be a long, often painful walk down a path I didn't always know how to navigate, but I guess that was the way I chose to learn my lessons, awaken to my personal myth, and evolve.

19

We're All
Unique Snowflakes

In a meeting I had with Maya shortly before she passed, she looked at my palms and said, "You will have a very strange life." She told me she could see many "fishes" in my hands that to her indicated my work was with a "different type of energy healing." She told me she saw me writing a book about this work, which at the time made me laugh as I really could not visualize that happening. She said, "Whatever you visualize can come, but you need to visualize it as coming in the now, not in the future." She counseled me, as she had in past sessions, that I should dream it into being. "As you are waking up from your dreamtime, your conscious mind is coming up while your unconscious mind is going back down, and where they cross, in that moment, you can send a message to Spirit about what you wish to accomplish."

I lost this dear mentor in 1998, Grandmother Kitty shortly thereafter, and significant others during the period 2004 to 2008: John Mack in September 2004, don Mariano in 2005, and Gram Twylah in August 2007.* Each was a sad good-bye. After Gram "dropped her

---

*While writing revisions to this manuscript for my new publisher, Inner Traditions, I learned Tlakaelel had passed on July 26, 2012.

robes" I remembered something that she had once told me early on in our time together: "There will come a time when you must take the work I am teaching you and stand on my shoulders, teaching others so someday they will stand on your shoulders. That is how we all ascend together up the ladder."

In this book I have only given the flavor of pieces of my journey into the mystical and shamanic realms. I have worked with the teachings of my Native mentors for over thirty years and in the Andean tradition for more than twenty, and I continue to have sporadic contact experiences. My dreams continue to offer me moments of clarity and awareness, and reflect back to me where tension or confusion is impacting my waking world. Bringing all of these paths together in one book has not been easy, but neither was the journey at times. Learning to blend my spiritual work with the mundane requirements of my daily routines has at times been an effort while also stretching my personal view of what it means to be human.

When I was driving aimlessly in the night, numb from the loss of Callie, I had no clue my path back to life would be so strange. The multidimensional shamanic realms take us both inward and outward, and that is their gift. The lens of any shamanic experience is through the self, and that lens is often clouded. That's why teachers, mentors, spiritual guides, and even our children are so important, as they can mirror the best of who we are, although ultimately we have to be accountable for the teachings and personal changes they elicit if we are to stand in the power of who we have come here to be.

I have been blessed to have had many extraordinary mentors, some have touched me profoundly, albeit momentarily and we have never crossed paths again. Others have lingered longer and been powerful examples of generosity and dignity as they shared their cultural teachings. I trust you can appreciate their wisdom through some of what I have shared in this book, as I am sure each one of you, once you look around, will recognize those who have helped guide you. As Maya suggested, "Everyone is a teacher for someone and the teachings can come in the simplest of ways if we listen with our hearts." There are other paths I have walked that are not included in these pages because of space constraints, yet they too helped me steer the course toward a more integrated sense of selfhood. The lifelong journey of restoring the Self requires maneuvering between the known and the unknown, the expected and the unexpected.

In some regard, the signposts on my personal path have been deaths: of people I've loved, relationships, and beliefs. All of these breaks in the fabric of life have forced me to walk between the darkness and the daylight, through the terrain of the middle distances. As I bring this book to publication, the most recent death has been my twelve-year relationship with Frank, which has been painfully challenging for me to let go of. The teachings are helping me as I work to heal this hurt as well. The teachings can be crystallized to one core message—something we all know in our hearts but tend not to live so well—and it is best stated by Rumi: "Your task is not to seek for love, but merely to seek and find all the barriers within yourself that you have built against it."

The way toward opening ourselves to love is through forgiveness, although the path of forgiveness can be strewn with rocks. All of our feelings, as we learn to forgive ourselves and others, become stepping-stones toward finding inner peace, because the definition of who we are and what we experience comes from what we choose to release or what we choose to hold on to. As Maya once said, with every person we forgive, including ourselves, we heal another cell in our body. Being able to forgive those who we feel have hurt, disrespected, or betrayed us—or even died to us—starts with the realization that something we desired has not happened for us, but has instead provided the mirror for a lesson—a very human lesson. Many times throughout the years, I railed, cried, and placed blame, but the truth is that the only person I had to open my heart in forgiveness to was myself. Ultimately what I had learned to forgive was how I had chosen to experience my life's lessons, and realized that this Earthwalk is merely one of many on the path to evolve the Self. As Maya had reminded me many times, "Everything is perfect just the way it unfolds."

When we lose our personal connection to our truth we are at the mercy of learning from pain, a process Gram Twylah called "learning from opposites." She taught that "if you avoid your inner truth, it affects your inner love and your inner peace, and the pain will last longer." The charge we carry energetically when we don't release our pain, our sins, each other, or even our fear of death holds us from the experiences our soul incarnated to master. As human beings we often project our separation from Self onto someone or something else. Projection has its basis in self-justifications, distortions, and even acts of injustice and cruelty—which are the reactions of the ego—and, at its worst, supports unconscious living. Although we need a healthy ego to negotiate our everyday reality, the wounded ego can confine us within a false, fixed reality.

As Oh Shinnah has suggested, our ability to "confront fixed realities" demands a practice, not necessarily a shamanic one, but some kind of discipline that allows us to develop the sensitivities to trust our inner knowing and to be responsible, accountable adults; and to surrender to the challenges that may guide us towards personal change, and ultimately more fulfillment. Gram Twy's words still ring in my ears, "If you are not living your truth, open and humble to learn, you can't be in service to others, because you have not been in service to yourself. As human beings we need to learn to face our challenges in increments; this is not always convenient or comfortable, but learning is better than not trying at all."

The work continues as I keep learning new lessons and relearning old ones. I returned to Peru in May 2011, leading a group of thirteen wonderful women, ages eighteen to seventy-four, many of whom shared a bond—as sisters, cousins, mothers and daughters, or best friends. We went as an *ayllu,* a spiritual family united in purpose, to do the work of the Self. I welcomed the smell of the land, the reunions with old friends, and the joy of once again being in a country I have always felt a deep heart connection with.

In part this trip was a birthday gift to myself as I moved into another new year on my personal cycle around the wisdom wheel. In addition, it took place as the one-year anniversary of the divorce was approaching, so I saw it as an opportunity to once again release "my story" and start anew with a fresh spirit. While there, I had a coca leaf reading with Nicholas, the son of one of my teachers who is now crossed. I was seeking clarity on three questions. The first was about where I should move, as during the divorce I had relocated from Texas to Montana, which I knew would be only a temporary, soft place to land. The second was how I could continue to write this book from a place of humility and honesty when I felt the words wouldn't form and the story was blocked. And the third was how I could rise above the lingering hurt from the dishonesty and deep rejection I felt through the divorce.

Nicholas threw the coca leaves onto his mesa cloth, which was spread out on the table top, and asked me to select one from the pile. I pointed to the tip of one that was deeply buried. Nicholas pulled out a large, unblemished leaf and tapped his index finger next to it for several seconds. Through translation, he began the reading, saying the leaf showed that I had a lot of strengths to draw on and my ability to work with people was among those strengths. The size of the leaf indicated that I had learned how to accumulate personal power through facing significant personal challenges. Learning my own lessons would help me to empathize with others as they faced their own challenges. Empathy was what would keep me in my heart. As far as moving, he said I should not to look for a location, but for a feeling. I would be giving a workshop or visiting someone and intuitively know I had found my place.

He then pointed out a series of leaves stretched in a line across the mesa cloth. "The reason you are blocked in the writing of your book," he said, "is you have not included certain accountings because you believe others will laugh at you or ridicule you. The book itself has stopped you, until you are willing to include those parts of your story. These experiences, though many of them will sound outrageous to some, were the way of your life, so write about them—and those who are meant to hear will read and understand." As I took in his messages, I thought of Gram Twy's comment that moths would be called to my flame when I was finally willing to stand in my own light; ironically and humbly, I had come to realize that I was the largest moth to my own flame.

Nicholas next drew my attention to two coca leaves that had fallen side by side on the far left of the mesa cloth, sitting as if they were a pair. "These two leaves show me you know your partnership with your ex-husband was not just of this plane, but beyond this time and place. You know love is multidimensional. Let go of what no longer serves you on this earth plane—and the relationship with him no longer serves you—but hold to a higher vibration where the two of you are actually one; where we are all One."

The messages from the coca leaf reading helped me realize what I needed to do to continue to magnetize into my reality the new life I sought. When explaining magnetism, Gram had said, "You need to learn how to draw to yourself the people, places, and things that help you grow; and learn to release from yourself the people, places, and things that no longer contribute to your growing." In the wisdom wheel work, magnetism is also about drawing boundaries. As Gram made sure to point out, "Boundaries are not walls. You can draw your boundaries in and out with people, but you can't do that with walls." Her discussion was analogous to Americo's about discernment and Juan's about decisions needing to come from my qosqo, my spiritual stomach and primary energy center. Boundaries in this way are about the choices we make as to how we stand in our power.

Our true inner self is always in a place of quiet nondoing. Our physical body is the material aspect through which we each live our life experience. It is the template in which we get to practice and express our divinity here on the earth plane. The body is subject to cycles and the universal laws, the most significant for all of us being birth and death. Throughout one's life, what affects the physical is both emotional awareness and mental consciousness. The emotional body is subject to the energy absorbed through our experiences with each other and how we feel about and incorporate those experiences. The mental body is affected not just by our thinking, but by how we evaluate what we feel and the set of moral values we live by. The spiritual self is what brings order, information, and unification to all three aspects of the self, often through flashes of insight, creativity, or purpose and even through what we can learn of our self through loss or pain. The consciousness we develop in ourselves in each lifetime extends beyond the physical body. It exists prior to being born and after we die. Therefore, our obligation is to live the truth encoded in us to the best of our ability, and our contribution is to evolve our individual consciousness in a way that uplifts humanity's collective consciousness.

As is obvious in all of our lives, given the decisions we make as we stumble to evolve, we can chose to exhibit either the best or the worst of our humanness. The foundational teaching of all my mentors is that in order to live as conscientious human beings we must hold ourselves accountable for our inner state, and thus for what we project back out into the world around us. And so, as we learn from and acknowledge those weaknesses and frailties that have broken the bonds of loving ourselves, we can stop blaming others and instead choose to do our best to overcome the obstacles that stand in the way of loving ourselves as we move forward.

When we live authentically in connection with Oneness, we do not need to take from another, be the target for others' problems and insecurities, or make ourselves small, as many of us do. To be in alignment with Oneness guides us toward two major realizations: we are able to glimpse, if only momentarily, the capacity of our personal power, and we get a peek at the reality that humanity belongs to the Legions of Light. When we live with the awareness that our actions affect not only us but seven generations forward, we can more easily shift from the selfish, narcissistic *me* to the magnanimous *we.* I struggle to live this promise day to day, not only for myself and for my daughter, Nyssa, but for all those who will follow, who will inherit a world fashioned from the impact of my—and your—decisions and actions.

If, as I believe is true, a developing paqo must learn to live in perfect ayni and the universe reciprocates our every action, then living "impeccably" takes on a whole new depth of meaning. Impeccability is something we have to continually strive for, doing our best moment to moment, not lying to ourselves or to others. This also means reaching for objectivity and balance, over self-serving beliefs and actions.

As Gram taught, our gifts of birth help us to discover the truth of the meaning in our individual Earthwalk, whereas our fears serve as a warning system about what we still need to awaken to in that walk. Angst is a lie put forth by our emotional body when we don't recognize that our fear of separation is both a wound we carried in with us when we separated from our divine memory and a forgetting of our connection to Source.

As religion, spirituality, and metaphysics teach, the way to divine radiance is through the intent to work from unconditional love: first, because it is based in the collective unconscious and, second, because our thoughts are what cause our reality. Gram suggested, "We have to start wherever we find ourselves. We, and all life, are part of Great Mystery, and the Mystery loves all equally and unconditionally in every moment." This present moment is the point in time in which we create our future reality; it is our gift to the Universal Self in each Earthwalk. What I have also had to learn while walking this path is that the form that ayni or reciprocity for actions, thoughts, and intentions—whether positive or negative—takes cannot be determined by anyone other than Great Mystery. While we might not like the form of the reciprocity, or think it's fair, by cultivating awareness we rest in the certainty that it is perfect for us in that moment for our personal growth and soul evolution.

If what my anomalous experiences have taught me is true—that our reality is not only defined by what we can perceive through our normal senses—then there is much more to reality than most of us have ever imagined. For instance, human eyes can only perceive objects in the visible light spectrum, but some animals can see beyond that spectrum to the infrared and ultraviolet. Their visual reality is greatly expanded. This analogy holds true for what are called anomalous experiences: some people can perceive the frequencies and wavelengths at which fairies, ghosts, angels, orbs, and even UFO's vibrate. Not being able to perceive these entities is more about conforming to the consensus opinion of what is possible and "real" than to what reality actually is. Again quoting Jung, "Prejudice cripples and injures the full phenomenon of psychic life."

If what my contactee encounters have taught me also is true—that we each are merely a particle of light or a molecule of developing consciousness in some greater unified whole—then our painful limitations and separations, and even death, are merely illusions, and how we fill the space between birth and death is of supreme importance because it is the imprint of our having been here. What these contacts have also impressed upon me is that what we co-create *this* day makes an imprint on the changing dynamics occurring on Mother Earth. What we as a global entity envision and project, and our accountability for thoughts and actions, or even nonactions, becomes the reality we will manifest as our future. What we conceive of as someday or *that* day is actually today. This lesson of the heart is twofold: the perfection we seek is already within and there really is no time except the present moment.

One of the gifts of being in the third dimension is that we get to take on a physical body, creatively bringing the formlessness of the One into form. If, as many cultural traditions teach, life is a circle, then the journey back toward Oneness—by expanding our consciousness—means reconnecting to all of our multiple selves and to other beings who are part of the divine spectrum of the All That Is. Awakening, thus, is both work and an act of grace. And it doesn't take much of a leap after that to see that if our lives are not encased in linear time, then it is quite possible that all our lives occur simultaneously, allowing each aspect of the Self many opportunites to learn, grow, and heal, because our infinite selves are all connected.

As Gram so eloquently taught, from the moment we are born until the moment we die, we are faced with challenge, change, choice, and commitment. We deal with these in a mature way through the power of the Silence, what Gram called our Vibral Core. To me, the power in the Silence is the ability to tap what we are ultimately made of— the knowledge, intuition, and possibilities that lie within each of us as we take in our life's experiences and learn from them. Thus aligning with our Vibral Core enables us to remember the experience called Oneness. When we are able to enter this Oneness we commit to join our Spirit self with our earth identity. From this state of awareness, we discover that our inner and outer worlds and our connection to everything in the cosmos are linked with what I can best describe as intent. And new clarity of purpose and further awareness come from consistently cleansing the heavy energy from the filaments of our intent. In this way, we help keep the wheel turning forward, not backward.

Once again quoting Gram, "All creatures are Relations, one family, but humans are the only relation unaware of this familial association." I believe relationship—honest, giving relationship—is one of the hardest paths for human beings to travel well. It is difficult to stay in the power of the heart, especially when hearts become wounded or grow apart. Our hearts keep us connected to life, and every relationship we have is moderated by the heart.

In my challenge to stay in the power of the heart during the recent dissolution of my marriage, I faced a choice: I could feel regret and anger or I could hold the person I fell in love with in nonjudgment and support his Earthwalk. I am still using mikhuy to digest my heavy, unresolved feelings concerning the divorce, so I can continue to mend my heart and learn to fill the space between my ex-husband and me with a softer, more refined energy. It is true, as Pio suggested, that I only have control over how I show up in the process, without any expectation of how, or even if, my ex-husband will choose to be present.

I do not wish to imply that this has been easy or that I don't still slip into dark, angry places. Gram Kitty once said, "When fear or darkness comes into your life, look past your confusion to your options and find the path that contains heart energy. The path of the heart is the only road home." This, too, was the teaching of don Mariano about munay, moving past where the ego defines, to forgive. While it is true that in a relationship we are responsible only for our half of the equation, it not quite accurate energetically, for, as grandiose as this might sound, the condition of each of our hearts in a cumulative way affects the web of the world.

Imagine what we could finally accomplish if we committed to coming from the power of the heart to alleviate our own suffering and that of those closest to us before we tackle it in larger spheres of relationship. How can we possibly expect opposing countries or diverse religious groups to honor and respect each other if we can't find the means to accomplish that within the inner circle of our partnerships or family units? The intimacy we seek with anything or anyone cannot evolve honestly or fully become manifest without first finding it within the Self. That is cosmic law. Thus our outer world is shaped by each of us doing our inner work, and although that is not easy, it is necessary for our life is the prayer we offer while here.

We have chosen our individual Earthwalk in order to find our *dharma*, our spiritual purpose in physical form. How we negotiate our Earthwalk determines our individual path toward enlightenment and also defines what karmic seeds will exist in future lifetimes. It is not karma that creates our next Earthwalk, but our innate god-expression that chooses to pass through those karmic conditions or life experiences, seeking divine realization. Almost universally, part of any individual dharma is learning forgiveness and love. In this regard, as Gram taught, "The beauty of every lesson is invested with the Eternal Flame and its secret is revealed through understanding the Language of Love."

Dr. J. J. Hurtak defined love in *The Book of Knowledge: The Keys of Enoch* as "the substance of eternal life." As we approach the shift of the ages, it is our success or not in learning this Language of Love that will either move us toward unity consciousness or keep us in separateness.

As a very young but wise friend of mine recently said, "We're all just unique snowflakes, aren't we, Sandy?" My challenge through all my losses was not to let my snowflake crystallize in my heart as ice, but rather to let it melt, helping to feed my Inca seed. Over the years, I have come to the realization that no matter how often I slip off course, it does not mean I have failed myself, or the teachings, but is just one more opportunity from the universe to honestly show up and participate in the game. It is a cliché in metaphysical circles to say we are all both teachers and students, but there is real truth to that. As Juan put it to me once, "I see you are the teacher taught." And that is true for all of us—we are either teaching or being taught.

Just as there are no mistakes, only learning curves, there is also no right or wrong way to live your Earthwalk as long as you are moving forward in a way that does not contribute to the chaos. To enrich our lives none of us need crystals, a mesa, ayahuasca, rosary beads, sacred sites, or anything else. Any shamanic or spiritual practice shows us, ultimately, that the richness of this life is found in the living of it. We are asked to cultivate compassion, first for ourselves and then for others, removing the patterns or restrictions that separate us from both our self and each other, instead of learning how to merge.

Living through compassion is both the service we offer each other and the challenge we face as we walk between our personal darkness and daylight. One of the ways I have learned to do this is not to say, "This is the truth," but to gratefully ask, "What is true for me in this moment?" Gram suggested that if we say "This is *the* truth," we limit ourselves from evolving and connecting to higher levels of knowing. Even when we choose to avoid or deny it, at a core level, our hearts know when we are limiting ourselves, for we eventually feel a disconnect in our Vibral Core when we are not aligned in a good way with truth.

When we finally come to understand we are, at our Source point, one being living different expressions of Itself, then we can more easily embrace the truth of Oneness. For it is in that Oneness that we find our connection. Then, we can take to heart the words of Alfred Lord Tennyson, who said, "I am part of all I've met." Or as the traditional Maya people say, "I am another yourself."

Epilogue

Dreams are ordinary in the sense that we all have them; however, they become extraordinary when we become informed by their metaphorical gifts. Once again on that special October date that has made itself significant to me throughout these past twelve years, on the night before I finished the final edit of this book, and only two days before I start my drive to Massachusetts to begin yet another "new life," I had this dream. It is a dream within a dream—much as this life is a dream within the larger scope of our divine lives—and I am grateful to my dreaming self as its content gives me more than one perspective in which to consider my present, through my past, as I walk in to my future. It is a poignant message to me about where I have been and where I am headed and as such is an unexpected conclusion to this book.

October 23, 2011, Dream Journal Entry

I am sitting on a wooden bench in a hallway, waiting for something or someone. A woman comes out of a door from across the hall and says, "The shaman will see you now."

I get up and enter a totally white room—white walls, white carpeting, and no furniture of any sort, so there is no place to sit. I wonder momentarily if this room is full of light or is in fact just all white.

The door opens and a short dark-skinned man with coarse, curly black hair and wearing a white shirt, black pants, and a colorful cape enters the room. He smiles and walks over to me. Silently he places both of his hands on my head, as if to give me a blessing or an initiation. I feel myself slipping out of consciousness, as if I am going under anesthesia. I feel myself lean to the right and then I slide to the floor, face down on the carpet.

I dream I am now standing alone in a long corridor of what I perceive is a totally different building. Behind me is a long cement passageway with barbed wire and broken steel beams and I know it is somehow part of a jail. Just ahead of me there is a small group of women. I join them. There are two white women, one younger with blonde hair and one older, and a tall statuesque Ethiopian-looking woman; I seem to intimately know each of them.

A short black man who I know is the jail guard comes through the door in front of us, and says, "You are free to go now." I look back down the long corridor and say, "Are you sure all the others are out? I don't want to leave any of them behind." The guard says, "You must hurry. You all need to go now; there is not a lot of time. You are the last ones."

We follow him out the door and enter what seems to be a processing room. There is a long, old wooden bench in front of a counter where people are processing the paperwork for the last of us who are being released. I am sitting next to a well-dressed woman who tells me, "It's all okay. They're just finalizing our freedom." I think how curious all this is and wonder how long I have been here.

One of the woman processors calls my name. I go up to the counter and she hands me some type of form. It has a number of questions and personal information on it. The first question asks me to fill in the last place that I lived. I write down my Texas address. The next question asks me where I started. I tell the processing lady "I do not remember all the details that got me to this jail." She says, "That's okay. Just sign here and you are free to go."

I am back in my body and begin to feel my face on the rug. I try to rouse myself and try without success to open my eyes. I am having a hard time regaining full consciousness. I drift off again. I vaguely hear Nyssa ask me a question, but I cannot see her or respond. I hear a door open, and I am barely able to turn my face in the direction of the door. Opening my eyes slightly, I see the shaman entering the room again. This time he does not have his cape on. He comes over to me and props my loose-limbed body up against his. Then reaching his hands from behind me, over my shoulders, he places his hands on my collar bones and begins massaging those points in small circular movements. The points are sore, but the pain is diminishing. I drift off again.

I am standing outside the jail compound now, holding a small leather suitcase in my hand. I am by myself looking back to the gates. I don't know which way to walk from here, but I know I am free and can go anywhere I please. I feel excited.

Once again, I am back in the white room trying to wake myself. With great effort I slowly open my eyes. The shaman walks back in through the door, and it sounds like he is talking gibberish or maybe a foreign language I do not understand. He gestures to his knees while making a wobbly motion with his legs, indicating to me that he realizes I am still weak. I try to speak, but cannot yet. He says, in the same gibberish, which I now inexplicably understand, "You've been gone a very long time." I finally find my voice and respond softly, "I have been alone."

With a gentle smile he produces an eleven-by-fourteen-inch glossy photograph and hands it to me.

The photo is a collage of faces: family, friends, lovers, people from my past, and still others I do not recognize at all. In the center of the picture sit six or seven people all glowing, a distinct aura around each. I clearly see I am one of them and the shaman is another. We all have our eyes shut and are sitting cross-legged around what I at first think is a fire pit. As I look closer, I see that each of us has what seems to be a flame coming out of the tops of our heads. They each are spinning, like wafts of smoke would, forming individual columns above our heads that all merge together creating what appears to be a central fire high above us. I look from the photo to the shaman, who kindly says, "You were never alone, Sandy." He then gently pats me on the back three times and walks out the door.

The room is no longer white. I can see large floor-to-ceiling windows and a huge old wooden door in front of me. I have a small leather suitcase in my hand, and I know I have more ground to cover. I feel excited.

I wake up.

About the Author

Sandra Corcoran, M.Ed., is a shamanic counselor and body-oriented psychotherapist trained for thirty years in traditional and esoteric healing techniques. Working with indigenous mentors throughout the Americas, she was initiated as a teacher in the Wolf Clan Teaching Lodge, is a dream decoder and ceremonialist, and is a fourth-level paqo and chunpi paqo trained in the Andean Mystical tradition. She is cofounder of the STAR Process (a soul retrieval healing method), a contactee experiencer, and Thoth tarot reader, and she leads workshops and sacred journeys nationally and internationally. For more information on her work, practice, and worshops please visit

www.starwalkervisions.com

BOOKS OF RELATED INTEREST

Shamanic Breathwork
Journeying beyond the Limits of the Self
by Linda Star Wolf

Bird Medicine
The Sacred Power of Bird Shamanism
by Evan T. Pritchard

Shapeshifting
Techniques for Global and Personal Transformation
by John Perkins

Black Smoke
Healing and Ayahuasca Shamanism in the Amazon
by Margaret De Wys

Ecstatic Healing
A Journey into the Shamanic World of Spirit Possession
and Miraculous Medicine
by Margaret De Wys

Shamanic Spirit
A Practical Guide to Personal Fulfillment
by Kenneth Meadows

The Voice of Rolling Thunder
A Medicine Man's Wisdom for Walking the Red Road
by Sidian Morning Star Jones and Stanley Krippner, Ph.D.

The Power of Ecstatic Trance
Practices for Healing, Spiritual Growth, and
Accessing the Universal Mind
by Nicholas E. Brink, Ph.D.

INNER TRADITIONS • BEAR & COMPANY
P.O. Box 388 • Rochester, VT 05767
1-800-246-8648
www.InnerTraditions.com

Or contact your local bookseller